A Critical Introduction to Syntax

Also available from Continuum

Critical Introduction to Phonetics, Ken Lodge
Critical Introduction to Phonology, Daniel Silverman
Critical Introduction to Translation Studies, Jean Boase-Beier (forthcoming)
Introduction to Syntactic Theory, Edith A. Moravcsik
Introduction to Syntax, Edith A. Moravcsik

A Critical Introduction to Syntax

Jim Miller

Continuum Critical Introductions to Linguistics

BLOOMSBURY
NEW DELHI • LONDON • OXFORD • NEW YORK • SYDNEY

First published in India 2017
First published by Continuum in 2011

This edition published with permission from Bloomsbury Publishing Plc
50 Bedford Square, London WC1B 3DP

British Library Cataloguing-in-Publication Data
A catalogue record for this book is available from the British Library.

Library of Congress Cataloging-in-Publication Data
Miller, J. E. (James Edward), 1942–
A critical introduction to syntax / Jim Miller.
p. cm. – (Continuum critical introductions to linguistics) ISBN: 978-0-8264-9703-1 (hardcover)
ISBN: 978-0-8264-9704-8 (pbk.)
1. Grammar, Comparative and general–Syntax. I. Title. II. Series.
P291.M498 2011 415–dc22
2009051952

ISBN : 978 93 86349 91 0
10 9 8 7 6 5 4 3
For sale in the Indian subcontinent only

Bloomsbury Publishing India Pvt. Ltd
Second Floor, Building No.4
DDA Complex LSC, Pocket C – 6 & 7
Vasant Kunj, New Delhi 110070
www.bloomsbury.com

Exclusively distributed in the Indian subcontinent by
Manohar Publishers & Distributors
4753/23, Ansari Road
Darya Ganj, New Delhi 110002
Tel.: 23284848, 23289100
Email: sales@manoharbooks.com, manoharbooks@gmail.com

Typeset by JS Typesetting Ltd, Porthcawl, Mid Glamorgan
Printed and bound in India by Replika Press Pvt. Ltd.

Contents

Introduction and Acknowledgements

This book has a slightly unorthodox perspective, reflecting my particular experience of syntax, the teaching of syntax and the various audiences for syntax. Several long-held ideas underpin and connect the different chapters and topics. The one that will perhaps be most obvious is that spoken language must be taken seriously, or rather spontaneous spoken language; that is, spoken language produced by speakers in circumstances that allow a minimum of planning time. Not that written language is downgraded; rather, spoken and written language are treated as equally worthy of attention, although speech has priority for early first language acquisition.

The above idea is ranked first because spontaneous spoken language and formal written language (to take the two poles of a continuum of text types) are not just different but profoundly different. This affects core syntactic theory (no sentences; different ways of combining clauses; different constructions and so on) and bears directly on theories of first language acquisition (Chapter 12), language complexity (Chapter 11) and evolution of language. The last topic is not included in the book, but theories of language evolution must take account of the fact that humans spoke long before they began to write. Indeed, even today, once they finish formal schooling, the majority of humans use spoken language more than they use written language.

A second idea is that grammar and meaning are closely connected, to the extent that all grammatical morphemes carry meaning and that for most users of grammar, especially non-native learners of any language, the most satisfying explanation of some grammatical point is a semantic one that works. This idea informed my doctoral research in the late 1960s on aspect in Russian, working within a localist framework. Here, the relation between grammar and semantics is discussed via four topics, in Chapters 7–10: the *get* passive, *wh* words, parts of speech and thematic roles.

A third idea, discussed in Chapter 1 on theory, data and analysis, is that it is essential to have insightful, reliable descriptive grammar as well as formal models. Both approaches to language are theoretical and formal models go astray without solid descriptive support. (See, for example, the discussion of strong and weak features and Indirect Questions in Chapter 1.) The audience for good descriptive grammars and grammar is enormous; the market and range of applications for descriptive grammar is far bigger than the specialist market for formal models. It must be emphasized that descriptive grammar does not stand still, just as formal models do not stand still. Good descriptive grammars draw on the vast amount of work that has been done inside and outside formal models over the past fifty years or so and a descriptive grammar produced in 2010 is not at all the same as a descriptive grammar produced in 1950.

The discussion of the various topics has also been influenced by the importance of collecting reliable data. As a user of databases and a collector of spoken data, JM is aware of the limitations on any one speaker's experience of language and intuitions about syntax and of the need to keep testing formal rules and principles against naturally occurring data as opposed to invented examples. This topic is central to Chapter 6, on usage-based models.

Some of the chapter topics might seem to be only indirectly related to syntax. What are complexity, grammaticality and configurationality doing in this book? Complexity is included because it is central to the differences between spontaneous spoken language and written language, especially the written language required at school and university and in many professions. (We leave on one side the question of whether and in what respect one language might be more complex than another.) It is directly relevant to theories of first language acquisition and to theories of the evolution of language. The concept of grammaticality is central to all generative grammar, to descriptive grammar, to theories of first language acquisition, to the teaching of English as an additional language and to the practice of speech therapy. To determine whether a patient has some speech deficit or is simply using a spoken-language construction, standard or non-standard, speech therapists need a thorough knowledge of spoken and written English and of the non-standard variety spoken in the area where they practise.

Configurationality has to do with whether heads and modifiers, particularly nouns and modifying demonstratives and adjectives, are adjacent or separated by other constituents of a clause. There are languages in which they are not adjacent; the question is how the facts are to be interpreted, and this in turn ties in with work on spontaneous spoken language. The facts also bear on the question of constituent structure and the extent to which analysts investigating spoken language have simply applied the structures familiar to them from written language (mainly the written varieties of languages spoken in Europe).

Naturally occurring examples of spontaneous spoken language are scattered throughout the book. The Russian ones are taken from Zemskaja (1973). The English ones come from various corpuses.

- The Miller–Brown Corpus, established as part of a research project on the syntax of Scottish English between January 1978 and June 1980. (The project was funded by the old Social Science Research Council, the Principal Investigators were Jim Miller and Keith Brown and the data was collected by Martin Millar and Bill Watson.) The project was carried out in the Department of Linguistics, the University of Edinburgh. The corpus consists of approximately 250,000 words split into 100 conversations. The corpus is stored in the Department of Linguistics and English Language at the University of Edinburgh. Another copy is in the Scottish Texts Archive, supervised by the Department of English Language, University of Glasgow.
- The Wellington Corpus of Spoken New Zealand English was collected between 1988 and 1994 by researchers in the Department of Linguistics and Applied Language Studies at the Victoria University of Wellington, New Zealand. The corpus consists of one million words made up of 2,000-word extracts. It contains formal, semi-formal and informal speech, both monologue and dialogue, and includes broadcast material as well as private interactions in a range of settings. Together with the Wellington Written Corpus, it was made available to the public in 1998 in the form of a CD entitled *Wellington Corpora of New Zealand English*. The website is at *http://www.vuw.ac.nz/lals*. Examples from this corpus are labelled 'WSC', for 'Wellington Spoken Corpus'.

The transcriptions in the WSC and the Miller–Brown Corpus have no punctuation and no capital letters. To help readers, longer spaces have been inserted to signal the ends and beginnings of what are taken to be clauses.

- Some examples come from the Macquarie Corpus, specifically from the Australian component of the International Corpus of English, which is abbreviated to 'Australian ICE' in the labels on the examples. The data come from texts categorized as unscripted dialogue, coded by 'S1A' in the Macquarie Corpus. One or two examples come from the New Zealand component of ICE, also part of the Macquarie Archive. I am grateful to Pam Peters and Adam Smith for giving me access to the archive.
- One or two examples are taken from Carter and McCarthy (1997), transcripts of various interactions. The data were collected and transcribed as part of the CANCODE project.

- One example comes from a transcript of a conversation between a doctoral researcher, Gillian Foy, and the mother of a school student, one of the subjects taking part in GF's work on literacy.
- Two examples of resultatives in Chapter 6 come from Ron Macaulay's book *Locating Dialect in Discourse*.

I close this very short introduction by acknowledging my debt to various friends and colleagues. My general outlook on language and linguistics was much influenced by people I worked with at the University of Edinburgh: the late Dennis Ward (in the Russian Department), John Lyons, Keith Brown and Keith Mitchell in Linguistics, John Anderson in English Language. Latterly, I have learned much from Rosanna Sornicola at the University Federico II in Naples and have been inspired by the work of Claire Blanche-Benveniste in Paris and Aix-en-Provence. During the last four years of my career, at the University of Auckland, I had many illuminating discussions with Andreea Calude, Jim Feist, Keith Montgomery and Helen Charters. (They probably did not realize at the time how illuminating their comments and questions were.) Andreea Calude, Jim Feist and Winifred Bauer have commented on parts of the book and answered questions. Of course, I alone am responsible for any unorthodoxies and mistakes.

1 Theory, Data and Analysis

Chapter Outline

Introduction

What counts as doing syntax? Some might insert the word 'real': what counts as doing real syntax? There are two main camps: those linguists for whom real syntax focuses on theories of first language acquisition and those who see syntax as focusing on concepts for the analysis and description of languages. Linguists who practise the first kind of syntax like to see it as explanatory, with the second kind being 'merely' descriptive. In this chapter, we argue that all syntactic work involves theory, though not necessarily formal models, and that data are important. Theory resting on incorrect data or unsatisfactory analyses of correct data might be coherent and internally consistent, but cannot be accepted without reliable supporting evidence. Gathering sufficient evidence is not a simple matter, even for written language, while obtaining good spoken data is difficult, its transcription is time-consuming and its analysis is tricky. (See Chapter 5 for a discussion of data and grammaticality.)

The need to check the data on which pieces of theory are based is demonstrated in pp. 4–7 via an account of indirect or embedded questions. Just how difficult it is to analyse the syntax of spontaneous spoken language is demonstrated in pp. 13–20 via an examination of transcription problems, *except* clauses (main or subordinate?) and the *be sat/be stood* structures, all from Carter and McCarthy (1997), and via a discussion of constructions typical of spoken language: NP-Clause (NP = Noun Phrase), V–Direct Object NP–Complement Clause, WH cleft (the spoken construction rather than the written one) and the 'thing-is' construction.

Explanation and description

The concepts and methods of syntax are two of the set of tools for the analysis and description of languages. The smallest units of syntax are words. They combine into phrases, phrases into clauses and clauses into sentences. Sentences combine into longer texts, but the discourse links over chunks of text are different from the links between words, phrases and clauses. The structure of phrases and clauses is different from the structure of sentences; the classical criteria for determining constituent structure apply neatly to phrases and clauses but much less neatly to sentences. That is to say, phrases and clauses require different techniques of analysis from sentences, and longer texts require very different analytical techniques. (The structure of words is likewise different from the structure of phrases and clauses and will not be dealt with in this book except in passing.)

What do linguists describe with syntax? They produce reference grammars of individual languages, descriptions that try to encompass all the structures found in all the different types of text in a given language: conversation, lectures, poetry, novels, newspapers, research monographs, textbooks for school and university and so on. Examples of such reference grammars are Quirk et al. (1985) for English, Grevisse-Goosse (1993) and Bauer (1997). The second in the list is entitled *Le bon usage* (*Good Usage*), but in fact covers patterns and *hapax legomena* from all sorts of texts and takes a relaxed view of norms. The last in the list has the aim of recording and analysing constructions used by older speakers of Maori whose usage was less affected by English than the usage of younger speakers. Grammatical descriptions may focus more narrowly, not on English in general but, say, on the language of Jane Austen's novels or of legal documents or court proceedings.

Linguists also produce grammars for non-native learners of particular languages. To do so, they decide what set of learners they are writing for, whether complete beginners, learners with some knowledge of the language or learners with a lot of knowledge, and select accordingly the areas of grammar (and vocabulary), the amount of detail and the level of explanation. A third set of grammars is written for native users of a language. For example, speech therapists treat children and adults who have difficulty producing language, whether because of an accident or stroke, in the case of adults, or because of some developmental problem, in the case of children. Therapists have to know what constructions (and vocabulary and discourse organization) their patients might be trying to produce, and they must be able to describe the language of their patients in clinical reports. Much forensic linguistic work for court cases deals with the sounds of language, but some work deals with grammar and discourse organization. People undertaking forensic work have to be able to analyse and compare the syntax of different texts, and they need to be able to describe their findings accurately and consistently.

The word 'describe' occurs several times in the earlier paragraphs, along with the word 'description'. The linguistics that is used in reference grammars and in grammars for speech therapists and forensic linguists is known as descriptive linguistics. Opposed to it, or at least presented by some linguists as opposed to it, is theoretical, explanatory linguistics, a choice of title that presupposes that descriptive linguistics is not theoretical and not explanatory. We will see that, whatever the opposition between the two approaches, it is not clear-cut and in fact is not recognized by a good number of practitioners.

Anderson (2008) sets out clearly the distinction between merely describing (Clark, 2005, p. 232) and explaining. For generative linguists, explaining means developing a small number of very general principles governing the arrangements of syntactic structure, the 'movement' of constituents, co-reference relations between anaphors and antecedents and the mapping of syntactic structure onto semantic interpretations. It also means providing a theory of how children acquire their native language without (according to the Chomskyans) instruction and with exposure to degenerate data. (For a different view, see the discussion of first language acquisition in Chapter 12.) Anderson (2008, p. 796) sets out this influential perspective very firmly: the object of study is not sets of sounds, or words, or sentences, or texts for their own sakes, but rather the system of knowledge and the cognitive capacity that underlies the ability of human beings to produce and understand these things.

Linguists are concerned with the nature and structure of the cognitive faculty that supports Language.

It would have been more accurate to say that *one* object of study is the cognitive capacity underlying the production and interpretation of utterances. The majority of scholars engaged in research on language are probably not directly concerned with the nature and structure of the cognitive capacity. But neither do they study words, sentences and texts for their own sakes but to understand why some texts are successful and others are not, to elucidate language practices and attitudes in groups of users, to write software-enabling computers to handle natural language and, as mentioned earlier, to describe, diagnose and treat the linguistic problems affecting patients in need of speech therapy, to undertake forensic linguistic work and even, in an ideal world, to teach languages at all levels of education.

Anderson does not say what counts as studying words, sentences and texts for their own sake, and his statement invites the inference that, whatever such study might be, it is not relevant to the study of cognitive capacity. We will argue in Chapter 12 that the study of language data, in particular spoken data, has revealed serious defects in the Chomskyan theory of first language acquisition and raised fundamental questions: What about fixed phrases and clauses? What about clause and phrase templates that allow some manipulation of patterns? What about phrase, clause and sentence structures that can be generated by rule (or controlled by simple constraints)? These issues lead to questions about the role of memory and rote learning and about the relationship between spontaneous spoken language in, say, informal conversation, produced with little or no time for detailed planning and written language produced and interpreted with time for planning, editing and revising.

We can question the distinction drawn so clearly by Anderson. Börjars (2006, p. 14) and Green (2005) point out that description and theory are interconnected and interdependent. Description of language requires a set of concepts and, crucially, generalization and abstraction. Even observation requires some theory to enable observers to pick out relevant data. For instance, the observer coming across the example in (1) would not appreciate the significance of the part in bold unless they knew that according to reference grammars of English indirect or embedded questions have the structure of a declarative sentence, a declaration that is repeated in all the generative grammars of English. According to these accounts, (1) should have the structure in (2).

(1) I'd love to know how much better a player is Tiger Woods than Tom Morris.
The Herald, Midweek Sport, 16 April 2008, p. 16

(2) I'd love to know how much better a player Tiger Woods is than Tom Morris.

In (1), the indirect or embedded question has the structure of a direct question: *How much better a player is Tiger Woods than Tom Morris?* The wh phrase *how much better* is in first position and subject–auxiliary inversion has changed *Tigers Woods is* to *is Tiger Woods.* (2) has the constituent order of a declarative clause. The wh phrase is at the front of the clause, this being a key property of indirect questions, but the subject NP precedes the auxiliary, *Tiger Woods is.* The latter order is a key property of declarative clauses.

Observers informed about Minimalism would also know that the example runs counter to the idea that such examples can be 'straightforwardly' analysed as arising from the lexical specification of the embedded C (complement), which would have a weak feature [Q] (for 'Question') rather than a strong [Q]. Furthermore, since the analysis of embedded questions and the analysis of wh-questions is syntactically parallel, 'we correctly predict that we do not find inversion in embedded wh-questions' (Adger, 2003, p. 357). (1) and many other examples from written and spoken English show that the prediction is wrong and cast doubt on the distinction between a weak and strong feature [Q].

It is important to have a number of examples to show that what the analyst has come across is not a one-off but perhaps a regular feature of one speaker's utterances. Even better is to have a range of examples from different text types, as in (3)–(7). The fact that (3)–(7) are from written texts is important, since that indicates clearly that we are not dealing with performance errors:

(3) The question remains of **what is the grant-giving body**.
Department Meeting, University of Edinburgh
(not Scottish English, as the speaker was English)

(4) This issue about **how are we preparing students to flow on seems to me quite important**.
Associate Deans Meeting, University of Auckland, unplanned

(5) No one is sure **how long are the passages leading off from this centre**.
Scotland on Sunday, 13 November 1988. Travel article by Doreen Taylor

(6) Log on at the BBC World Service AIDS site to find out **how much do you know about condoms**.
BBC webpage 2006

(7) You have to ask **why is it necessary to raise this very delicate and difficult subject in the fraught and febrile context of a general campaign**.

New Zealand Herald, 17 February 2005, written

(8) The biggest uncertainty hanging over the economy is **how red will things get**. [Ref to map showing areas of house-price decreases in red]

The Economist, 10–16 May 2008, 'American housing. Map of misery', p. 97

The history of a construction may be relevant, given a propensity among many professional linguists and ordinary users of a given language to dismiss constructions that are supposedly confined to one (or more) non-standard variety or to spontaneous speech or that are (supposedly) of recent origin. With respect to the indirect question construction exemplified earlier, Denison (1998, p. 246), following Henry (1995), asserts that the construction is normal in Ulster English, in Welsh English, in recent American English (note the *recent*) and in the New Englishes. (3)–(8) show that Denison does not cast his net wide enough, and we would add that the construction has been in existence since at least the first half of the nineteenth century, witness the example from Esther Summerson's narrative in *Bleak House*: '*I had thought beforehand that I knew its purport, and I did. It asked me* ***would I be the mistress of Bleak House***' (*Bleak House*, Part 14, Chapter 44). (9) is a written example of the construction from the early 1940s.

(9) They think that what happened in Poland could never happen here, but I sometimes wonder. **Have just asked one man did he hear this programme**, and he replied, 'No, we turned off.'

Mass-Observation, Britain in the Second World War, **Folio Society 2007**, Doris Melling, p. 21

The importance of good, detailed description is recognized by many linguists who would describe themselves as dealing with theory and not description; one major exception is Chomsky, who stated (Chomsky, 1980, p. 11) that substantial coverage of data is not significant and directed his particular explanatory theory towards I-language (internal and abstract) and away from E-language (external and observable). It will be argued in Chapter 12 that this neglect of E-language has important negative consequences for Chomsky's theory of first language acquisition.

Börjars (2006, p. 16) draws attention to disagreement among linguists over what counts as explanation. In the Chomskyan approach, analyses are deemed explanatory if they accord with certain general and universal principles that are innate (part of the language faculty) and enable children to acquire their native language, whatever it might be. Quite apart from current controversy over first language acquisition, a very large number of linguists consider analyses to be explanatory only if they provide semantic or pragmatic motivation for patterns of syntax. (See the discussion of the *get* passive in Chapter 7 and case in Chapter 10.) Associating semantic interpretations with syntactic structures is crucial to the development of an adequate theory of first language acquisition. Humans find it very difficult – in fact many find it impossible – to remember and use meaningless sequences of symbols such as PIN numbers and telephone numbers. Children are no exception.

It is not a simple matter to set out the syntactic and morphosyntactic patterns of a given language, demonstrate how they interact and what their semantic interpretations are. For instance, the Simple Present and the Progressive Present in English interact in a complex way, as do the Simple Past, the Progressive Past and the (Present) Perfect. The Imperfective aspect of Russian is used in main and subordinate clauses and in finite and infinitive clauses. Is there a connection between the finite and non-finite patterns? An adequate explanation is one that offers a semantic–pragmatic account which demonstrates convincingly that the patterns and usages are not arbitrary but are rooted in semantics. Another type of explanation is required for, say, the patterns of relative clause formation that are found in human languages, in particular which nouns in a clause can be modified by a relative clause. Keenan and Comrie's (1977) classic work on a hierarchy of grammatical functions and the possibility of relativization connects the concepts of complement and adjunct with the concepts of the core of a clause – subject, direct object and verb – and its periphery – oblique object. Like the work by Givon and others on the accessibility of reference, their research produced a hierarchy of accessibility to relativization and a pleasing set of implicational relations along the lines of 'If a language can relativize a direct object, it can also relativize subjects (but not necessarily oblique objects).'

It should be emphasized that not all formal models deal with the cognitive capacity underlying language. Börjars (2006, p. 13) cites Gazdar et al. (1985) stating plainly that it would be irresponsible to claim that their formal grammar of English (and by invited inference, any formal grammar of English) is a psychological theory or a biological theory of the structure of 'an as-yet-unidentified mental organ'. Generalized phrase structure grammar was overtaken by the very similar head-driven phrase structure grammar, which has served as a framework for some of the most explicit accounts of particular areas of English grammar – see Ginzburg and Sag (2001). No claims are made for psychological reality there either, though the account could be the basis for a computer program handling such data. And other models, such as Dik's Functional Grammar and Van Valin's (originally Foley and Van Valin's) Role and Reference Grammar, make no claim to psychological reality either.

Data and theory

Good, reliable data are equally crucial to descriptive syntax and to formal syntax. (We will use 'formal' rather than 'theoretical'; we have been arguing that descriptive linguistics also rests on theory and what all the different schools of 'theoretical linguistics' have in common is the application of some formal framework.) What counts as good reliable data? Not just the intuitions of the analyst or of native speakers who are asked if they find particular sentences acceptable or not. The analyst's intuitions can be led astray by preferences for this or that analysis or theory.

Much of the following discussion deals with English structures, but one goal of linguistics is to develop concepts that apply to all languages. It is extremely difficult to collect reliable data and analyses from languages that one does not know well, or does not know at all, and for which one relies on other people's descriptions. For example, when analysing the concept of 'head' in connection with cognitive/construction grammar, Croft (2001, p. 246) comments that agreement gives conflicting evidence for headhood across languages. In some languages, he says that the head noun agrees with the Genitive Modifier (initial capitals as in Croft's text), while in others the Genitive Modifier agrees with the head noun. This distinction will be discussed in the section on heads and dependents/modifiers; what is relevant here is the Bulgarian phrase used by Croft to exemplify a Genitive Modifier agreeing with the head noun. Consider (10).

(10) Sestr-ina-ta kŭšta
sister-gen.fsg-art.fsg house
the sister's house

The word *sestrinata* is not a Genitive Modifier. It is not a noun but an adjective, albeit a possessive adjective, and it is not in the genitive case. (Such possessive adjectives are found in the Slavic languages generally. They occur regularly, though not frequently, in writing, but are rare in spontaneous speech, at least in Russian and Bulgarian.) As an adjective, *sestrina* follows the Indo-European pattern of agreeing with its head noun. Scatton (1984, pp. 316–17), the source of Croft's example, labels *sestrinata* 'a possessive adjective derived from a noun'. As he notes, another possessive construction consists of the possessed noun followed by a prepositional phrase containing the possessor noun: *kŭšta na sestrata* house-the of sister-the, 'the sister's house'.

Sampson (2007, pp. 16–18) highlights the way in which erroneous intuitions can become data that other linguists take as solid. He cites the claim by Ross that when a verb in English has a prefix it cannot take a non-nominal complement, a claim that was taken up by Roeper and Siegel and then by Aronoff and others. A search with Google showed Sampson that Ross' claim was wrong; examples such as *overindulge in something* and *reaffirm that such and such* turned out to be quite frequent.

People's intuitions are even less reliable for spoken language. Labov (1975, pp. 34–6) interviewed speakers of Philadelphia English whom he had observed using examples such as *John is smoking a lot any more*, in which *any more* is equivalent to 'is continuing to' or 'these days'. The speakers denied using such examples and declared that they would have no idea what they might mean if they heard them. Relative clauses such as *There are some people can't stop talking* are standard in presentative–existential constructions in spoken English all over the English-speaking world. They are peculiar in that the relative clause *can't stop talking* has no relativizer, although the missing *who* would be the subject of the relative clause. The standard story is that such relative clauses must be introduced by a wh word such as *who* or *which* or by *that*. The author asked several tutorial groups of students in the 1980s whether they had heard such examples or thought they were possible structures of English. All the students denied having heard them and were of the opinion that they were not possible structures of English.

The particular difficulty here is that speakers of English (and presumably this applies to the speakers of other languages that have spoken and written varieties) do not have reliable intuitions about regular syntactic patterns in the spontaneous speech of speakers of standard English, never mind non-standard varieties. An example which the author has discussed elsewhere (Miller, 2010) concerns the use of *sat* versus *sitting* and *stood* versus *standing*. Commenting on the utterance *the pilot was sat in one of the seats*, Carter and McCarthy (1997, p. 34) remark that the speaker spoke Yorkshire dialect and that standard English requires *was sitting*. In contrast, the research by Cheshire et al. (1993, pp. 70 and 71) showed that BE *sat/stood* was widespread and characteristic of 'a general non-standard or semi-standard variety of English'. The unclear status of the construction is reflected in Trask's (2001, pp. 252, 273) description of *was sat* as 'colloquial British English' and of *was stood* as 'regional British English'.

Burchfield (1981), writing for the BBC, declared *was sat/stood there* unacceptable in any circumstances; 20 years on, the structure is widely used by, for example, reporters on the BBC *News at Ten* (though not by the presenters, who read from autocues) and seems to be characteristic of unplanned speech (including that produced by speakers of standard English, contrary to the opinion of Cheshire et al.) Many structures considered 'non-standard' may be misclassified; rather than being non-standard, they may be normal in the spontaneous speech of all speakers.

The construction has reached newspaper writing, as shown by the examples in (11) and (12).

(11) **Sat** between a beaming Tony Blair and Sir Bob Geldof, Ethiopia's Prime Minister, Meles Zenawi, pictured, could hardly have wished for a stronger endorsement.

The Independent, 17 October 2007
('From West's favourite leader to grave-digger of democracy')

(12) The same could not have been said for John Fleck, **sat** alongside him on the bench.

The Herald, Friday Sport, 23 May 2008, p. 5

(13) is from a dialogue in a novel set in the early 1930s. The speaker is the wife of a Church of England vicar and definitely a speaker of standard English. (As Jim and Lesley Milroy have repeatedly said, there is far more variation in *standard* English than the arbiters of usage imagine.)

(13) 'My dear Hilary, how kind of you! Yes, indeed - I can do with all the white flowers I can get. These are beautiful and *what* a delicious scent! Dear things! I thought of having some of our plants **stood** along there in front of Abbot Thomas, with some tall vases among them . . . '

Dorothy Sayers (1934), *The Nine Tailors*, p. 59
in the Hodder and Stoughton edition, first published
as a Four Square edition, 1959, 14th impression 1987

Getting the data right is important for various enterprises, not just Minimalism. The indirect question construction exemplified in (2)–(8) figured in tests given to non-native speakers of English in 2003–04 as part of a research project in New Zealand. The participants in the experiment were counted as having made a mistake if they used that construction. Participants who 'made a mistake' might infer that many native speakers also made that mistake or would be left puzzling over why they could not use in the ESOL classroom a construction that they regularly heard and saw. And the results of the experiment and their interpretation would not be of the most reliable.

Data and analysis

TH clefts without wh words

The collection of good spoken data via good recordings and reliable transcriptions is the first step in analysing the syntax of spontaneous speech. The second step, actually analysing the syntax, is beset with traps. In this section, we consider three sets of tricky constructions that occur regularly, even frequently, in spontaneous spoken language: TH clefts, *except* clauses and reported speech. To arrive at an analysis based on evidence, it is essential to know the syntax of spontaneous spoken English in detail and to be able to apply the recognized criteria for, in the second case, subordinate clauses. Even an analysis produced under these conditions may not be rock solid. Consider the following excerpt from a dialogue in Carter and McCarthy (1997, p. 73). The last line contains a construction that will be treated as a TH cleft. The TH clefts studied in the literature are of the form *That's where Andrew works, That's why you should phone her* and *This is what I was talking about.* (See Calude 2008 for an overview of recent work on TH clefts.)

(14) A: Is it not er nice at all?
B: Oh some of the things are delicious yes. But it's a long way from here.
A: Just got to be careful what you choose.
B: . . . You can't choose. He just cooks them a meal. If they ring up and say they're going, he serves a meal.
A: Where is it then?
B: Battersea.
A: **Is that Sally lives there or something?**

Commenting on the last line, Carter and McCarthy (1997, p. 76) state that the chunk *Is that Sally lives there or something*? is a combination of three questions: (a) *Is that* (*where Sally lives*)? – a false start; (b) *Does Sally live there*? – not fully formed as a result of the previous false start; (c) *Is* (*it*) *Sally* (*who*) *lives there*? Carter and McCarthy's analysis is mistaken. Note first that they say nothing about the intonation and rhythm. Are there hesitations? How do they know the speaker makes a false start? What do they mean by their remark that (b) is not fully formed? What evidence do they have that the yes–no question is in the speaker's mind, given that *lives* agrees in person and number with *Sally* and that the utterance contains nothing corresponding to *does* or a part of *does*?

Is that Sally lives there or something? is a regular construction of spoken English. *That* contrasts with *it*, as illustrated in (15) from Swan (2005, pp. 584–85).

(15) a. So she decided to paint her house pink. It upset the neighbours a bit.
b. So she decided to paint her house pink. That upset the neighbours a bit.

Swan comments that *that* is more emphatic than *it*, not surprising given that it is a deictic for pointing at entities distant from the speaker. It is used to highlight situations conveyed by a NP plus a participle, as in (16)–(18). With a past participle, *that* points at the result of some action or process. (See the discussion of Perfect and Resultatives in Chapter 6.)

(16) A: that1 it started now?
B: that1's it that1's it going

Miller–Brown Corpus, conversation 71

(17) That's dinner sorted.

TV advertisement, ITV, autumn 2009

(18) **S1A**-015(B):6 Yeah what we thought we'd do is Oxford ends on I think the tenth and um Edinburgh usually starts about two days after Oxford so what I thought we'd do is travel up and see if maybe stay maybe in one place on the way up to Edinburgh and then take about three days to come back and look at a couple of places
S1A-015(A):12 **Is that by train**
S1A-015(B):13 No bus

Macquarie Corpus, Australian ICE,
S1A private dialogue, conversation 15

Is that by train is an embryo cleft, equivalent to *Is that by train that you're going to Edinburgh*, with the cleft highlighting trains as opposed to cars, buses and planes or even bikes. (19) contains a full cleft with *that*.

(19) S1A-020(B):146 No I'm not the one that's depriving you
S1A-020(B):147 X is the one that's depriving you
S1A-020(A):149 She's not depriving me of anything
S1A-020(B):150 Well so you're getting it more than a- once or twice a week
S1A-020(A):152 Oh no no ever
S1A-020(B):154 Ever
S1A-020(A):155 Yeah Problem of timing this week
S1A-020(B):156 Oh right **was that only last week that she came over for dinner**

Macquarie Corpus, Australian ICE,
S1A private dialogue, conversation 20

The interrogative cleft *was that only last week that she came over for dinner* is related to the declarative cleft *that was only last week that she came over for dinner*. The annex clause, to use Quirk et al.'s term (Quirk et al., 1985, pp. 1386–7), has the complementizer *that*: *that she came over for dinner*. In contrast, the *that* cleft in (20) has an annex clause with no complementizer.

(20) **S1A**-084(A):151 Start at the beginning Her her first husband Who's X's father was a bit of a bastard really
S1A-084(A):154 He was really um really tight
S1A-084(B):155 Oh rightie oh
S1A-084(B):156 Is that the one who died or did her husband die
S1A-084(A):157 Yeah
S1A-084(A):158 No Well **that was both of them died**

Macquarie Corpus, Australian ICE,
S1A private dialogue, conversation 84

The chunk *that was both of them died* is equivalent to *It was both of them who died*, which in the context is to be interpreted as 'It wasn't the case that one husband left her and the other one died – they both died.' (Cf. *That was both of them* ***that*** *died.*) Going back to Carter and McCarthy's dialogue, we can now interpret *Is that Sally lives there or something?* as the interrogative of *that is Sally lives there.* The relative clause *lives there* lacks a relativizer, but this is typical of spoken English. There is no need to appeal to a false start and a mixing-up of three structures.

Except clauses: main or subordinate?

The same dialogue contains another sequence of words whose syntactic status is not straightforward. It is in (21).

(21) A: I suppose it's a long way to go for dinner though isn't it?
B: It is on a week d week night
A: **Except he can go straight from work**

Carter and McCarthy (1997, p. 76) treat *Except he can go straight from work* as a subordinate clause standing on its own but do not explain why they consider it subordinate. At this point, we make a noticeable detour to look at the syntactic properties of subordinate clauses and then at their discourse properties. The outcome of the examination will be that *Except he can go straight from work* is to be analysed as a main clause. The finite subordinate clauses in a given sentence are to some extent grammatically independent of the main clause; the main clause does not control the choice of verb and other constituents nor the choice of participant roles, tense, aspect and modal verbs. (The choices must make semantic sense, but that is a different question.) Compare the variants of the complement clause in (22).

(22) We heard that their team will win the league/is winning the league/has won the league/might win the league/must have won the league/had been beaten in the final/was demoralized

In (22), the last complement clause is a copula construction, the penultimate one is passive and the rest are active, but with different tenses and aspects. None of this depends on the main clause. Subordinate clauses are however subject to a number of constraints that do not apply to main clauses. For instance, main clauses can be declarative, interrogative or imperative, as shown in (23).

(23) a. The secretary sent an e-mail to my colleague.
b. Did the secretary sent an e-mail to my colleague?
c. Send an e-mail to my colleague!

Relative clauses, adverbial clauses and most types of complement clause must have declarative syntax, as shown in (24).

(24) a. ***Because did the secretary send that e-mail**, my colleague resigned. [Because the secretary sent . . .]
b. *The e-mail **which did the secretary send** was very abrasive. [. . . which the secretary sent . . .]
c. *I feared **that would the secretary send the e-mail**. [I feared that the secretary would send the e-mail.]

One type of complement clause is the indirect question. The classic indirect yes–no questions of written English have the word order of declarative clauses – *We asked if the secretary had sent the e-mail.* In more formal texts *if* can be replaced by *whether*, and the subordinate clause becomes partly interrogative in its word order, having a wh word at the front. The classic indirect wh questions also have declarative word order apart from the wh word at the front: *We asked who had sent the e-mail.* (1)–(8) are examples of indirect questions from modern spontaneous spoken English and certain written text types. They have the word order of interrogative clauses. This raises the question of how subordinate these clauses are, but our concern here is simply to signal that construction as an exception to the rule that subordinate clauses have declarative word order.

Subordinate clauses are limited in other respects and exclude certain constructions. Consider (25).

Prepositional phrase fronting

(25) a. **Into the room** came the secretary. [Cf. The secretary came into the room.]
b. She said ***that into the room*** came the secretary.
c. *The person who into the room came was the secretary.
d. *Because **into the room** came the secretary, everyone stopped talking.
e. *When **into the room** came the secretary, everyone stopped talking.

The construction has a prepositional phrase in first position followed by the main verb followed by the subject NP. It can occur in declarative main clauses as in (25a), complement clauses as in (25b), but not in relative clauses as in (25c) nor in adverbial clauses as in (25d,e).

Negative fronting

(26) a. **Never** had he been so offended. (He had never been so offended.)
b. They realized that **never** had he been so offended.
c. *The person who **never** had been so offended was Sir Thomas.
d. *Because **never** had Sir Thomas been so offended, even Mr Yates left.

In (26a), *never* is at the front of the clause, followed by the finite verb *had* and the subject NP *he.* The construction is acceptable in main clauses as in (26a) and complement clauses as in (26b), but not in relative clauses as in (26c) nor adverbial clauses as in (26d).

Tag Questions

(27) a. The Chairman habitually ate too much rich food, **didn't he**?
b. *We realized that the Chairman habitually ate too much rich food, **didn't he**?
c. *The person who ate too much food **didn't he** was the Chairman.
d. *Because the Chairman ate too much food **didn't he**, he was dangerously obese.

The structure in (27a) consists of a declarative clause, *We realized that the Chairman habitually ate too much rich food*, with a question tagged on at the end, *didn't he?* Tag questions do not occur in any type of subordinate clause. Note that in an example such as *Edmund knew that the Chairman was dangerously obese, didn't he?* the tag question relates to part of the main clause, *Edmund knew*, and not to *was dangerously obese*. Note also that the examples in (27) are to be taken as written language and that spoken utterances must be supposed to carry a single intonation pattern and to have no breaks. The latter stipulation is necessary because speakers do produce utterances such as *because he was dangerously obese* or *because he ate too much food*, break off the utterance, ask the tag question *isn't he* or *didn't he* and then, having received an answer, go back to the main clause. That type of interrupted syntax is not relevant for present purposes.

The data in (23)–(27) suggest that there is a hierarchy of subordination. Complement clauses are the least subordinate and allow Preposition Fronting, Negative Fronting and, depending on the head verb, interrogative structures. Relative clauses and adverbial clauses are most subordinate. They exclude all the constructions in (23)–(27), together with interrogative and imperative structures.

The extent to which adverbial clauses are subordinate is affected by their type and by their position in sentences. As (28) shows, adverbial clauses of reason can precede or follow the main clause. When they precede the main clause, they exclude negative fronting and preposition fronting but not when they follow it. This suggests that in the former position they are more subordinate.

(28) a. Everyone stopped talking because in came the secretary.
b. *Because in came the secretary everyone stopped talking.

Adverbial clauses of concession do not behave the same way: compare **Although in came the secretary, everyone continued talking* and **Everyone* *continued talking although in came the secretary*. Adverbial clauses of time introduced by *when* present a different problem, as shown by (29) and (30).

(29) a. *When into the room came the secretary everyone was talking.
     b. Everyone was talking when into the room came the secretary.

(30) a. *When into the room came the secretary, everyone had just stopped talking.
     b. Everyone had just stopped talking when into the room came the secretary.

It has been proposed that sequences of main clause + adverbial clause of reason or adverbial clause of time (*when*) come close to being conjoined clauses, that is, clauses of equal status. This proposal seems on the right lines, particularly when, as in the (b) examples, *when* can be replaced by *and then*, that is, by an expression that overtly conjoins the two clauses and fits with the notion of main clause + adverbial clause as two conjoined clauses.

We can now return to the dialogue in (21), repeated below as (31).

(31) A: I suppose it's a long way to go for dinner though isn't it?
     B: It is on a week d week night
     A: Except he can go straight from work.

To apply the above criteria for subordinate clauses we adapt the last line to (32).

(32) It would be too far for a week night except he can go straight from work.

In (31), the *except* clause excludes imperative constructions, as shown by (33).

(33) *It would be too far for you on a week night except go straight from work.

Whether except clauses exclude interrogative clauses is not clear. (34) sounds acceptable if there is a long pause between *except* and the following clause.

(34) It would be too far for a week night except can he go straight from work?

Except clauses do allow Prepositional Phrase Fronting and Negative Fronting, but not Tag Questions. This is shown in (35a–c), devised for the purpose of demonstration. (35c) is acceptable only if the tag is addressed to someone else and the speaker is appealing to that third person for confirmation.

(35) a. I would have enjoyed the trip except into the carriage came a crowd of noisy rugby fans.
b. I might have bought the house except never have I seen such a neglected building.
c. We had a good time, except two boys got lost in the park, didn't they?

What the examples given in (35) show is that *except* clauses following a main clause are not even semi-subordinate, since they meet many of the criteria for main clauses. What about the *except* clause in the dialogue in (31), which was abandoned to apply the criteria for subordination to more amenable examples?

(31) A: I suppose it's a long way to go for dinner though isn't it?
B: It is on a week d week night
A: Except he can go straight from work.

The above *except* clause behaves differently. It is on its own, not immediately preceded by a main clause in the same turn. It allows interrogative constructions, tag question, preposition fronting and negative fronting, as shown by (36) and (37).

(36) A: I suppose it's a long way to go for dinner though isn't it?
B: It is on a week d week night
A: Except who would want to travel in the rush hour?
A: Except nowhere can you find better haggis (negative fronting).

(37) A: I suppose it's a long way to go for dinner though isn't it?
B: Except he likes driving in London, doesn't he?

Given the data (regrettably, devised by JM for the purpose, so further exploration is required), it looks as though the *except* clause in (21/31) is a main clause and that *except* is not a subordinating conjunction, but a discourse particle roughly with the force 'You're not entirely wrong but there's another fact that works against your assertion.'

Indirect questions and anacoluthon

Matthews (2007, p. 17) defines *anacoluthon* as 'a sentence which switches from one construction to another', as in (38).

(38) He told me that he was desperate and could I please help.

The clause *could I please help* does not construe with the complementizer *that* in *He told me that*... Matthews' remarks apply to the classic construction of indirect or reported speech typical of formal written English, but the example is typical of spontaneous spoken English. The classic indirect speech construction would be as in (39).

(39) He told me that he was desperate and asked if I could help.

The key properties of indirect speech are these. Instances of someone's direct speech or the contents of a written or spoken message – statement, question or command – are reported by means of construction containing a verb of saying or asking followed by a complement clause: *He said that he was desperate* and *He asked if he could help.* A direct statement keeps its word order, but changes the tense of the verb from present to past and the person of pronouns from first or second to third: *I am desperate* becomes *He was desperate.* A direct question acquires the word order of declarative clauses and may also acquire a complementizer that was not in the original question: *Can you help* becomes *if I could help.*

The indirect speech constructions are required in formal written English, but many users have difficulty meeting the requirement. One reason for this is that the classic indirect speech constructions occur very infrequently in spontaneous spoken English. (40) is an example of the classic construction. The speaker is a woman in her mid-twenties.

(40) he said that they didn't even send white policemen down there and he wasn't going to take me

Miller–Brown Corpus, conversation 2

In contrast, (41) is an example of the typical spontaneous spoken construction in which the speaker purports to reproduce the original speaker's words (spoken or written). This means that the verb does not change to past tense nor the pronouns to third person. Moreover, the speaker typically changes pitch and/or voice quality to signal where the reported speech begins and ends. The speaker in (41) is an 18-year-old schoolgirl.

(41) Brenda passed the message over to me when I kick you knock the cup into Andrew's face

Miller–Brown Corpus, conversation 12

Speakers produce examples of a mixed construction in which they use, for example, *X said* and/or transpose first into third person, but, that apart, purport to reproduce X's exact words. Cf. (42).

(42) they said if they get us there again they're going to wrap the air-rifle round my neck

Miller–Brown Corpus, conversation 8

Miller and Weinert (2009) examined a subset of 14 conversations from the Miller–Brown Corpus for instances of direct and indirect speech. There were 22 instances of the direct speech construction exemplified in (41), 3 instances of the indirect speech construction exemplified in (40), and 1 instance of the mixed construction exemplified in (42). The indirect speech examples include *we thought he was going away*, which could have been expressed as *we thought – 'he's going away'*. Two of the three classic indirect speech examples are produced by an older speaker, the woman in her mid-twenties from whose narrative (40) comes. (43) is a good example of a mixed construction.

(43) there was this note pinned on the common room notice board . . . and it was a mr. c. lyon had phoned and would you phone him back . . .

The first clause in the note is introduced by *it was*, and the tense is changed from Perfect or Simple Past to Past Perfect. The indefinite article might have been in the original or might have been added: that is, *Mr C Lyon (has) phoned* becomes *a mr c lyon had phoned*. The second clause in the reported message is as it was in the original: *would you phone him back*, a request addressed to the recipient of the note. The classic indirect speech construction would be *the message said that a mr c lyon had phoned and asked her if she would phone him back*.

Consider now Matthews' example *He told me that he was desperate and could I please help*. Anacoluthon is not just switching from one construction to another, but switching incorrectly. The example would be correctly labelled 'anacoluthon' if the speaker intended to produce two complement clauses, but was sidetracked into a direct question. On the other hand, if the speaker was following the typical pattern of spontaneous spoken English as exemplified above, the interrogative clause does not modify *told*, but is an independent clause conveying the construction and words used by the original speaker, apart from the substitution of *I* for *you*: presumably the original utterance would be *Could you please help*? As an example of spontaneous spoken language, Matthews' example is not anacoluthon.

Clause and sentence

Cheshire (2005, p. 81) observes that digital corpora of transcribed speech are readily available, and analysts have no excuse for avoiding spontaneous speech. She also observes that we cannot easily understand the nature of spontaneous spoken language in terms of the standard linguistic descriptors. To these remarks must be added a third point of crucial importance: a given transcription represents the perceptions and analyses of a given transcriber or team of transcribers and it is quite insufficient to work just with the transcription. The original audio recording must also be listened to. This is why Miller and Weinert (2009) worked with the small corpuses containing Map Task dialogues and the Miller–Brown conversations: the original audio recordings were available and portions had been listened to in depth and their syntax analysed.

Ochs (1979), very early in the study of syntax and discourse organization of spontaneous spoken language, drew attention to the fact that transcription becomes data; Leech et al. (1995) add that nowadays both transcription and coding become data. It is very convenient to have transcriptions of spontaneous speech but also dangerous, for the simple reason that the analyst is prisoner of the transcribers' (possibly incorrect) decisions. This is why the Miller–Brown Corpus of spontaneous conversation was transcribed (in 1977–80) without capital letters, without punctuation and with no indication of lengths of pauses or of non-linguistic noises and presumably why the Wellington Corpus is similarly transcribed.

Importantly, the corpuses are not just transcriptions, but transcriptions together with tape recordings. This is why, in spite of detailed coding of long pauses and non-linguistic noises such as grunts, in-breaths, laughs and so on, the Wellington Corpus of Spoken New Zealand English and the Macquarie Corpus of Australian Spoken English are not easy to work with. The author was given recordings of individual conversations in the Macquarie Corpus in connection with Peters et al. (2009), the editors being the compilers and managers of the corpus, but to listen to the audio recordings on which the New Zealand Corpus is based, researchers have to travel to Wellington.

Crucially, the more information in a transcription, the further away users are from the original data and the more they are hemmed in by someone else's analysis. This point is underlined by recent methodological reflections on the role of prosody in conversation. In her review of research over the last 15 years, Selting (2007) lists many aspects for future investigation, including the use of prosody in the segmentation of turn constructional and other interactional units, as well as its relevance for the categorization of grammatical constructions. Selting (2007) and Gilles (2007) comment that they and other highly experienced analysts have questioned the aspects of the GAT system designed to mark prosody and units, and the reliability of decisions based on the system. While GAT represented a vast improvement in transcription (especially German) and offered a relatively unobtrusive and consistent set of transcription conventions, the next generation of public spoken corpuses will come with transcriptions and sound aligned. This will render the corpuses more transparent, by making visible the theory behind the methodology and enabling all users to make up their own minds about the best analysis of the original data. In the meantime, caution is required when using standardized and annotated transcriptions, whatever the model.

Cheshire's remark on the inapplicability of the standard linguistic descriptors is particularly apt with respect to 'sentence'. Many analysts working on spontaneous speech have abandoned the sentence as a unit of analysis, a move that seems to have been first proposed, at least for spoken English, by Crystal (1976). We review the reasons for this below, but first we must distinguish the two concepts to which the label 'sentence' is attached. Following Lyons (1977a, pp. 29–31), we work with text sentences and system sentences. System sentences are abstract, idealized units of linguistic analysis that derive historically from the work by Greek and Roman philosophers on language conceived as a system for expressing propositions. Text sentences are the chunks of utterances that typically correspond to some kind of system sentence. The problem for analysts is that while mature writers usually signal where their text sentences begin and end, in spontaneous speech not even mature speakers signal consistently, or even at all, where putative sentences might begin and end. (As we will see in Chapter 12, this gap between writing and spontaneous speech poses grave problems for the Chomskyan theory of language acquisition.)

Sentences, then, are out but other descriptors such as 'word', 'clause', 'head' and 'modifier/dependent' are applicable to spoken language. However, other problems are lying in wait. After the discussion of sentences below, we will see that the assignment of syntactic structure to spontaneous speech is far from straightforward. Indeed, we have already seen the problems in connection with TH clefts and *except* clauses. To take an example that bears on the abandonment of sentences, the cores of clauses can be established by recognizing a verb and its complements, while the placement of adjuncts is not obvious. Suppose a speaker produces the utterance *the garage is in Broughton*

Place Lane . . . just round the corner from Broughton Place. Suppose the phrase *just round the corner from Broughton Place* is separated from *Broughton Place Lane* by a long pause, so long that it has clearly been added as an afterthought. Does *just round the corner from Broughton Place* belong in the clause *the garage is in Broughton Place Lane*? Or is it outside the clause, although modifying *garage*?

To handle this kind of data, making the fewest assumptions about structure, we need to invoke the notion of rhetorical relations holding across sentence and clause boundaries. In the above example, the afterthought *just round the corner from Broughton Place* is not a constituent of the clause, but is connected with it by the interpretative mechanisms of rhetorical relations theory and discourse representation theory. Along with other analysts of spontaneous speech, we recognize that clauses may combine into clause complexes in which the clauses are interrelated, but this is not a good reason for assuming that such groups of clauses are organized into sentences. Sentences are units of written language and reflect (more or less) conscious decisions taken by writers.

The earlier example about the garage in Broughton Place Lane is typical of, but at the 'modest' end of, the data that led other leading analysts to a similar view of spontaneous spoken language. In her classic work on spoken Italian, Sornicola (1981) presents data from Neapolitan Italian, demonstrating that spontaneous spoken language may have a very fragmentary syntax. (For a sample, see Miller and Weinert, 2009, pp. 58–9.) She opposes any approach in which such fragmentary syntax is analysed in terms of underlying integrated clauses and phrases distorted by performance error. Sornicola suggests that many spontaneous spoken utterances are to be analysed, not as coherently organized pieces of syntax but as resulting from the juxtaposition of information blocks. (Such sequences of information blocks can only be interpreted by discourse interpretation mechanisms that are designed to handle separate chunks of syntax, beginning with separate sentences.) Linell (1988, p. 54) reaffirms the lack of clear-cut sentences in spoken language and adds that talk consists of phrases and clauses loosely related to each other and combining into structures less clear and hierarchical than the structures dealt with in grammar books. Similar points are made in Brown et al. (1984, p. 16–18), for Russian in Zemskaja (1973) and for French in Blanche-Benveniste (1991). (For a detailed discussion, see Miller and Weinert, 2009, pp. 22–71.)

Miller and Weinert (2009, pp. 28–71) provide a detailed argument for why the sentence is inappropriate in the analysis of spoken language. (They recognize that the sentence is central to the analysis of written language.) We summarize the argument, adding new points and new data. One argument rests on the difficulty of recognizing sentential beginnings and endings, since they are not signalled consistently by pauses and since pauses occur in other positions too. Another argument is based on Wackernagel-Jolles' (1971) work on German. She demonstrated that even listening to texts uttered by slow and careful speakers, regardless of whether the texts were conversation or the re-telling of a well-known tale, senior university students in Germany disagreed about how to divide transcriptions into sentences. (The transcriptions had no punctuation and no divisions into sentences or indeed clauses.)

A third argument was based on the fact that young children have to learn at school how to combine clauses into sentences, the task being easier the greater the exposure of a given child to written materials. An argument from the study of syntax is that the central concepts of dependency relations and constituent structure apply most straightforwardly inside single clauses and that the densest networks of dependency relations are to be found inside single clauses. (This is not to deny that dependency relations can occur across clause boundaries. See the discussion of dependencies and constituent structure on pp. 41–57.) Miller and Weinert (2009) adopt Halliday's idea of clause complexes, an idea that is supported by the work of Sornicola, Linell, Brown and others referred to earlier in connection with fragments of syntax.

Wackernagel-Jolles' work has not been replicated, but the problems she revealed and explored are neatly illustrated by texts in Carter and McCarthy (1997). Consider (44), an excerpt from a local radio programme in Birmingham, UK (Carter and McCarthy, 1997, p. 111).

(44) Presenter: . . . I'd have thought the first thing you do when it gets as dark and as wet and as miserable as this. You turn your lights on and I don't mean the parkers. I mean the lights.

The chunk transcribed as a sentence ending in *the first thing you do when it gets as dark and as wet and as miserable as this* is not a complete sentence of written English. The written construction is *the first thing you do . . . is to turn your lights on.* In spoken English, the NP the *first thing you do when it gets as dark and as wet and as miserable as this* is simply juxtaposed with *you turn your lights on.* There is no copula, though there is one in the corresponding written construction: *The first thing you do when it gets as dark and as wet and as miserable as this* **is** *you turn your lights on.* (See the discussion on WH clefts below.) If Carter and McCarthy want to insist on sentences, a more accurate transcription, taking account of the constructions of spoken English, is *I'd have thought the first thing you do when it gets as dark and as wet and as miserable as this — you turn your lights on. And I don't mean the parkers. I mean the lights.*

The transcription in Carter and McCarthy is inconsistent. In contrast to the treatment of (44), a chunk of text on p. 142 of their book is not divided into sentences, although it easily could be. The text is in (45):

(45) Because originally when we thought we were going I thought we were just going to Amsterdam and that was it we were just spending our week in Amsterdam cos there's loads to do [No full stop in the original. JM]

The pausing and intonation would allow *we were just spending our week in Amsterdam* and *cos there's loads to do* as separate text sentences.

Inconsistency in transcription is one thing, but lack of attention to the audio recording leads Carter and McCarthy to mis-analyse a LIKE construction. The relevant chunk is in (46).

(46) A . . . you'd like to have a building where you could go yourselves, would you?
B Yeah . . . in the nights, like, when, it's cold.

The transcription of the utterance from Speaker B fails to show that *like* goes with *in the nights*, as is clear from the intonation. This indicates that, contra Carter and McCarthy (1997, p. 126), *like* is not equivalent to 'for example'. Rather, it is an instance of the utterance-final *like* that is associated with giving or asking for explanations (see Miller, 2009). Speaker B explains why they would like a building where they could go themselves; presumably, a leisure centre would not be open at the right hours or would not welcome teenagers who just wanted to sit and chat.

Miller and Weinert (2009) consider the sentence a low-level discourse unit and that idea is retained here. They appeal to the fact that what counts as a well-formed and well-organized sentence differs across languages and within a given language differs from one period to another over its history. These arguments are still valid. An additional argument is that for stylistic reasons, authors can produce very untypical text sentences – untypical with respect to the injunctions in grammars and style manuals. These stylistic manipulations suggest discourse arrangements rather than clause syntax.

Dickens opens *Bleak House* with the paragraph in (47) containing text sentences with no finite verbs at all. Two of the text sentences consist of NPs,

London and *Implacable November weather*. The one clause with a finite verb is a subordinate clause, *as if the waters had but newly retired from the face of the earth.*

(47) London. Michaelmas Term lately over, and the Lord Chancellor sitting in Lincoln's Inn Hall. Implacable November weather. As much mud on the streets, as if the waters had but newly retired from the face of the earth . . . Smoke lowering down from chimney-pots . . . Foot passengers, jostling one another's umbrellas, in a general infection of ill-temper. Fog everywhere. Fog up the river . . . Fog down the river.

Lee Child opens his novel *One Shot* with two paragraphs in which sentences consist of NPs, prepositional phrases, participial phrases and subordinate clauses, with the odd main clause. Consider (48).

(48) Friday. Five o'clock in the afternoon. Maybe the hardest time to move unobserved through a city.' Or, maybe the easiest. Because at five o'clock on a Friday afternoon nobody pays attention to anything. Except the road ahead.

The man with the rifle drove north. Not fast, not slow. Not drawing attention. Not standing out. He was in a light-coloured minivan that had seen better days. He was alone behind the wheel . . .

The text has text sentences consisting of NPs, *Friday*, *Five o'clock in the afternoon*, and *Maybe the hardest time to move unobserved through a city*. Other text sentences consist of adverbs, *Not fast, not slow*; participial phrases, *Not standing out*; and a prepositional phrase, *Except the road ahead.* Both Dickens and Child use the non-clausal text sentences to build up a background description detail by static detail. A finite main clause turns up only when actions begin to unfold: *The man with the rifle drove north.*

Tricky structures in spontaneous spoken English

Which: relative pronoun or discourse connective?

Even with close observation of rhythm and intonation the assignment of syntactic structures to particular utterances can be very difficult. The syntax of spontaneous speech, whether English, German, Russian, Japanese and so on, is not well understood. Consider the following example from Burchfield

(1996, p. 50). The example comes in an entry on anacoluthon, defined as 'a change or break in the grammatical construction of a sentence or phrase, e.g. a recapitulatory pronoun in casual speech . . .' The example is in (49).

(49) put little bits of bacon on which the fatter they are the better
The Victorian Kitchen, BBC2, 1989 (cook speaking)

The recapitulatory pronoun is presumably *they*, and the version without an anacoluthon would have been *put little bits of bacon on which the fatter the better*, although JM is distinctly uncomfortable with the construction. But the important point is that Burchfield sees *which* as beginning a relative clause, which is abandoned in favour of a main clause *the fatter they are the better*. An alternative analysis is that *which* in (49) is not a relative pronoun but a discourse connective and that (49) is not an example of anacoluthon at all, since there is no change in construction.

What evidence is there for this analysis? We begin with the observation that in spontaneous speech most relative clauses are introduced by *that* or by zero, that is, are contact clauses. (For numbers, see Miller and Weinert, 2009, p. 105, and Biber et al., 1999, pp. 610–615.) The relativizer *that* is not a pronoun but a conjunction. It is invariable (cf. the contrasts of form in the wh pronoun – *who* vs *whom*, *who* vs *which*, *whose*) and prepositions must be at the end of the clause: *the book in which I found the quote* versus *the book that I found the quote in* versus the incorrect **the book in that I found the quote*. Historically *that* was indeed a pronoun, but has been grammaticalized as a conjunction (and of course still functions as a demonstrative pronoun). *Which* likewise was originally a pronoun and still functions as a pronoun (see the discussion of wh pronouns as indefinite deictics on pp. 175–190). It has also followed *that* along the same route to the status of conjunction.

Burchfield (1996, p. 844) has an example of the construction in the entry for *which*, sub-entry 3. The sub-entry deals with *which* referring to propositions or states of affairs but at the end Burchfield comments 'These examples are perilously close to the type (18–19c) condemned by the OED as 'in vulgar use, as a mere connective or introductory particle.' He gives an example from an issue of the *Daily Chronicle* in 1905: *If anything 'appens to you – which God be between you and 'arm – I'll look after the kids.* Whether the construction was just in vulgar use or in general use in spontaneous speech among all classes of speakers, it is now widespread.

(50) and (51) are from Dickens (1853/1996). The speaker is Mr Snagsby, not a lawyer himself but an educated person who makes a living as a law-stationer,

arranging for legal documents to be copied and inspecting the copies to make sure they are correct and up to the expected standard.

(50) 'About a year and a half ago', says Mr Snagsby strengthened, 'he came into our place one morning after breakfast, and, finding my little woman (**which I name Mrs Snagsby** when I use that appellation) in our shop, produced a specimen of his handwriting and gave her to understand that he was in wants of copying work to do . . .'

Dickens, 1853/1996, p. 170

(51) 'I was only going to say, it's a curious fact, sir, that . . . that you should come and live here, and be one of my writers, too. **Which there is nothing derogatory**, but far from it in the appellation,' says Mr Snagsby . . . '

Dickens, 1853/1996, p. 508

An example from contemporary Scottish English is in (52).

(52) k13 this was what i wondered if it was basically these families that were still in the dumbiedykes

s13 no well actually there're one or two that went back in [= returned JM] **which so happens that i'm a member of the kirk** [= church] **just locally here** the kirk o'field church which is the parish of dumbiedykes area (uh huh)

Miller–Brown conversations, conversation 1
[recorded by Karen Currie for Brown et al. (1980)]

Burchfield relates the discourse connective construction to structures where *which* refers to propositions or states of affairs, but there is another construction that is even closer. It is frequently used in spontaneous spoken English among all types of speakers and is exemplified in (53), uttered by a senior accountant at the University of Edinburgh.

(53) You have a little keypad down here **which** you can use your mouse to click on the keys.

Presentation on Financial Information Systems,
Old College, University of Edinburgh, 1 May 1996

(53) is an example of an unintegrated relative clause, that is, a relative clause that has no wh word referring back to the antecedent of the clause and no gap that might have been filled by a wh word or *that*. *You can use your mouse to click on the keys* is a complete clause with subject NP *you* and direct object NP *your mouse*. An example with *that* is *a filing cabinet that you can only open one drawer at a time* (uttered by JM's wife). An integrated version would

be something like *a filing cabinet that only allows you to open one drawer at a time* or *a filing cabinet only one of whose drawers you can open at a time.* (The latter version is quite untypical of spontaneous speech, but would be in place in a very formal written text.) An example from New Zealand English is in (54).

(54) even if we have any meetings over here it's still just as long as those **that we go somewhere else**

Wellington Corpus of Spoken New Zealand English, DPC004:0385:IB

That links the clause to *those*, but the clause has a subject NP *we* and a directional phrase *somewhere else.* An integrated version would read along the lines of . . . *just as long as those for which/in connection with which we go somewhere else* or *those that we attend elsewhere.* The crucial example is (53), with *which.* Miller and Weinert (2009, pp. 110–11) treated it as a relative pronoun introducing an unintegrated relative clause, but it might be better treated as a discourse connective linking a following complete clause to the preceding chunk of discourse.

NP-Clause: one clause or one clause + extraneous NP?

The sequence of words in (55), typical of spoken English (and spoken French, Russian and German), has been given various analyses. We will call it the NP-Clause construction, the label reflecting the view that the initial NP is not part of the clause. New data has shed light on its textual function, and the construction bears on a moot point in typology. Because the clause is complete in its syntax, displaying no gaps, our analysis assumes that the initial NP is outside the clause and, in spite of the regularly-used label 'left dislocation', is not moved from a position inside the clause. This analysis is supported by recent detailed work on the French NP-Clause construction (de Cat 2007), which demonstrates that were the NP to be moved, it would violate various syntactic properties that otherwise block movement.

Miller and Weinert (2009, pp. 237–9 – but see also the discussion of French and Russian on pp. 239–42) analyse the NP-Clause construction as primarily a focus structure highlighting the NP and its referent. More data, presented in (55)–(58), indicate that speakers use the construction for contrasting one NP/entity with another. (Note that (55b,c)–(58) are from newspaper articles, but are transcribed directly from the audio recordings made by the journalists.) Quirk and Greenbaum (1985, pp. 1416–17) saw the construction as typical of loose and informal speech. In an utterance such as *This man I was telling you about – he used to live next door to me*, the initial NP, *This man I was telling you about*, was analysed as setting the 'point of departure' for the utterance. It was convenient for speaker and hearer, since neither had to process a clause containing a complex NP subject.

It is true that in spontaneous speech complex NP subjects are avoided and that complex NPs are more acceptable in object position. However, many left-dislocated NPs are simple, and many have a contrastive function, as in (55a–c).

(55) a. **this film** it does give a real close-up of what goes on behind the scenes.
Tom Brook, Talking Movies, BBC World, 19 April 2007

b. 'I like his [Keith Floyd's] style of cookery,' adds Fenton's wife Patricia. 'He just throws everything in. **Rick Stein – he's only copying Floyd, isn't he?**'
The Independent, 11 October 2007, Extra, pp. 2–3

c. '**My youngest daughter** gets embarrassed when she sees me on television,' says Stewart. '**My eldest**, she doesn't mind so much because it gives her extra street-cred at school.'
Dr Iain Stewart being interviewed by Susan Swarbrick – 'Preparing to rock your world', The Herald [Scotland], 13 November 2007, p. 17

But the construction can simultaneously ease the production of complex utterances and signal a contrast, as in (56)–(58).

(56) 'What struck me was that **people who behaved the way my ex and I did**, their children were fine, but **those who made more mistakes**, their children suffered more. That cause and effect was quite clear.'
'Divorce doesn't have to be a disaster,' *The Herald*, 3 December 2007, p. 15

(57) Contrasting the fortunes of different sub-sectors, he said: 'Electronics is performing particularly well. **The areas of industry that were being hit quite hard** – the one that stood out was the food industry.'
The Herald, 27 October 2007

(58) 'You know, it's an amazing building. **The one that was never built,** that would have been even more amazing. It was going to be over 550 feet in height, an unbelievable sight.'
Sir Terry Leahy, Interview in *The Tablet* by Chris Blackhurst, 22–29 December 2007

Three important points arise. The construction is not new; the following example is from Dickens: '***Your cousin, Mr Jarndyce. I owe so much to him.*** *Would you mind describing him to me*?' (Dickens, *Bleak House*, Penguin, 1996, Chapter 4). (The speaker is not addressing Mr Jarndyce. *Mr Jarndyce* is in apposition to *Your cousin.*) It appears to have become much more frequent in spoken English over the past 30 years. The construction is not just a means for dealing with hitches in syntactic planning. Examples (55b,c), (56) and (58) demonstrate that it is used for contrast: Rick Stein, in contrast with Keith Floyd, the eldest daughter in contrast with the youngest, the one that was never built in contrast with the one that was. Finally, with respect to typology, the NP-Clause construction brings into question the proposed typological difference between subject-prominent and topic-prominent languages and raises interesting issues concerning the typology of spontaneous spoken English and the typology of formal written English. (See Miller and Weinert, 2009, pp. 363–6)

Direct Object NP + Complement Clause

Another sequence of words whose constituent structure is a mystery is what will be called the NP-Complement Clause construction. It occurs regularly in spontaneous speech – see (59) from Scottish English, (60) from New Zealand English, and (61) from a novel by an American writer.

(59) Everyone knows Helen Liddell how hard she works.
Discussion programme on BBC Radio Scotland

(60) i can never **remember any of my family how old they are**.
New Zealand ICE, Macquarie Corpus

(61) everyone turned to [Stoichev] with a smile . . . I **remembered Rossi, how he'd listened so modestly** to the cheers and speeches
Elizabeth Kostova, 2005, *The Historian*

From a logical point of view (59) conveys the proposition that everyone knows something, namely how hard Helen Liddell works. The speaker who uttered (59) can be seen as achieving two goals. He – the speaker was male – avoids a subordinate clause with an exclamative construction – wh word + subject NP + verb – and a relatively complex subject NP. The construction also enables the speaker to re-establish Helen Liddell as the focus of attention and the principal actor in the situations being discussed. Having done that with the main clause, the speaker then moves on to the complement clause and highlights the new property, her capacity for work.

The reasons for speakers using the direct object NP–Complement Clause sequence are easy to see; less easy to see is the constituent structure. The NP is the direct object of the main verb. Is the clause, which complements the same verb, simply part of one and the same VP? What is the syntactic significance of the comma between the NP and the clause in the written example in (61)? The simplest solution would be to treat the sequence as a double-object construction.

WH clefts and the 'thing-is' construction

Finally, we look at WH clefts. The classic WH cleft from written English is exemplified in (62); (63)–(65) exemplify WH clefts from spontaneous speech.

(62) a. What you need most is a good rest.
b. What he's done is spoil the whole thing.

The classic WH cleft is introduced by a wh clause, the cleft clause – *What you need most* and *What he's done*. The last chunk in the structure is the cleft constituent, which is either a phrase, such as *a good rest* in (a), or a non-finite clause, such as *spoil the whole thing* in (b). The two chunks are connected by some form of the copula, *is* or *was* or *will be*. The chunk of particular interest here is the non-finite clause, which has no subject NP and only a bare verb stem, *spoil*. The lack of subject NP, tense and aspect signals a clause that is well integrated into the matrix main clause. Treating *what* as an indefinite deictic (see the detailed discussion on pp. 175–190), we can consider *what* as a noun modified by a relative clause *you need* [ ] or *he's done* [ ], where the gap contains an empty direct object NP co-indexed with *what*. It points forward to the cleft constituent specifying the referent of *what* – *a good rest* in (62a) and *spoil the whole thing* in (62b).

(62b) is of particular interest here because what regularly occurs in spontaneous spoken English is a WH cleft containing a cleft clause and a cleft constituent but in which the cleft constituent is a full clause with subject NP, tense and aspect and in which the cleft clause and the cleft constituent are typically not linked by *be* but simply juxtaposed. Examples from British English are in (63) and (64), and (65) is an example from New Zealand English.

(63) A What you do
B right

A you drop down then you go right

Map Task Dialogues

(64) And what you're doing now is you're going along to the right

Map Task Dialogues

(65) but i used to — like — what we'd do when I was a kid in the sounds we used to sometimes catch fish catch blue cod and th just head for the beach and light a fire on the beach

WSC, DPC079:0705:AC

Note the copula *is* in (64) – [*what you're going to do now*] + *is* + [*you're going to go along to the right*]. Note the absence of the copula in (63) and (65): [*what you do*] + [*you drop down*] and [*what we'd do . . .*] + [*we used to . . .*]. The constituent structure of each clause, whether finite or non-finite, is along the usual lines, whatever the analyst's usual lines are. How are the clauses combined? The cleft clause does not make a complete text on its own: *What you do, what you're doing now* and *what we'd do when I was a kid in the sounds* all require some continuation for the listener to construct a satisfactory interpretation. *What* is an indefinite deictic and its referent has to be specified for the listener. The analysis proposed here is that the two clauses are part of a larger construction, which can be labelled 'WH cleft 1'. ('WH cleft 2' might be the label for the classic WH cleft of written English exemplified in (62)). In fact, we need two labels for two constructions: 'WH cleft 1a' for the construction in which the cleft clause and the cleft constituent are linked by *be* and 'WH cleft 1b' for the construction in which they are simply juxtaposed. (This last comment anticipates the discussion in Chapter 4 of when different sequences of words are to be reckoned alternative realizations of one and the same general construction or realizations of two different constructions.)

In the earlier examples, there is continuity of subject referent, tense and aspect from the cleft clause to the cleft constituent, and this might suggest that examples such as (65) be analysed as having a copula which is empty. We take the view that, although it seems to be minor, the lack of a copula is a symptom of a significant difference. Consider (66) from British English and (67) from New Zealand English

(66) **What I thought I'd do** Chairman as you know, the most important issue at the moment is the poll-tax.

Member of Parliament addressing a meeting in Edinburgh

(67) yes i'm astonished and would very much have liked to ask him to question him more closely but **what we ARE going to do** he HAS spoken to one of our journalists and we're going to repla replay that for you in its entirety so that you can hear what he said but it does leave a lot of things unanswered

WSC, DGB005:0060:HS

What I thought I'd do and *what we ARE going to do* are not only unconnected by a copula to the following clause, but there is a break in the subject referent and in tense and aspect. In (66), the subject NP *I* is replaced by *the most important issue* and the past tense of *thought* is replaced by the present tense of *is*. In (67), the subject NP *we* is replaced by *he*, although *we* returns in the next again clause. In these examples, *What I thought I'd do* and *what we ARE going to do* function as complex, highlighting discourse particles and do not seem to be part of a WH cleft clause complex. *What* is still an indefinite deictic, but points forward to the entire following chunk of text, not necessarily to a single clause.

A trickier construction has appeared in spontaneous spoken English. Examples from New Zealand English are in (68) and (69), but the construction occurs regularly in British and American English.

(68) DN i cleaned out the cupboards with the mice pooh in them
AL you're nesting
DN oh yes very much so julia told me and since then i've been doing it
CH laughs
BT laughs
AL what nesting
DN **this is what you're meant to do is nest**

Wellington Corpus of Spoken New Zealand English, DPC066:1175–1210

(69) i mean kids ARE really cruel and roz **that's the reason roz had such ha had such a thing about HER ear was because she'd had such a hard time**

WSC, DPC062:0380:AL

The structure begins with a TH cleft: *that's the reason roz had such ha had such a thing about HER ear* and *this is what you're meant to do*. The TH cleft is linked by a second occurrence of *is* to a finite or non-finite clause – *nest* in (68) and *because she'd had such a hard time* in (69). Calude (2008, p. 113), citing Ross-Hagebaum (2004), regards the construction as an amalgam of the TH cleft and WH cleft structures, with an internal arrangement of constituents as in Figure 1.1. (Calude uses the term 'Demonstrative Cleft', but we keep the term 'TH Cleft'.)

Cleft Complex				
TH Cleft			Basic WH-Cleft	
Cleft constit	COP	Cleft Clause/Cleft constit	COP	Cleft constit
That	's	what you're meant to do	is	nest

Figure 1.1 Possible constituent structure for (68)

The amalgam hypothesis is compatible with a central characteristic of spontaneous spoken language noted by a number of analysts. Calude (2008) cites Brazil (1995), who commented that the constituents of spoken language are like beads on a string, and McCarthy (1998), who emphasized the linear nature of spoken language as opposed to the hierarchical organization of written language. Brazil's and McCarthy's ideas accord well with the views of Sornicola, Linell, Blanche-Benveniste, Zemskaja, and Miller and Weinert referred to earlier.

The general point is that the linear and disjointed organization of spontaneous spoken language (but beware of exaggerating the disjointedness) facilitates the formation of amalgams. The double clefts are not, however, performance phenomena. Like all changes in grammar, the double cleft construction has arisen during performance, but is now a regularly occurring construction in many varieties of English and recorded in the utterances of many speakers. Massam (1999, p. 336) reports that McConvell (1988) had found instances in essays by students and that Ellen Prince had found examples in electronic newsgroups.

Massam (1999) does not discuss TH clefts, but focuses on examples of the sort in (70a–e), which are taken from her paper. She labels the structure the 'thing-is' construction.

(70) a. The problem is, is that we can't find the evidence
b. My feeling was, was that she doesn't have a professional hold on the situation
c. The hitch is, is that it seems to be occurring in the opposite direction
d. The only thing is, is that I couldn't move down here because I don't drive.
e. The fact of the matter is, is that the policy is totally unclear.

Massam argues that the 'thing-is' construction shares with WH clefts (she uses the term 'pseudo-cleft') the important property of connectivity: although the constructions consist of two clauses, they behave in certain respects like a single clause. (See Massam, 1999, pp. 340–6.) The argument can be strengthened. Massam thinks that the 'thing-is' construction can occur without a linking *be* – *The thing is we got to have lunch together*, but that WH clefts must have a linking *be*. Examples (63) and (65) show that Massam was considering the wrong type of WH cleft: *What he saw was an apple* as opposed to *What he did was eat the apple* or *What he did was he ate the apple*. The latter type of WH cleft does not in fact need a linking *be*. (This part of Massam's paper relates to the point made earlier about correct theory depending on correct data. Massam declares that in *The thing is, is he can't be dismissed* [JM's example] the second *is* can be omitted – *The thing is he can't be dismissed* – because it is a focus marker rather than a verb. In *what he likes is marzipan*, the *is* is a verb and cannot be omitted. But of course it can be omitted in *what he does is he refuses to answer the phone*. Some other explanation must be sought.)

The rest of Massam's analysis need not concern us in detail. Briefly, working within a Principles and Parameters framework, she proposes a derivation involving an empty category and paralleling the derivation of WH clefts. The most basic structure is [[*the thing is* ec_i] *is* [*that I like you*]]. From this is derived [[that I like you $]_I$ [the thing is] is t_I]. This then yields the structure [t_i the thing is that I like you] is t_i. The *is* linking the two chunks inside square brackets is described as a focus/copular head and the nouns occurring inside the chunk [the ___ thing is] are said to belong to a small set of appositional nouns, such as *problem, thing, claim, feeling* and *hunch*. The second chunk in square brackets, *that I like you*, provides the content of the referent of the appositional noun. The appositional relation is supposed to explain why only *is* can link the two chunks; only *is* can signal an apposition.

Massam's account shows that there is a way to handle the 'thing-is' construction in the Principles and Parameters model, but does not address the question of how the construction arose, whereas the amalgam analysis provides both a reason and an appealing surface structure for the double 'is'. (Of course, what counts as appealing depends on an individual's theoretical preferences.) There is another way of looking at the data. As Massam points out, a limited set of nouns occur in the 'thing-is' construction: *problem, thing, claim, feeling* and *hunch*, to which can be added *fact* and, from Massam's examples, the phrase *fact of the matter*. From the perspective of constructions and formulae, the limited set of nouns suggests a template allowing limited modifications rather than a freely generated construction.

The construction shows signs of being grammaticalized, probably into a discourse particle, but the end-state is not yet in sight. The process can be glimpsed in examples such as (71), where *the thing is* has been reduced to *thing is*.

(71) B 117: yeah i mean he does tend to drop things an awful lot in fact
I 115: yeah he seems to take his eye
B 118: thing is he's watching the man he's not watching the ball
Miller–Brown Corpus, conversation 60.
The game being discussed is rugby.

Other reduced phrases that the author has heard are *fact is* and *problem is*, but not in recorded speech.

We return to (66), *What I thought I'd do Chairman as you know, the most important issue at the moment is the poll-tax.* As noted earlier, the wh clause is independent of what follows with respect to subject NP, tense and a cohesive link for *do*. Consider now (72). A produces the wh clause *what you're going to do* and the copula *is* and then pauses. After the short pause A specifies the content of *what you're going to do*. Massam treats such examples as single sentences, but from the perspective of clause complexes the wh clauses in (63) and (66) are quite separate clauses, which may, as in (66), be separated from the following clause by a shorter or longer pause. (Regina Weinert reported that the introductory *what I thought I'd do* was followed by a long pause.) In the following examples (from Miller and Weinert, 2009, pp. 292–3), the wh clauses look even more independent because of a change in mood from declarative to imperative.

(72) Eh, what you're going to do is go in between the camera shop and the lefthand side of the page, right.

(73) Okay. Now what we have to do is sort of v- veer to the left just a wee bit, . . .

(74) what we need to do is turn turn right . . . straight right . . .
Map Task dialogues

The difficulty with (72) is that the rhythm and pitch pattern is compatible with *go in between the camera shop and the lefthand side of the page* being an imperative main clause. The sequence *what you're going to do is* is spoken with a fastish tempo. There is no drop in pitch and amplitude on *is* (contrary to what happens in other examples), but between *is* and *go* there is a short pause, and the vowel of *go* is held so that it is realized as a double vowel with an increase in amplitude.

In (73), the sequence *what we have to do is sort of* is separated by a medium pause from *v- veer to the left*. In (74), the sequence *what we need to do is* is spoken with a fast tempo, whereas the following sequence *turn turn right* is spoken on a slow tempo. That is, in both (73) and (74), the pausing and the tempo also suggest an imperative clause analysis for the sequence following the headless relative.

Massam (1999, p. 344) presents two examples of the 'thing-is' construction with different patterns of pausing and intonation.

(75) The problem is, we can't find the evidence.

(76) The point is that she doesn't want to run for mayor any more.

In (75), there is a high/falling/rising intonation (M's description) on *is* followed by a pause. In (76), there is no varying intonation (M's description) and merely a slight pause after *point*. Massam assigns the two examples the same structure and proposes, on the basis of the pausing, that, given the basic sequences *the problem is is* and *the point is is*, the second *is* is missing in (75) and the first *is* is missing in (76). The difficulty here is that pauses are not a reliable guide to syntactic structure. As Crystal (1987, p. 94) pointed out long ago, pauses are not even a guide to the beginning and end of putative sentences. Brown et al. (1980) proposed three types of pause in their data: long pauses of between 1 and 1.8 seconds, which were associated with the end of topic phrases, a set of medium pauses, which they (1980, p. 68) identified as contour pauses, and a third set of very brief pauses, which seemed to be associated with lexical and syntactic searches. The difference between (75) and (76) might well be that (75) consists of a separate 'topic' clause plus second clause, constituting separate units of syntax and not part of a single sentence. (Of course, if, as argued earlier, the sentence is rejected as a unit of analysis for spontaneous spoken language, then a sentential analysis for (75) is not available.) (76) appears to consist of two clauses that are well-integrated into a clause complex.

Many of the WH clefts in the Map Task dialogues are organized into two bits by pitch and rhythm. The wh clauses were pronounced rapidly and on a low pitch, with the following clauses pronounced on a higher pitch (presumably each speaker's normal pitch). Some of the wh clauses were separated by a pause from the following clause; we assume for the moment that these wh clauses function as topic clauses, carrying given information (at least in the Map Task dialogues).

We conclude this part of the discussion with an example of the 'thing-is' construction, showing another well-integrated clause complex but with an adjective modifying *thing*.

(77) and i looked it up in the scottish national dictionary and it gave the — I cannae mind [= can't remember] how it gave it now — but **the strange thing is** that now it's more prevalent in the borders [area of Scotland next to the border with England, JM] than anywhere else

Miller–Brown Corpus, conversation 33

The 'thing-is' construction can be extended even where it constitutes a topic clause, as in (78).

(78) **the only thing is with Beth** — Beth'll not spend money she's mingy she's really mean she wouldn't give you two halfs for a one

Miller–Brown Corpus, Conversation 12

Finally, the 'thing-is' chunk can be part of a TH cleft, as in (79), which extends the parallelism between the 'thing-is' and WH clefts argued for by Massam.

(79) **that's the bad thing about the halls of residence** — there's always people knocking on your door

Miller–Brown Corpus, conversation 58

Conclusion: integrated and unintegrated structures

The above discussion deals with only a small number of constructions, but brings out various problems. One is the difficulty of deciding what is a regular construction as opposed to a performance error and then which regular constructions are standard or non-standard and even which are spoken-only and which also occur in writing. Another problem is how difficult it can be to resist imposing constructions of written language on transcriptions of spontaneous speech. It is only too tempting to collect phrases and clauses into a single sentence, and indeed such a move may be made unavoidable by models such as Principles and Parameters or Minimalism or perhaps any formal model of syntax. We all like to draw a clean boundary between syntax and discourse for the purpose of exposition in textbooks. In spontaneous speech, the boundary is very fluid, and many sequences of constituents probably require amalgams of discourse models and models of clause syntax.

Dependency Relations 2

Chapter Outline

What is a head?

Heads and modifiers

Our discussion of syntax begins with two central ideas. The first is that words are grouped into **phrases**; the second is that in each phrase one word, the **head**, controls the other words, the **modifiers**. A given head may have more than one modifier or may not have any modifier. In *the large dog*, the word *dog* is the head and *the* and *large* are its modifiers. In *barked loudly*, the word *barked* is the head and *loudly* the modifier. (Criteria for recognizing heads and modifiers will be given below.) Another idea, which is central for many syntax people but not for many others, is that a given clause has a verb as its head. In the written varieties of many languages, such as English, French, Russian, etc., heads and their modifiers occur next to each other, in phrases. The arrangement of words into phrases, of phrases into clauses, and of clauses into sentences is the subject matter of constituent structure analysis. 'Constituent' is a convenient label for the smaller bits that combine to build up a larger unit, whether phrase, clause or sentence. On pp. 53–57, we briefly discuss the analysis of constituent structure; all introductions to syntax cover the topic.

In Chapter 3, however, this being a critical introduction, we will discuss a major problem of constituent structure arising from the phenomenon of split NPs.

A phrase then is a group of interrelated words and every phrase represents some type of construction. (See the discussion of constructions in Chapter 4.) The head word in a phrase is the head of a construction. As we will see in Chapter 3, groups of interrelated words can be moved around inside **clauses** as a single unit; here, we concentrate on the fact that in such groups various links can be recognized among the words, between heads and their modifiers. This relationship of **modification** is fundamental in syntax. It will play an important role in the account of different types of clause and is crucial to discussions of word order in different languages.

Although the concept of head is widely used in syntax, both in 'descriptive' frameworks and in 'explanatory' formal models, analysts have tended to take it for granted. The criteria for heads were discussed extensively in the 1980s, with the exchange between Zwicky (1985) and Hudson (1987), the work by Abney advocating determiners as the heads of NPs (Abney, 1987) and the extended discussion by the contributors to Corbett et al. (1993). Matthews' (1981) generally recognized criteria are listed in Hudson (1990, pp. 106–7).

Complements and adjuncts

The basic criteria for recognizing the head of a syntactic construction are that the head is obligatory and controls certain other possible constituents (words) called modifiers. The modifiers are said to modify or depend on the head, and a distinction is drawn between modifiers that are controlled in some way by the head and those that are not controlled. The former are complements, the latter adjuncts. These concepts apply most clearly to main verbs in clauses, which control the number and type of constituents in the clause. Some main verbs require only a subject NP as in (1a); others also require a direct object NP as in (1b); a third set requires a subject NP, a direct object NP and a directional PP as in (1c) and a fourth set requires a subject NP and a directional NP as in (1d).

(1) a. The Cheshire Cat faded.
b. The dog chased some pheasants.
c. The lawyer put the deeds into his safe.
d. The boys dived into the pool.

Matthews (1981, pp. 121–45) makes the important point that control by a verb over a particular type of constituent manifests itself in two ways, requiring and excluding. The verb may require a constituent of a given type; for example, *put* must be accompanied by a directional phrase and *put the deeds* is not acceptable. In contrast, *dive* does not actually require a directional complement: *Do you know how to dive?* and *The boys spent ten minutes diving and splashing then went home.* The essential fact is not so much that *dive* typically requires a directional PP but in a few cases does not, as that *dive* permits directional PPs but many verbs exclude them: *discuss, exclude, play* (with the possible exception of the idioms *play into somebody's hands, play to the gallery*), *sit* (= *be sitting*), *lie* (= *be lying*), *stand* (= *be standing*) and so on.

Directional PPs are complements. Locational PPs and temporal PPs are adjuncts. They are optional modifiers and are not required or excluded by any verbs. (There are exceptions. *Be* requires some kind of complement, which can be a locational PP – *They were in France*, or a temporal PP – *The concert is on Friday. Stand, sit* and *lie* may require locational PPs – *The longcase clock stands in the dining room*, but not **The longcase clock stands*; *The castle sits on the ridge*, but not **The castle sits*; *The town lies in a sheltered valley*, but not **The town lies.*)

In many languages the verb determines the shape of its modifying nouns. In Russian, the verb *tolknul* 'pushed' requires an accusative case suffix on its direct object noun, while the verb *pomog* 'helped' requires a dative suffix, as in (2).

(2) a. Petr tolknul Ivana.
Petr push Ivan-acc 'Petr pushed Ivan.'
b. Petr pomog Ivanu.
Petr helped Ivan-dat 'Petr helped Ivan.'

In traditional terms, the verb is said to govern the noun in a particular case: *pomog* governs its object noun in the dative case. The governing constituent/word is the head of a given structure. The verb is also the morphosyntactic locus of a clause; that is, it carries the marking that indicates the relationship between a given clause and another clause, or in the case of phrases, between a given phrase and another phrase or a clause. In many languages, the verb takes one or another set of affixes depending on whether it is head of a main or a subordinate clause. For instance, in French, *est* 'is' is the form that typically occurs in main clauses, whereas *soit* 'is', the subjunctive form, occurs in certain types of complement clause and adverbial clause.

Number: agreement or government?

Two other properties of heads are that they control agreement and act as arguments for functors. Zwicky (1985) concluded that in the basic declarative clause construction of English, NP + VP, the NP controls agreement and adopted the traditional view of agreement between subject noun and verb, that is, the verb agrees with the noun. There are two issues here: what is the difference between agreement and government, and why regard the verb as agreeing with the noun? Lyons (1968, pp. 241–2) points out that the traditional distinction between agreement and government relates to the surface marking of constituents. In instances of government, the governing constituent does not change its shape, but the governed one does; in the classic Indo-European languages, verbs and prepositions impose particular case affixes on nouns, but are not themselves marked for case. But in both government and agreement there is a governing category. In the NP construction, the N assigns various features to modifying adjectives. In the Russian *širokaja reka* 'broad river', the noun *reka* is feminine, singular and in the nominative case. The traditional view is that the noun assigns these features to the adjective, which acquires the correct suffix. Compare *širokoe pole* 'broad field', in which *pole* is neuter, singular and in the nominative case, and *širokie reki,* in which *reki* is plural, feminine and in the nominative case. In the PP construction, the P is the head: in the Russian *za rekoj* 'beyond (the) river' *za* assigns instrumental case to *rekoj*, while in *iz reki* 'out-of (the) river' *iz* assigns genitive case.

What is the head of the NP + VP construction? Is it the N of the NP or the V of the VP that governs? Lyons (1968, pp. 241–2) states 'it would be incorrect to maintain (as some linguists have maintained) that the person and number of the subject is determined by the person and number of the verb.' His reason is that number and person are nominal categories, which may or may not be marked in the verb or verb phrase. In semantic terms, number and person are properties of entities, and prototypical entities are denoted by nouns, prototypical entities being concrete objects such as chairs, dogs, spoons, prams, shoes, cots, milk, juice, bread and the other entities that small children encounter in the first phase of their lives. Many such concrete entities are countable and may occur singly or plurally.

It is also true that human entities such as speaker, addressee and someone other than speaker and addressee are referred to by pronouns and nouns, but also by personal affixes on verbs, and in the spontaneous spoken varieties of many languages verbs are used without pronouns. (But rigorous research on the frequency of occurrence of verbs alone vs verbs plus pronoun subjects is still to be done.) A more important point is that the status of certain properties as inherent in nouns, or rather in the denotata of nouns, has to do with semantics. Person and number can be recognized as properties of entities in the semantic component of a model or description, and this attribution is not changed by making the verb in a clause assign person and number to its subject noun. In English, in fact, past-tense verbs and present-tense verbs, apart from third-person singular, allow any person or number, though the verb may require a subject noun with a particular type of denotatum; for example, FLOW can be regarded as requiring a subject noun denoting a liquid (in non-metaphorical usage).

A final and strong piece of evidence for the core position of verbs in clauses comes from languages in which a clause can consist of a single verb. Examples are given in (3)–(5).

(3) **Latin**

a. pugnatur.
is-fought 'There is fighting.'

b. tonuit.
thundered 'There was thunder.'

(4) **Turkish**

konuş	ul	maz.	[one word]
spoken	Passive	Negative	'It is not spoken.', that is 'No speaking'

(5) **Luganda** (Africa - Bantu language)

a	li	gi	goba.	[one word]
she	future	it	chase	'She will chase it.' (a chicken)

The Latin clause in (3) consists of the verb *pugnatur*. This verb is passive; while it might be thought that a subject NP has been ellipted, it is difficult to know what that NP might be. The same applies to the Turkish passive verb in (4). The Luganda verb in (5) is active. No independent NPs are needed because in context the person doing the chasing and the bird being chased are obvious to the hearer.

Croft on the concept of head

The concept of head, and in particular the status of the verb as head of verb phrase or clause, has been challenged by Croft (2001, pp. 246–9). Taking up the well-known property of verbs that any given verb may take one or more subcategorization frames, Croft (2001, p. 248) argues that it is difficult to maintain the mathematical function relationship between a verb and its subcategorization frame unless, for example, a verb such as *give* is treated as two distinct lexical items, one with the frame NP NP, *give the dog a bone*, and the other with the frame NP PP, *give a bone to the dog*. Croft proposes that there is no directionality between verb and its complements but a many-to-many mapping. How telling is Croft's objection? One response would be to organize lexical entries in terms of a single argument structure (where appropriate) with several associated subcategorization frames. The one–one mapping would then be between a given subcategorization frame and a given syntactic structure. For instance, GIVE has the conceptual structure [Cause [X move from Y to Z]]. Y is the Source and previous owner and Z is the Goal and new owner. (See the discussion of thematic roles in Chapter 10.) The associated subcategorization frames are NP PP and NP NP. The sorts of linking mechanisms that are required have been discussed by, for example, Goldberg (1995) and Levin and Rappaport-Hovav (2005).

This organization of the lexicon fits the facts of agreement and government, especially with respect to case marking – in Russian, for instance, the corresponding phrase is *dal sobake kost'* '(he/she) gave dog-dative bone', in which the verb *dal* assigns dative case to *sobake* and accusative case to *kost'* and various word orders are possible depending on the context: *dal kost sobake*, *sobake dal kost'* and *kost' dal sobake*; it fits with the general semantic relationship between head and modifiers described below; it fits with the large body of work on argument structure, which is successful because classes of verbs can be established and provide a link between syntax and vocabulary, and it fits with the fact that in many languages the sole obligatory constituent of a declarative clause is the verb.

Croft presents various other arguments, three of which we look at here. Using the Locative Alternation as an example, he mentions that subcategorization frames affect the meaning of clauses. *Mary sprayed paint on the wall* leaves it open whether the wall is entirely or partially covered with paint; *Mary sprayed the wall with pain* denotes a situation in which the wall is entirely covered. What Croft does not say is that the key to the different interpretations is the direct object. Unless signalled otherwise, it is assumed that the action referred to by a verb completely affects the referent of its direct object NP. If *the wall* is the direct object, it refers to the entity completely affected by the spraying. Add *partially* and the meaning changes: *Mary partially sprayed the wall with paint.* It has never been suggested in the verb-dependency literature that verbs determine the entire interpretation of clauses and it is not clear exactly how the idea of verbs as clause heads is undermined by the contribution of subcategorization frames to the interpretation of clauses. (See the discussion of such examples in connection with participant/thematic roles in Chapter 10.)

The second argument rests on Russian data, which Croft interprets as demonstrating that NPs are equivalent to VPs in copula constructions. He says 'But an NP can also be the distributional equivalent of the VP, if the language uses NPs in predicate nominal constructions without the addition of copulas or verbal inflections, as in Russian' (Croft, 2001, p. 251). The parallel distribution noted by Croft is in the examples in (6), where *čitala knigu* is in the same slot as *student.* (In (6b), *student* has been changed [by JM] to *studentka*, the feminine form.)

(6) a. Ona čitala knigu.
She read a-book.
b. Ona studentka.
She is a student.

The data is more complex than appears from Croft's account. He says 'if the language uses NPs in predicate nominal constructions without the addition of copulas or verbal inflections' (Croft, 2001, p. 251). The facts of Russian are that the copula is missing only in present-tense clauses; non-present tense clauses *require* some past-tense form of the copula – *byl, byla, bylo, byli* – or some future-tense form – *budu, budet*, etc. Croft mistakenly translates *ona student* (his original example) as 'She was a student.' The translation should have been 'She is a student'; 'She was a student' is *Ona byla studentka* – better, *studentkoj* in the instrumental case, which denotes a temporary state. In definitions, or where there is emphasis, the invariable present-tense form *est'* is used. The upshot of all this is that it is only in present-tense clauses that there is an apparent parallel between NP and VP, which reduces the force of Croft's argument. A possible treatment of the data, the traditional one in fact, is to regard present-tense clauses as containing a copula, which is realized as zero.

The third argument is that there are exocentric constructions, that is, constructions with no heads. Croft's examples are in (7).

(7) a. [What really bothers me] are all of those square brackets.
b. I said [(that) I was going to do it].

Using Cognitive Grammar terminology, Croft (2001, p. 256) says that in (7a,b) no element profiles the same thing as the whole construction. For (7a), Bresnan and Grimshaw (1978) proposed an alternative analysis, which provides the structure with a head. They suggest the analysis in (8), which is used in the discussion of wh words as deictics in Chapter 8.

(8) What [Ø really bothers me] are all of those square brackets.

Given this structure, we can say that *what* is a deictic pronoun pointing to *all of those square brackets.* That is, the traditionally labelled 'headless relative' does have a head and from a verb-dependency standpoint the head of the main clause is *are.* If the copula denotes an equivalence, the entire main clause construction denotes, in Halliday's terms, an equative equivalence (as opposed to an identificational or locational one). That is, *are* can be regarded as profiling the same abstract 'thing' as the whole construction.

The complement clause *I was going to do it* has a complex structure, since it contains a non-finite clause. If *was going* is treated as the head, it profiles an event of going, and the whole clause fills in details of this event. The non-finite clause has *do* as its head. *Was going* and *do* are internal heads, inside the complement clause, whereas Croft is presumably talking about an external head that would profile the whole complement clause as a thing said. The generally accepted hypothesis is that the complementizer *that* was originally just such an external head, but in English and many other languages subordinate clauses lack external heads. This does not affect the analysis of all clauses as having internal heads and can be seen as a consequence of the peculiar nature of sentences as low-level discourse units. (See the discussion of clauses and sentences in Chapter 1.)

Heads and meaning

As will be argued in Chapters 7–10, there is a close link between grammar and semantics; indeed, what many analysts and users of grammars count as explanation is the provision of a semantic property for a particular set of case suffixes or for a particular aspect of the verb, and so on. It is a pity that in the proposed treatment of agreement the noun is not the governing constituent, but this does not require us to deny that person and number are properties of concrete entities that are denoted by nouns. And we get a treatment of syntactic relations within the clause in which the verb controls all the other constituents. We do get a pleasing semantic property: in all structures, whether clause, NP, PP or AP, we can consider the head as conveying a central piece of information and the modifiers as conveying extra information. Thus in the phrase *expensive books* the head word *books* indicates the very large set of things that count as books, while *expensive* indicates that the speaker is drawing attention not to the whole set but to the subset of books that are expensive. In the longer phrase *the expensive books*, the word *the* signals that the speaker is referring to a set of books which have already been mentioned or are otherwise obvious in a particular context.

The same narrowing down of meaning applies to clauses. Consider the examples *drove* and *drove a Volvo*. *Drove* indicates driving in general; *drove a Volvo* narrows down the activity to driving a particular make of car. Consider further the phrase *on the plate*. The first word *on* signals a relationship between some entity, say a piece of toast or a knife, and the surface of something; *the plate* tells us what that something is, that is, it narrows down the meaning 'being on' to 'being on a particular plate'. Modifiers that are adjuncts have the same effect. The clause *Juliet bought a book for Jennifer in Berwick last Tuesday* contains four modifiers of *bought* – *a book*, *for Jennifer*, *in Berwick* and *last Tuesday*. *A book* signals what was bought and narrows down the activity from just buying to buying a book, as opposed, say, to buying the weekly groceries. *For Jennifer* narrows the meaning further – not just 'buy a book' but 'buy a book for Jennifer,' and similarly for the phrases *in Berwick* and *last Tuesday*.

Heads of PP and NP

Nothing has been said so far about PPs and NPs, though they have been mentioned in passing. The head of a PP is a preposition. Prepositions link nouns to nouns (*books about antiques*), adjectives to nouns (*rich in minerals*) and verbs to nouns (*aimed at the target*). Most prepositions must be followed by a group of words containing a noun, or by a noun on its own, as in *(They sat) round the table*, *(Claude painted) with this paintbrush* and *(I've bought a present) for Freya*. That prepositions are heads and control what occurs in prepositional phrases is shown by the fact that in English a small number of prepositions allow another preposition between them and the noun: *In behind the woodpile (was a hedgehog)* and *(An owl swooped on the rabbit) from up in the beech tree*.

In allows *behind* and *from* allows *up*. Another aspect of this control is that in standard English prepositions can be followed by pronouns, but they exclude *I, he, she, we* and *they* and require *me, him, her, us* and *them*: **I've bought a present for she* and *I've bought a present for her*. In a number of Indo-European languages, prepositions govern nouns in a particular case. For example, in Russian, *v* 'in/into' assigns accusative or locative case depending on whether it denotes movement or location, *iz* 'out of' assigns the genitive case and *pod* 'under' assigns the instrumental case.

The head of a NP is the subject of some controversy. Until the mid-1980s, it was generally assumed that NPs are headed by nouns, although Lyons (1975/1991) had proposed deictics as the primary constituents of NPs and suggested, in almost throw-away remarks, that the heads of NPs were not nouns but determiners (Lyons, 1977b, pp. 391–2; 1981, pp. 222–3). Since the publication of Abney (1987) it has been taken for granted by most generative linguists that the heads of NPs are determiners, and NPs have been relabelled 'DP' (determiner phrase). One pleasing consequence of this re-analysis is that DPs and VPs have a parallel structure: determiners are seen as analogous to auxiliary verbs. The latter are taken to be the head of VPs when they occur because they carry person and number, and also indicative or subjunctive mood in languages for which that distinction is valid.

Analyses taken for granted usually benefit from re-examination. Many such analyses are intuitively appealing and based on irreproachable data and arguments but some, including DPs, are open to challenge. (See Sampson's comments on the quality of data on pp. 118–139.) One drawback is the loss of the semantic parallel between VPs and NPs, whereby the modifiers of a verb narrow down the type of event denoted and the modifiers of a noun narrow down the type of entity denoted. The modifiers of a determiner do not narrow down its meaning. Apart from the syntactic parallel between VP and DP, what syntactic arguments are given for working with DPs?

Hudson (1990, pp. 271–2), but not Hudson (2007), lists the following points. In phrases such as *any student* the optional word is *student*: cf. *I haven't insulted any student* versus *I haven't insulted any* (*student, colleague, policeman,* etc., understood from context). This can be countered with the observation that *any* in *any student* can be analysed as a quantifier–determiner, but in *I haven't insulted any*, it can be analysed as a pronoun. Similarly, *This* in *This project is fascinating* can be considered a determiner, whereas in *This is fascinating* it can be considered a pronoun. It is worthwhile drawing attention to the fact that this point only applies to NPs containing singular count nouns.

In NPs containing mass nouns or plural nouns, for example, *any coffee* and *any projects*, the determiner is omissible too: *Did you find (any) coffee in the kitchen?* and *Have you (any) projects in preparation just now?*

Hudson's second point is that the determiner – in English, but he is dealing with the grammar of English – is the locus of number, negation and definiteness, which are crucial for the distribution of any whole phrase containing a noun. The point is valid for negation and definiteness, but, with the exception of a few invariable nouns, the determiner is never the sole locus of number: in *these books*, both *these* and *books* carry number. Hudson's comment on negation and definiteness raises the point that the distribution of *the book* is different from that of *book*: *book* combines with *the*, *the book* cannot – **the the book* is unacceptable.

Hudson's third point is that determiners vary lexically and arbitrarily with respect to whether a noun is optional: *There were several houses to choose from, and each had its attractions* but not **and every had its attractions.* This property, he says, is typical of heads, which have different valencies. Another way of looking at the data is that *each* can be a determiner or a pronoun, that is, can occur in a determiner position or a pronoun position, whereas *every* can only function as a determiner. At issue here is a certain tension between the basic lexical class of a word and the syntactic slots it can occupy. An instructive example is afforded by words such as *remarkable*, *delicate* and *sharp*, which are basically adjectives and typically occur in adjective slots in syntactic structures. But *The Remarkables* are a mountain range in the South Island of New Zealand; in *We passed The Remarkables just before Queenstown*, *The Remarkables* is a NP and its head is *Remarkables.* The word is not an adjective functioning as the head of a NP; it has a plural suffix and has to be analysed as a noun. In *Wash delicates by hand*, *delicates* is the sole and therefore head word in the direct object NP. It too has a plural suffix and has to be analysed as a noun, although *delicate* is basically an adjective and typically occurs in adjective slots. (Other adjectives that are converted to nouns in the context of instructions for washing machines are *woollen* and *cotton*, and in the days before *tights* women wore *nylons.*) *Sharp*, likewise, is basically an adjective, but in *No sharps in this container* (notice in a hospital) it is a noun with a plural suffix. That is, the phenomenon of a form that is basically an X but functions occasionally or even frequently as a Y is not unknown in the grammar of English.

Hudson's fourth point is that the determiner is always on the periphery of the noun phrase, which is easy to explain if it is the head. The rest of the NP can be regarded as the complement of the determiner (Hudson's fifth point), and in English complements follow their head. A semantic–pragmatic explanation is that, for example, *the*, *this*, and *that* pick out a particular member of a particular subset of entities. For instance, in *the blue car with alloy wheels and bald tyres*, *the* picks out the entity denoted by *blue car with alloy wheels and bald tyres*. *The* modifies or applies to the entire sequence, and this is what is signalled by its position on the extreme periphery.

Hudson's sixth point concerns the parallels in relation between determiner and noun and between auxiliary verb and main verb. The parallel lies in the following properties: the determiner and auxiliary carry much less semantic content than the noun or main verb; the determiner and auxiliary verb are sometimes required for purely syntactic reasons; the noun and main verb are generally optional; determiner and auxiliary verb define different parts of the meaning of the same concept. These points are correct but what weight is to be given to each of these points? This depends on the analyst's theoretical preferences; none of the points is compelling by itself and neither is their union. The phrase 'define different parts of the meaning of the same concept' is difficult to interpret. If it came to a choice between the above parallel and the semantic parallel in the narrowing down of denotata, JM would choose the latter.

Payne (1993), working with data from Russian, Greek, Farsi, Chukchi, Warlbiri and other languages, provides other reasons for regarding nouns as heads of NPs. The reasons are these: nouns, not determiners (and verbs, not auxiliaries), are the constituents that accept incorporated material; the subcategorization of verbs (i.e., the constituents whose occurrence in clauses is controlled by verbs) is determined by nouns and their modifiers, not by determiners and their modifiers; nouns control agreement (are the governors) in NPs; nouns are the structural pivots in appositional structures. (The point about nouns controlling agreement in NPs does not contradict our argument earlier that verbs control number agreement in clauses. What happens inside NPs is indeed controlled by nouns.)

Incorporation of nouns into verbs is illustrated by the example from Southern Tiwa in (9a,b).

(9) a. Wisi seuan-in bi-mu –ban.
two man-PL 1.SG-see-PST
I saw two men.

b. Wisi bi-seuan-mu-ban.
two 1.SG-man-see-PST
I saw two men.

Seuan 'man' loses the plural marker *in* and the roots *seuan* 'man' and *mu* 'see' combine to form a complex root with a person-number prefix *bi* and a tense suffix *ban*. Payne points to a parallel process in the Palaeo-Siberian languages Chukchi and Koryak by which adjectives are incorporated into nouns. He gives the Chukchi example in (10a,b).

(10) a. ne-tur-qine-te kupre-te
new - INST net-INST
with a new net
b. tur-kupre-te
new-net-INST
with a new net

In (10a), *ne* and *qine* mark the adjective root *tur* 'new' as a free lexical item. Both the adjective and the noun root *kupre* 'net' have the instrumental suffix -*te*. In (10b), *tur* 'new' is no longer a free lexical item, as signalled by the absence of *ne*- and -*qine*, and the combination of *tur* and *kupre* has a single instrumental suffix -*te*. The parallel between incorporation into verbs and incorporation into nouns is clear. Verbs are the heads of clauses, and if the parallel is to be extended, nouns should be the heads of NPs.

Payne's point about subcategorization hardly needs to be argued here. Any discussion of the subcategorization of verbs deals with nouns and NPs, prepositions and prepositional phrases, adjectives and adjective phrases, but not with different types of determiner, say *each* versus *every*, *all* versus *some*, *this* versus *the*, *the* versus *a*.

Dependency and constituent structure

The central idea in dependency theory is that every phrase has a head word, which is obligatory and determines what other constituents can occur in the phrase. The other constituents are the modifiers of the head, and heads and modifiers typically occur next to each other – but see the discussion of split NPs on pp. 74–98. Combinations of head and modifier(s) 'move around' together, that is, occur together in different constructions and in different places in one and the same construction. They can be replaced by a single word and can be ellipted. These points are illustrated in (11).

(11) The Ethel that we knew and loved has left – just packed her bags and walked out.

As a proper noun, *Ethel* typically does not allow the definite article *the.* Proper nouns do allow definite articles, however, provided they are also modified by a relative clause. Presumably, the speaker who utters (11) is thinking of Ethel not as a single individual but as a bundle of individuals or personae who appear and disappear depending on the situation. The phrase *The Ethel that we knew and loved* picks out one of these individuals (as opposed, say, to *the Ethel that ate administrative staff for breakfast*). In the lexicon, we must include in the subcategorization of proper nouns the information that they do allow a definite article but only along with a relative clause. *Ethel* is the head of the NP *The Ethel that we knew and loved*; inside the NP it controls the occurrence of the word *the* and of the relative clause *that we knew and loved.*

That whole sequence of words can be replaced by the single word *she.* The phenomenon of ellipsis is shown in the second clause *just packed her bags and left.* This clause has no subject; if there were one, it would be *she* or *The Ethel that we knew and loved.* Either the long sequence of words is replaced by a pronoun or it is ellipted, as in the second clause above.

Verb phrases

The manipulations described earlier apply neatly to adjective phrases, prepositional phrases and adverb phrases: *very difficult, in the garden* and *amazingly quickly.* In the discussion earlier of semantic parallels in which modifiers narrow the meaning of heads, whether nouns, verbs, prepositions or adjectives, a connection was made between verbs and clauses, not between verbs and verb phrases. Many descriptions of English and other languages use a type of phrase known as the Verb Phrase, but the view adopted here is that verbs are the heads of clauses. The concept of verb phrase is not supported by solid evidence in English and is inapplicable many languages, for instance, those in which the major active declarative construction has the unmarked order of constituents Verb – Subject NP – Direct Object NP.

The strongest criteria for recognizing a sequence of words as hanging together to form a phrase are transposition and substitution. These do not apply straightforwardly to possible verb phrases. The occurrence of *do so* is one of the criteria, as in (12).

(12) Norman Lemming jumped off the cliff and William Lemming did so too.

did so indeed substitutes for *jumped off the cliff*, but two words are involved and it seems clear that the verb *did* substitutes for *jumped* and that *so* substitutes for the complements of *jumped.* (12) is the sort of example that turns up in discussions of American linguists, but it is not the normal construction in British English, where (13) is the common construction. In (13), the sequence is *so did*, which is not even a straightforward substitution of *did* for *jumped* and *so* for *off the cliff* because the verb and its complement would have to be transposed to yield *so did.*

(13) George Lemming jumped off the cliff and so did Anthony Lemming.

The one structure from spontaneous spoken English that might fit is shown in (14).

(14) Came right in he did without so much as a knock.

Unfortunately, the structure of (14) is not clear. *Came right in he did* could be seen as a rearrangement of *He did come right in*, except that in the latter *come* has no tense whereas in (14) *came* is in past tense. Moreover, new electronic bodies of spoken English are yielding examples such as *They complained about it all the time they did*, which has two clauses, *They complained about it all the time* and the tagged-on clause *they did.* So (14) can be analysed as having a two-clause structure in which the first clause, as happens regularly in spontaneous speech, is lacking a subject. That is, (14) can be considered not a basic construction but the result of ellipsis.

Examples such as *Walking the dog is good exercise* and *Buying his son a car was a mistake* are regularly invoked in support of verb phrases, along with *He likes walking the dog* and *He regretted buying his son a car.* The argument is that *Walking the dog* and *Buying his son a car* show that a verb and its complements (and adjuncts) can occur in different positions in clauses. This argument is not rock-solid. *Walking* and *Buying* are certainly derived from verbs, but they are nominals. The supposed verb phrases can be replaced by *it*, a substitute for NPs, but not by *did so* or *does so*: *It is good exercise, It was a mistake*, etc. In formal written English, the *-ing* forms can be preceded by possessive pronouns: *His walking the dog four times a day is a bit excessive, Their buying their son a car was a mistake*, etc.

How exactly does the operation of transposition apply? In examples such as *The documents were in his desk* and *In his desk were the documents*, the sequence *in his desk* occurs in different positions without any change of form. Similarly, in the following examples, the sequence *the latest documents from the developer* occurs in different positions in different constructions with no change in form: *We need the latest documents from the developer, What we need is the latest documents from the developer, The information is in the latest documents from the developer, The latest documents from the developer are what we need*, etc. (Similar comments apply to adjective phrases and adverb phrases.) If transposition is to apply without any change of form, the gerunds do not count as evidence for verb phrases. (This line of argument extends to sequences with infinitives and free participles.) If minor changes of form were allowed, gerunds could count as evidence, but that would leave the evidence for verb phrases weaker than the evidence for NPs, prepositional phrases, adjective phrases and adverb phrases.

Other arguments for verb phrases turn on examples of the sort in (15) and (16).

(15) Harriet couldn't marry Mr Knightley but Emma could.

(16) What Harriet did was marry Mr Martin.

The argument is that in (15) the sequence *marry Mr Knightley* has been ellipted – *Emma could marry Mr Knightley* is reduced to *could.* Since ellipsis applies to phrases, the sequence is regarded as a phrase. In (16), *was* has the WH clause *What Harriet did* as its subject and *marry Mr Martin* as its complement. That is, the sequences *marry Mr Knightley* and *marry Mr Martin* turn up in different slots and in (16) can even be genuinely transposed to the front to give (17).

(17) Marry Mr Martin was what Harriet did.

The trouble is that *marry Mr Martin* cannot occur as a verb phrase in the basic active clause: **Harriet marry Mr Martin* is incorrect as a declarative clause. In (16) and (17), *marry Mr Martin* is cross-referenced by *what* not by *did.* We end up with the same question that was asked about gerunds: does transposition allow changes of form? Depending on the answer to that question we have either no evidence for verb phrases or weaker evidence than for other types of phrase.

In contrast, the evidence that verbs are the heads of clauses is more solid. Descriptions focusing on dependency relations do not devote much time to the arguments for and against verb phrases, but incorporate the view that other divisions of the clause, based on dependencies, are more important. Clauses are analysed as having a nucleus and a periphery. The nucleus contains the verb and its complements (subject, direct object, indirect object and oblique objects–adverbs of direction); the periphery consists of oblique objects that are adverbs of time or adverbs of location, and some other types of adverb. (Adverbs are a very large and heterogeneous class and in at least one construction – the middle construction – adverbs of manner seem to be obligatory with some verbs, for example, *Her new book reads well* is quite acceptable, but **Her new book reads* is not acceptable.)

The split between nucleus and periphery is sometimes replaced by a three-way split between core, nucleus and periphery, as in Foley and van Valin (1984) and Van Valin and LaPolla (1997). The core of a clause is the verb, the nucleus is the verb plus complements as described earlier and the periphery is as described earlier. The idea that the verb is the core of a clause fits with the analysis of verbs as controlling the other constituents in clauses.

Dependency relations and subordinate clauses

Dependency relations are important in another area of syntactic analysis, the recognition of different types of subordinate clause, both finite and non-finite. We begin with two types of finite clause in English, relative clauses and complement clauses. Relative clauses are exemplified in (18) and complement clauses in (19).

(18) a. the car she drives
b. the car that she drives
c. the car which she drives
d. the car that she drove to Spain in
e. *the car in that she drove to Spain
f. the car which she drove to Spain in
g. the car in which she drove to Spain
h. the car she drove to Spain in
i. *the car in she drove to Spain

(19) a. She said that she drove to Spain.
b. She asked who drove to Spain.
c. She inquired whether/if we were driving to Spain.
d. She asked when we were leaving.
e. *She said which she drove to Spain.

The two types of subordinate clause possess different formal properties. Relative clauses are introduced by *that*, *who*/*which*/*whom*, etc., and Ø.

Complement clauses are introduced by *that* and Ø, but also by wh words such as *who* in (19b) and *whether* in (19c). Complement clauses have a complete set of constituents, subject, direct object, verb, oblique object, etc. Relative clauses have a gap; (18b) can be analysed as *the car [that she drives Ø]*, *that* being a subordinating conjunction/relativizer but not a pronoun, as shown by the unacceptability of (18e). In relative clauses, the relativizer *that* cannot be preceded by a preposition, whereas *which and who(m)* can be. The latter are pronouns which also function as relativizers.

Relative clauses are typically, but not always, inside NPs, and most complement clauses are the subject or object of verbs that are typically, but not necessarily, adjacent to them: cf. *The manager announced yesterday in a meeting convened with little notice that she was making half the workforce redundant.* The complement clause *that she was making half the workforce redundant* is at some distance from the verb but is still its direct object. A key distinction between relative clauses and complement clauses is that the former modify nouns, whereas the latter modify verbs. This relation of modification is independent of other formal properties or position in a sentence. Of course, some complement clauses modify nouns, as in *the proposal that we accept the offer*, *the hypothesis that the temperature will not rise more than 3 degrees* and *the idea that she is the right person for the job.* For these examples, we have to ask if *which* can be substituted for *that* or Ø. If it cannot, the clause is a complement: cf. *the proposal that we accept the offer* versus **the proposal which we accept the offer.* Another clue is that the complement clause conveys the content of an idea, plan, theory, hypothesis, proposal and so on.

Clauses introduced by *when* can be relative clauses, as in (20a), complement clauses, as in (20b), and adverbial clauses, as in (20c).

(20) a. the time when you left your briefcase on the train
b. I asked when she was leaving.
c. When she announced her resignation, there was a long silence.

Adverbial clauses modify complete clauses. In (20c), *When she announced her resignation* modifies *there was a long silence*; that is, it provides more information about the situation of there being a silence, namely the time at which it came into existence. Clauses introduced by *if* may be complement clauses – *Can you tell me if you have read that book* – or adverbial clauses – *If you have read that book, please take it back to the library.* As a complement clause *if you have read that book* modifies *tell* and as an adverbial clause it modifies the entire clause *please take it back to the library.*

The question of what a clause modifies is particularly important for non-finite clauses. Huddleston and Pullum (2002) abandon the distinction between gerunds and free participles on the ground that it is next to impossible to distinguish them formally. They refer to them as *-ing* clauses and *to* clauses. The view taken here is that these different types of non-finite clause are perfectly distinguishable when attention is paid to what they modify and that it is worthwhile taking the trouble to make the distinctions because the different non-finite clauses have different discourse functions.

Gerunds modify nouns and can be the subject or object of a verb: cf. the above examples *I like walking the dog* – *walking the dog* is the object of *like*, and *walking the dog is good exercise* – *walking the dog* is the subject of *is (good exercise)*. Free-participle non-finite clauses also contain verbs with the suffix *-ing*, but, unlike gerunds, they modify whole clauses. (In this respect, they resemble finite adverbial clauses. In *Drinking his coffee and brandy, Sir Louis felt better, Drinking his coffee and brandy* modifies *Sir Louis felt better.* It gives information about when the situation arose, as he was drinking the coffee and brandy. In *Knowing the country like the back of her hand, she was able to find the shortest route, Knowing the country like the back of her hand* modifies *she was able to find the shortest route.* It gives the reason for this ability and is equivalent to an adverbial clause of reason – *because/as she knew the country like the back of her hand.*

There is a second type of gerund which is found in examples like those in (21).

(21) a. I saw the burglar climbing in the window.
b. I caught him opening the safe.
c. I found Cordelia sitting on the terrace.
d. We heard the boys driving off in the car.

The *-ing* chunks – *climbing in the window* and *driving off in the car* – could on the face of it be reduced relative clauses, but this analysis does not fit (21c), with the proper noun, Cordelia. *The burglar climbing in the window got stuck* could be analysed as containing a reduced relative clause – *I saw the burglar who was climbing in the window. The burglar climbing in the window* could be a subject NP – *The burglar climbing in the window was seen by everybody.* In contrast, **Cordelia sitting on the terrace looked woebegone* is unacceptable. The examples can, some of them at least, be made passive by moving the direct object noun to the front of the sentence and leaving the *-ing* chunk behind, as in (22).

(22) a. The boys were heard (by us) driving off in the car.
b. Cordelia was found (by me) sitting on the terrace.
c. The burglar was seen (by me) opening the safe.

I saw the burglar climbing in the window can be expanded to *I saw the burglar who was climbing in the window*, which is a good answer to the question *Who did you see? The burglar was seen (by me) climbing in the window* cannot be expanded into **The burglar was seen (by me) who was climbing in the window*. These passive versions show that the *-ing* chunks do not modify a noun, *burglar* or *boys*, but a clause: *the boys were heard by us*, *the burglar was seen by me* and *Cordelia was found by me*. This accords with the fact that *I saw the burglar climbing in the window* is also an answer to the question *What was the burglar doing when you saw him*? The fact is that (21a) is grammatically ambiguous and the *-ing* chunk can be interpreted either as a reduced relative clause or as another construction, which we will call a type II gerund. This second construction allows a different set of paraphrases: *We heard the boys in the act of driving off in the car* or *We heard the boys as they were driving off in the car*.

Saying there is another construction is one thing; justifying it as a gerund is another. We appeal to historical evidence. The construction in (21a) derives historically from *I saw the burglar a-climbing in the window*, where *a* derives from *on* and the *-ing* chunk is a nominal. The head–modifier relationship is not crucial to the earlier discussion, but the essential point is that it is quite inadequate to lump all the *-ing* sequences together. It is important to distinguish the different *-ing* constructions, the gerund, the free participle and the type II gerund, and dependency relations save the day.

3 Noun Phrases and Non-configurationality

Chapter Outline

Non-configurationality: Warlbiri, Russian and spontaneous spoken language

In the previous chapter, we looked at some examples of how modifiers cluster round their heads, forming a single constituent which can be recognized by applying the major criteria of transposition and substitution and the minor criteria of ellipsis and conjoining. The classic phrasal constituent is the NP, but there are languages in which the words that could be gathered together into a single phrase are scattered throughout the clause. Languages displaying this phenomenon are said to be non-configurational; the potential constituents of NPs do not have to come together into the configuration of a NP. We will see that, although English is not a non-configurational language, speakers speaking off the cuff either use constructions that enable them to avoid processing complex NPs inside clauses or use very simple NPs. The non-configurational phenomena can be interpreted as means for achieving the same goal, the avoidance of complex NPs.

Since the 1980s the topic of non-configurational languages has been regularly, though not frequently, discussed. (See the references throughout the chapter.) Non-configurationality came to the attention of generative linguists through the work of Ken Hale on the Native Australian language Warlpiri in the late 1970s – see especially Hale (1983). Hale realized that Warlpiri and a number of other Native Australian languages posed a problem for formal models of syntax, which take hierarchical constituent structure as central. Languages such as English gather together into one group of adjacent constituents items such as nouns, demonstratives, numerals and adjectives, whereas languages such as Warlpiri can have the constituents combined into a single phrase but also regularly have them distributed throughout clauses producing unintegrated structures in which demonstratives and adjectives are not adjacent to the nouns they modify. (See examples (1)–(11) below.) Hale (1983) proposed that this property of non-configurationality (or the property of having syntactically discontinuous expressions) goes with free word order and null anaphora.

Several key questions are raised by the data from Warlpiri and other Native Australian languages. Do they form a unique set of non-configurational languages with 'split NPs', the head noun being separated from its modifiers? Baker (1996) demonstrates that they do not, since Mohawk also has non-configurational sequences. Zemskaja (1973, p. 383–93), who may have been the first to comment on the phenomenon, observed that in spoken Russian heads and modifiers are not necessarily adjacent, whereas they are always adjacent in what she called 'scientific Russian' (i.e., the formal written Russian of academic monographs, but also of, for example, official documents and serious newspaper discussions). Spoken (and indeed written) Russian texts also display much null anaphora and flexible word order. (The word order is not free, but governed by information structure, and it is a reasonable conjecture that word order in Native Australian languages is controlled in the same fashion.)

Zemskaja's observation leads to a very interesting perspective. Not only are Warlpiri and its like not typologically unique, the treatment of nouns and their modifiers (to use these terms for convenience) may be different in the spoken varieties and written varieties of a given language, particularly in the spontaneous spoken variety that is found, for example, in impromptu conversation in relaxed circumstances. Thus, there are similarities (and that is the strongest statement we can make) between spontaneous spoken Russian and Warlpiri but not between written Russian and Warlpiri.

The Warlpiri and Russian data raise problems for constituent structure analyses. One problem has to do with the free order of verb, agent NP and patient NP. Jelinek (1984) proposes that the Warlpiri auxiliary contains fully referential clitic pronouns which bear theta roles and case and that any nouns that do occur in Warlpiri clauses are merely optional adjuncts linked to the pronouns. (A very similar analysis was applied by Elson and Pickett (1967, p. 72) to a Mixe-Zoque language, Sierra Popoluca – now called Highland Popoluca.) Another problem has to do with the 'split NPs': are nouns, demonstratives, adjectives, numerals and possessor nouns to be thought of as generated adjacent to each other in sequences to be labelled 'NP' and then moved apart – whatever is meant by 'move'? Or are they to be generated in situ, are clauses to be assigned a highly unintegrated structure and are the nouns, demonstratives and so on to be connected (i.e. are their contents to be connected) via a formal system such as Discourse Representation Theory (DRT)? The discussion below opts for the latter approach, in contrast with Pereltsvaig (2008), who offers a movement analysis of Russian 'split NPs'.

The final issue is one that affects the spontaneous spoken varieties of all languages. The structures in Warlpiri and spoken Russian can be seen as one ramification of a general problem, the processing of NPs in spontaneous speech. English has very different syntax and morphology from Warlpiri, but an examination of spoken English shows that speakers avoid complex NPs (and for many speakers, in spontaneous speech even an NP with one adjective is complex – witness the small percentage of such NPs in spontaneous speech) and use large numbers of personal and other pronouns. (See ( )–( ).) English also has constructions with various syntactic and discoursal functions, but which serve to isolate NPs from clauses; that is, they allow speakers to process NPs, which may be simple or complex, separately from the processing of clause structures. The Warlpiri and Sierra Popoluca clauses with clitic pronouns on the verb and optional nouns can be seen as a way of dealing with the same problem.

Simple NPs and successful reference

All the examples presented below and by other analysts are, potentially or actually, components of texts. A more general issue on which the earlier questions bear is how speakers and writers construct successful referential descriptions of entities. Depending on the type of text they are composing and what type of audience they are addressing, writers produce simple structures or very complex structures, especially very complex NPs. Speakers, especially those speaking impromptu and producing spontaneous speech, typically do not produce complex NPs. This explains why in the texts of the Australian languages Diyari and Ngiyambaa included in Austin (1981) and Donaldson (1980), respectively, it is difficult to find a NP containing one adjective let alone three or four. This discrepancy is mentioned by Dixon (1972, p. 60), who notes that a NP can in principle contain any number of adjectives, although in actual texts few NPs involve more than one adjective. The small number of adjectives is actually surprising given that the texts are not conversation but narrative; specific tales are told again and again and become scripted, and new tales can be rehearsed. However, these narratives do have one special property; they were almost lost before being elicited by the analysts and are not regularly recited in the original language. This circumstance precludes the polishing up and elaboration of texts and would explain the simple syntax. It does raise the question of what intuitions the analysts were tapping into when they found evidence for complex NPs.

NPs, complexity and text type

Research into naturally occurring data has brought out large differences in the types of NP that occur and their complexity. In the late 1960s, Hawkins (1969) and Coulthard and Robinson (1968) concluded that the structure of NPs ('nominal groups' in their terminology) in written language is more complex than the structure of NPs in spoken language, modifiers of all types being rare in the former but typical in the latter. (They do not distinguish different types of written text or different types of spoken text, but it is clear from the context that the significant contrast is between formal writing and spontaneous speech.)

Biber (1988, pp. 89, 104–8) establishes various 'dimensions' for the recognition and comparison of different English text types. He emphasizes a point accepted by all researchers of spoken and written language: it is NOT the case that all types of spoken text are different from all types of written text.

There are structures that occur in both spoken and written texts. Nonetheless, it is clear from Biber's discussion of the six dimensions that spontaneous spoken English, in particular conversation, is very different from other text types. For instance, one dimension has to do with involved versus informational production. Involved production is discourse produced under real-time conditions, which typically exclude the time-consuming processes of making precise lexical choices and packing a lot of information into a small amount of text. The latter task requires the use of adjectives, prepositional phrases and participial phrases, all of which have a high negative weighting in this dimension. That is, they are not found in spontaneous spoken English. This is supported by the data in Biber et al. (1999), which also shows that among written text types academic writing is the densest and most complex; it offers intricate sentence structures with much embedding of subordinate clauses, complex subject NPs and an abundance of Greco-Latinate vocabulary with dense derivational morphology. With respect to NPs, the general picture is that the most complex structures are found in dense technical texts (such as academic monographs, legal documents, encyclopaedia articles and broadsheet newspapers), with the least complex structures in tabloid newspapers, comics and books for young children.

One striking feature of spontaneous spoken language is the simplicity of NPs in comparison with the NPs that occur in the aforementioned types of written text. What do we mean by 'simplicity'? For written English (and written Russian, written German and so on), a relatively simple NP consists of a noun modified by one or two adjectives (*an impressive performance*), or a numeral/quantifier (*some showers*), or a prepositional phrase (*the branches of the tree*), or some combination of these modifiers (*some heavy showers* and *the highest branches of the tree*). In spontaneous spoken English, the simplest NPs consist of just a noun or pronoun. Miller and Weinert (2009, pp. 133–76) examined various spontaneous spoken texts and found that they contained relatively high proportions of NPs consisting of a personal pronoun: 44.9 per cent in English narrative and 48.9 per cent in English conversation. In contrast, the proportion in the readers' letters to the upmarket newspaper *The Independent* was 14.1 per cent. For Russian conversation the figure was only 21.9 per cent, but this is almost twice the percentage in Russian newspaper and academic monograph texts – 11.9 per cent and 12.1 per cent, respectively. It is not however much higher than the figure for the extracts from a Russian novel, where 16.8 per cent of the NPs consisted of personal pronouns. For German, in telephone conversation, single-pronoun NPs accounted for 43.9 per cent of

NPs, 38.7 per cent in face-to-face conversation and 52.4 per cent in map-task dialogue. In a German newspaper text, only 6.6 per cent of the NPs were single pronouns. When NPs consisting of single constituents such as demonstratives, interrogative pronouns, quantifiers, proper nouns, mass nouns and plural nouns are taken into account, the proportion of NPs with just one constituent rose to 62.5 per cent for the English conversations and to 64 per cent for the English narrative. (These figures chime with the figures for extracts from the Australian component of ICE to be discussed below.)

In both the English narrative and the English conversation, there were NPs containing adjectives, 5.6 per cent in the former and 6 per cent in the latter. But there was only one adjective per NP. In the narrative, 3.2 per cent of NPs contained a relative clause, 3.8 per cent in the conversation; the relative clauses were mainly contact ones – *the cup I broke* (*can be replaced*) – or ones with *that* as complementizer – *the cup that I broke.* (For a more detailed account, see Miller and Weinert, 2009, pp. 143–59.)

The English narrative and conversation contained no instances at all of complex NPs such as these two from readers' letters to *The Independent*: *a rigorous and valid examination on applied economics that consists of three papers* and *the desire of Oftel to retain the geographic significance of the area code despite the fact that this is already being attenuated.* Such NPs occur in, and may even be considered typical of, academic writing, legal documents, local authority documents and so on. Such text types also contain smaller NPs, which still have more than one adjective or reduced relative clauses as in *the beautiful marble gates* and *a wild apricot tree red on the bare slopes*, from Thubron (1987). The English narrative and conversation examined by Miller and Weinert offered no examples of these either. An NP with just one adjective counts as complex.

One other feature of complex NPs deserves mention. Even in written texts they tend not to occur preceding the verb in subject position, and in spontaneous speech subject NPs are typically pronouns, single nouns or at most Det–N. (See Quirk et al., 1985, pp. 1350–2, Jucker, 1992, and Thompson, 1988.)

NPs in two types of spoken text

How do speakers get away with it? How do they communication successfully yet avoid what experienced readers and writers would consider straightforward and necessary structures? Clues are offered by the excerpt of 1,000 words in Appendix 3.1. It comes from the Australian component of ICE, the section labelled 'private dialogue', and consists of impromptu conversation. Like the

British English conversation analysed by Miller and Weinert in the early 1990s, this one has a very large percentage of NPs consisting of one constituent: personal pronouns – 52.3 per cent, Proper Nouns – 15 per cent, single common nouns – 3.4 per cent, making 70.7 per cent. NPs consisting of two constituents, Det–N, make up 16.5 per cent, taking the percentage figure for very simple NPs to 87.2 per cent. The two relative clauses are *about three bunches of flowers* ***that we bought them*** *and some little plastic containers* ***to out it in*** and the compound nouns are all much used in everyday life both in Australia and in the United Kingdom, though *harbour bridge* may be peculiar to Sydney (and also to Auckland): for example, *fire extinguisher, fire brigade, peak hour* (*rush hour* in the United Kingdom), *freezing compartment* (of fridge), *deep freeze, pumpkin soup* (3 exx), *news flash* and *harbour bridge* (2 exx).

Consider the following small chunk of conversation, an excerpt from the excerpt in Appendix 3.2.

(1)	**S1A**-057(A):55	So who else was ov who who was firstname6 and firstname7 there were they
	S1A-057(B):57	Yes
	S1A-057(A):58	Oh and how's firstname1 Is he alright today
	S1A-057(B):60	Yes He's sitting out on the chair and
	S1A-057(A):61	Has he still got a drip
	S1A-057(B):62	No He didn't have the drip Well I don't think so
	S1A-057(B):64	I didn't see any drip but I didn't stay I just went sort of in and out and when they were all there I took the flowers and put them in water for them
	S1A-057(A):68	Oh
	S1A-057(A):69	Did mum
	S1A-057(A):70	Ho what flowers
	S1A-057(B):71	We got about three bunches of flowers that we bought them
	S1A-057(A):73	What did ah mum have a drip in
	S1A-057(B):74	Yes She's still got it
	S1A-057(A):7	Did they say how long she's gonna be in hospital for
	S1A-057(B):76	Well I really wasn't talking to anybody this morning but see they've gotta get her back on food and see how that goes

Chunk 55 is syntactically broken up. The speaker begins two wh interrogatives before settling for the yes–no interrogative *was firstname6 and firstname7 there*? The next interrogative, at 58, is a sequence of wh and yes–no. The proper noun is introduced as the second post-copula NP, *how's firstname*, and the yes–no question simply has a personal pronoun – *Is he alright today*?

This sequence keeps the subject NP in the second clause simple, an apparently trivial result here but in keeping with the general patterns in spontaneous speech. All the human actors in this little narrative about a hospital visit are known to (and possibly are related to) the interlocutors, who have no need of full NPs to refer to them. When some referential help is required, it comes via lexical nouns – *chair*, *drip*, *flowers* and *three bunches of flowers* – but as soon as the referent is established the speakers revert to personal pronouns.

The 500-word excerpt in Appendix 3.2 is from a TV commentary for a programme on snakes. The linguistic features worth commenting on are the big drop in the percentage of NPs that consist of personal pronouns from 52.3 to 22.5, a modest rise in the Det–N NPs from 16.5 to 24 and a large rise in the percentage of NPs with the structure Det–Adj–N from 2.3 to 20.3. The two excerpts have about the same percentage of compound nouns, but the commentary has more complex ones, such as *a strike and release method of attack* and *taipan anti-venom*. The commentary also has a number of complex NPs: for example, *one of the last to be developed*, *the longest of the venomous snakes*, *their preferred diet of small rodents, birds and the occasional bandicoot*, *the most densely populated corner of the continent*, *the process of breaking down the food* and so on.

In Biber's terms (Biber, 1988, pp. 129–69), the conversation results from involved production (being discourse with interactional and affective purposes) and exhibits situation-dependent reference (outsiders with no knowledge of the situation would be at a loss) and on-line informational elaboration (the speakers produce one piece of information per clause or chunk of syntax and add information by producing a sequence of clauses and phrases). In contrast, the commentary is informational (being carefully composed and edited), it exhibits explicit reference (the speaker takes nothing for granted about the audience's world knowledge or memory of previously mentioned entities) and it does not involve on-line informational elaboration. The information about the various snakes and their habitat, prey, physical characteristics and behaviour is presented via highly integrated and dense NPs.

Complex NPs in clauses: avoidance techniques

Spoken English has two constructions that can be considered as devices for helping speakers and listeners to process NPs. As we will see shortly, however, the NP-Clause construction has acquired specific discourse functions and the other construction, Direct Object NP–Complement Clause, also seems to have a discourse function. We begin with the NP-Clause construction, which many analysts handle as left dislocation. Our view is that not only is nothing dislocated to the left (the terminology of transformational grammar and all its descendants is dynamic but the dynamism is metaphorical), but there is no evidence that the NP is actually part of the following complete clause, in spite of the typical transcription. An example of the construction is (2), which Quirk et al. (1985, pp. 1416–17) assign to loose, informal speech.

(2) This man I was telling you about – well, he used live next door to me

They analyse *This man I was telling you about* as setting the 'point of departure' for the utterance as a whole and as enabling speakers to avoid the tricky processing of clauses containing complex NPs. Speakers do avoid complex subject NPs in spontaneous speech, but many left-dislocated NPs are simple. The key point, which Quirk et al. do not make, is that the construction is used to highlight entities or to contrast entities. In (3a), the speaker re-establishes the topic of the discussion, *this film*, and moves on to the important comment *it does give a real close-up of what goes on behind the scenes.* In (3b), Rick Stein is contrasted with Keith Floyd, and in (3c) the youngest and the eldest daughters are contrasted.

(3) a. **this film** it does give a real close-up of what goes on behind the scenes.
Tom Brook, *Talking Movies*, BBC World, 19 April 2007

b. 'I like his [Keith Floyd's] style of cookery,' adds Fenton's wife Patricia. 'He just throws everything in. **Rick Stein –** he's only copying Floyd**, isn't he?**'
The Independent, 11 October 2007, *Extra*, pp. 2–3

c. '**My youngest daughter** gets embarrassed when she sees me on television,' says Stewart. '**My eldest**, she doesn't mind so much . . .'
Dr Iain Stewart being interviewed by Susan Swarbrick – 'Preparing to rock your world', *The Herald*, 13 November 2007, p. 17

The construction can simply signal a contrast, as in (3b,c), or simultaneously ease the production of complex utterances and signal a contrast, as in (4) and (5).

(4) 'What struck me was that **people who behaved the way my ex and I did**, their children were fine, but **those who made more mistakes**, their children suffered more.'
'Divorce doesn't have to be a Disaster,' *The Herald*, 3 December 2007, p.15

(5) 'You know, it's an amazing building. **The one that was never built,** that would have been even more amazing. It was going to be over 550 feet in height, an unbelievable sight.'

Sir Terry Leahy, interview in *The Tablet* by Chris Blackhurst, 22–9 December 2007

In (6), information identifying a set of referents is supplied in three chunks of syntax, three NPs: *the rest of them*, then *the mill lasses* specifying the referent of *them*, then *some of them*, specifying that a subset of the mill lasses dressed up or carried balloons and followed the couple. In an edited written text we might find *Some of the other mill lasses* or *some of the remaining mill lasses.*

(6) and then the rest of them, the mill lasses, some of them dressed up wi funny hats or they'd carry balloons and follow them, just singin.

Bennett, 1992, p. 108

In (7), the NP *people who say they don't like bats* is used to highlight this particular set of people and to say that even they find the bats astonishing. A written text might have *When we take people who say they don't like bats out to meet them, even they stand there with grins . . .* The written version is unsatisfactory because *take* has a very complex direct object NP, *people who say they don't like bats*, which leaves the directional phrase and the infinitive, *out to meet them*, stranded at the end of the *when* clause.

(7) Mr Tomlinson said: 'Possibly, they once flew around the heads of dinosaurs, which is a mind-blowing thought. **Even people who say they don't like bats**, when we take them out to meet them, they stand there with grins that if they got any bigger would split their heads in two.

The Independent, Friday, 5 October 2007, p. 26

In (8), a written text might have *Of the areas of industry that were being hit quite hard the one that stood out was the food industry.* This version involves a pre-posed prepositional phrase, which is itself made complex by the relative clause *that were being hit quite hard.*

(8) Contrasting the fortunes of different sub-sectors, he said: 'Electronics is performing particularly well. **The areas of industry that were being hit quite hard** – the one that stood out was the food industry.'

The Herald, 27 October 2007

At this point, the reader is reminded in passing of the three important points mentioned in the previous discussion of these examples in Chapter 1.

The construction is not new, it has a contrastive discourse function, and it raises interesting questions about the typological difference between subject-prominent and topic-prominent languages.

The NP-Clause construction has processing and discourse functions and is widespread in all types of spoken text except completely scripted ones such as the rehearsed commentary accompanying a programme on snakes. The construction does turn up in literary texts too, an example being the excerpt from *Little Dorrit* in (9). Not surprisingly, given that the text is literary and written and that the author is Charles Dickens, the construction is exploited and stretched, with eight NPs (in bold) preceding the main clause in the second text sentence and picked up by the direct object *these* in the main clause and with rather complex NPs preceding the main clauses in the third and fourth text sentences. And the main clauses are all wh interrogatives, which is unusual in spontaneous speech.

(9) Everybody knows how like the street the two dinner-rows of people who stand by the street will be . . . **The house so drearily out of repair**, **the occasional bow-window**, **the stuccoed house**, **the newly-fronted house**, **the corner house with nothing but angular rooms**, **the house with the blinds always down**, **the house with the hatchment always up**, **the house where the collector has called for one quarter of an Idea, and found nobody at home** – who has not dined with **these**? The house that nobody will take, and is to be had a bargain - who does not know her? The showy house that was taken for life by the disappointed gentleman, and which does not suit him at all – who is unacquainted with that haunted habitation?

Charles Dickens, 1967, *Little Dorrit*, Penguin edn, Chapter 21, (p. 292)

We close this discussion of the NP-Clause construction by noting that it is not confined to English. French has a very similar structure, and in fact also has a construction that we will label Clause-NP. The following dialogue is taken from Vargas (2008, p. 114).

(10) — Il a bossé, ton chien
— he has worked-hard, your dog
— 'He's been working hard, your dog'

— La bave de chien, c'est antiseptique
— The saliva of dog, it is antiseptique
— 'Dog saliva is antiseptic'

The first part of the dialogue shows how French speakers have the option of keeping full NPs out of a clause by tacking them on at the end of the utterance. (10) is from written dialogue and Vargas has chosen to put a comma between *il a bossé* and *ton chien*, indicating that she has placed them in the same text sentence. If we were transcribing spoken dialogue, the intonation pattern might suggest that the two chunks of syntax are not part of a single sentence – particularly if we accept the idea that sentences are not appropriate for the analysis of spontaneous spoken language. Instead, we would opt to have just two pieces of syntax side by side, with the connections being made via the sort of procedure used in DRT.

The second part of the dialogue has been translated (by JM) as an ordinary clause because the context does not justify the NP-Clause construction in English. The speaker is not highlighting anything or drawing a contrast. He is simply making an unemphatic statement. The French construction looks like the English one, but functions differently in discourse. It is like the English one in allowing speakers to process NPs, possibly complex, independently and then to process a main clause with a simple pronominal subject or object. The French NP-Clause construction is quite frequent. According to Ball (2000, p. 1301) 'the frequency of dislocated sentences in familiar and popular French can be as high as 50%' and they are a noteworthy feature of the usage of younger speakers of whatever social category. Certainly 22 years ago the author was addressed by a 3-year-old native speaker of French who said, as her baby brother lay screaming on the floor: *il n'aime pas être par terre, Ranald.* The use of the construction by a 3-year-old was a good indication that it was frequently used by her parents.

The King James Bible translates Matthew VI.28 as 'Consider the lilies of the field how they grow.' Imitating the Greek (See the discussion in Miller and Weinert, 2009, p. 362), the construction has the merit of making central the lilies of the field, as the referent of the direct object in a simple clause, and stating their relevant property in a separate complement clause. The constituent structure is not clear, though *the lilies of the field* and *How they grow* both modify *consider.* Other translators have been unhappy with the construction: the Revised English Bible has 'Consider how the lilies of the field grow', with *the lilies of the field* as subject of the complement clause. This structure sanitizes the syntax, but removes the lilies of the field from prominence and the focus of attention.

The construction has been noticeable in spontaneous spoken English for some time; (11) was uttered in 1978 by a 17-year-old Scottish male in Edinburgh, with no pause between *religion* and *the damage* . . .

(11) i was brought up a catholic and i hate religion the damage it does to human people . . .

Miller–Brown Corpus, conversation 13

Here, the direct object of *hate* is *religion* and the complement clause conveying the relevant property of *religion* is *the damage it does to human people.* (12) is from the New Zealand component of ICE, again with no pause.

(12) i can never remember any of my family how old they are.

NZ ICE, Macquarie Corpus

The direct object of *remember* is *any of my family* and the relevant property is conveyed by *how old they are.*

(13) was uttered in November 2008 by the prosecuting counsel in a court case in Britain (The transcription of the words appeared on the TV screen and the words were spoken by actors).

(13) Did you threaten Michael X at any time that you would have him killed?

The direct object of *threaten* is *Michael X* and the clause *that you would have him killed* conveys, not a property of Michael X, but the content of the putative threat. A written version might be *Did you threaten to have Michael X killed . . .* ? (The *OED* lists a superficially similar construction from the Wycliffe Bible of 1380: *And he threatenyde hem, that thei schulden not seie to any man of him.* However, the clause *that thei . . .* is a clause of purpose. The people were threatened so that they would not say anything.)

This sub-section closes with an example of the construction from writing. *Remembered* has *Rossi* as its immediate direct object and *how he'd listened so modestly to the cheers and speeches* as a second direct object, or at least as a second modifier.

(14) everyone turned to [Stoichev] with a smile . . . I remembered Rossi, how he'd listened so modestly to the cheers and speeches

Elizabeth Kostova, 2005, *The Historian*

The constituent structure and dependency relations are not obvious. The spoken examples could be analysed as consisting of two paratactic clauses: for example, in (11), *i can never remember any of my family* and *how old they are.* On this analysis, the clauses are linked by adjacency and by the anaphoric pronoun *they* picking up the referent of *any of my family.* Writers using the construction have to decide how they are going to organize the clauses on the page. It would be possible, if unusual, to write (14) as (15); this organization would fit in with, for example, the excerpts from Lee Child's novel quoted on p. 26. Kostova, being a less inventive writer than Child, has chosen not to have a text sentence consisting only of a complement clause, but in writing (14) she invites an analysis in which *Rossi* and *how he'd listened so modestly to the cheers and speeches* are both direct objects of *remembered*; that is, in one representation, she invites the constituent structure VP [V NP Comp Clause].

(15) I remembered Rossi. How he'd listened so modestly to the cheers and speeches.

Non-configurationality in Native Australian languages

We turn now to the non-configurational structures of Native Australian languages. Bowe (1990) offers a good account of the phenomenon in the Native Australian language Pitjantjatjara. She observes (1990, p. 53) that in Pitjantjatjara nouns and attributive modifiers combine in two different ways. First of all, either a noun or a modifier can be the sole constituent in a NP, as in (16).

(16) a. minyma-ngku-ni nya-ngu.
woman-Erg-1SgAcc see-Past
'the woman saw me.'

b. wara-ngku-ni nya-ngu.
tall-Erg-1SgAcc see-Past
'the tall one saw me.'

A first-person singular direct object is signalled by the clitic *-ni*, which attaches to the subject noun. *Minyma* and *wara* can combine to give the NP in (17).

(17) minyma wara-ngku-ni nya-ngu.
woman tall-Erg-1SgAcc see-Past
'the tall woman saw me.'

Wara and *minyma* constitute a single NP, witness the single case affix on *wara*, but both can carry a case affix and can occur in either order, as in (18a,b).

(18) a. minyma-ngku wara-ngku-ni nya-ngu.
woman- Erg tall-Erg-me see-Past
'The woman, the tall one, saw me.'

b. wara-ngku minyma-ngku-ni nya-ngu.
tall-one - Erg woman-me see-Past
'The tall one, the woman, saw me.'

The apparently disjointed nature of the Pitjantjatjara NP is further brought out by the typical relative clause construction as exemplified in (19).

(19) wati-ngku panya kuka ngalya-kati-ngu.
man-Erg Anaphor meat back-bring-Past
'that man brought the meat back.'

panya paluru mutaka palya-ngu.
Anaph 3sgNom car fix-Past
'that one fixed the car.'

This construction is strongly reminiscent of the unintegrated clause structures discussed in Chapter 00 whose key property is that, instead of a clause embedded inside an NP, as in the relative clause construction of written English, two clauses are juxtaposed and the relationship between them is signalled by means of deictics. Bowe describes *panya* as an 'anaphoric demonstrative'.

Interestingly, Bowe (1990, p. 101) says that Pitjantjatjara does have a strategy for forming relative clauses, by which she means a construction that is more integrated in having two verbs and therefore two clauses but only one overt subject NP, as in (20).

(20) wati panya waru atu-ntja-lu ngayu-nya u-ngu.
man Anaphor wood chop-Inf-Erg 1Sg-Acc give-Past
'the man who chops wood gave me some.'

The central features of this construction are the lack of a case marker on *wati* 'man' and the presence of a case marker on the verb *atu* (chop). This case marker, according to Bowe, indicates that the head of the relative clause is the transitive subject of the main verb *ungu* (gave). A further feature is the lack of a tense marker on the verb in the relative clause. We can assume that the integrated structure in (20) is not typical of Pitjantjatjara, since Bowe describes it as 'not used very often in narrative'. A reasonable hypothesis (given that conversation is typically not pre-planned whereas narrative is) is that it is not used in conversation either and may be a construction that was used in planned or rehearsed speech. Elsewhere Bowe (1990, p. 30) comments that any number of attributives may modify a head noun, although in practice the number is limited – a comment that raises questions about the nature of the data. From the work on NPs mentioned on pp. 165, 193–194, we expect few or no adjectives in NPs in spontaneous speech.

Jelinek (1984, p. 40) cites the data in (21) as exemplifying null anaphora.

(21) a. Ngarrka- ngku ka panti-rni.
man Erg Aux spear-Non-Past
'The man is spearing him/her/it.'

b. Wawirri ka panti-rni.
kangaroo AUX spear-Non-Past
'He/she is spearing the kangaroo.'

c. panti-rni ka.
spear-Non-Past AUX
'He/she is spearing him/her.'

In (21a), the agent noun plus ergative suffix, *ngarrka—ngku*, is present, but there is no overt patient noun. In (21b), there is an overt patient noun, *wawirri*, but no Agent noun. In (21c), there is neither agent nor patient noun. This is a very frequent pattern across languages, whereby third-person agents and patients have zero realization in surface syntax. In contrast, first- and second-person agents and patients are realized by overt surface morphs, as in (22)–(24).

(22) ngajulu-rlu ka- rna- ngku nyuntu-Ø nya-nyi.
I – Erg Pres- 1sgNom- 2sgAcc you-Abs see - Non-Past
'I see you.'

(23) nyuntulu-rlu ka- npa- ju ngaju- Ø nya-nyi.
you- Erg Pres -2sgNom- 1sgAcc me- Abs see-Non-Past
'You see me.'

(24) nyuntu- Ø ka-npa purla-mi.
you- Abs Pres -2sgNom shout-Non-Past
'You are shouting.'

The examples in (22) and (23) have independent first- and second-person pronouns, *ngajulu* and *nyuntu* plus ergative suffix for the agent and absolutive suffix for the patient. In addition, the auxiliary *ka* has two suffixes, nominative for agent and accusative for patient. (24), with an intransitive construction, has one independent pronoun with the absolutive suffix and the auxiliary *ka* with one suffix, the nominative.

Free word order is exemplified by (25). The auxiliary *ka* must be in second position, but the other constituents can occur in any order. (26) shows how two apparent constituents of an NP are not only not adjacent but at either end of the clause.

(25)	Ngarrka-ngku	ka	wawirri-	panti-rni.
	man-Erg	Aux	kangaroo	spear-Non-Past

'The man is spearing the kangaroo.'

(26)	Wawirri	kapi-rni	panti-rni	yalumpu.
	Kangaroo	Future-1sg	spear-Non-Past	that

'I will spear that kangaroo.'

All the attempts at analyzing examples like (26) have begun from the perspective of a Chomskyan formal model. Hale (1983) handled the data within the Government and Binding framework, where the Projection Principle precluded structures with missing nominals in the analysis of clauses such as (21a–c). To make the Projection Principle work, GB analyses of English allowed empty NPs to be assigned theta roles and the category *pro* was introduced for the structures of clauses (e.g. in Italian or Russian) where the deictic suffix on the verb was enough to establish reference to an agent and made subject NPs unnecessary. *Pro* had independent deictic reference. Hale suggested that non-configurationality arose from the relationship between phrase structure and lexical structure (predicates and their arguments). Lexical verbs assigned theta roles and case to their arguments. These stipulated arrays of cases specified what cases optional nominals would carry if present in the surface syntax. A particular argument might not be assigned to any nominal, as in (21a–c), and an argument might be assigned to more than one nominal, as in (26). The reason for recognizing more than one nominal is exemplified in (18), repeated below for convenience.

(18)	a. minyma-ngku	wara-ngku-ni	nya-ngu.
	woman- Erg	tall-Erg-me	see-Past
	b. wara-ngku	minyma-ngku-ni	nya-ngu.
	tall-one - Erg	woman-me	see-Past

Words such as *wara* can function on their own as a nominal, as in (16b), or as the modifier of a noun, as in (16a). Like nominals, *wara* can occur in any position, but when it is in second position, it carries the double suffix, indicating the grammatical person assigned to each of the agent and patient. In other positions, it carries only one. Pensalfini (2004, p. 364) gives the example in (27), from the Native Australian language Jiwarli.

(27) **Kutharra-rru** **ngunha** ngurnta-inha **jiluru**.
two-now that lie Pres egg (Nom)
'Now those two eggs are lying there.'

Baker's take on examples such as (16b), (18) and (27) – see Baker (1996) – is that these languages collapse N and A into a single distributional and morphological class of nominals, case-bearing elements which appear freely ordered with respect to one another and the verb. These elements have the syntactic distribution of adjectives – they do not appear in argument position and appear to be predicated of true (null) arguments. As a result, any number of them can be construed with a single null arg and they need not be adjacent. (Baker considers the phenomenon unusual, but it is widespread; witness the discussion of Russian below.)

Jelinek (1984) argues that Hale was correct to propose no empty categories in his account of Warlpiri and optional nominals, but puts forward an alternative analysis incorporating Hale's key insight about empty categories while preserving the Projection Principle. Her solution (1984, pp. 43–5) is to have Auxiliary contain case-marked, fully referential clitic pronouns that serve as verbal arguments. Nominals do not bear grammatically relevant case marking, they do not realize grammatical functions and they never occur in argument positions. Like any pronouns, the clitics in the Warlpiri Auxiliary can have antecedents outside their governing category. (An analysis similar in its essence but perforce differing in technical concepts and vocabulary was proposed in Elson and Pickett (1967, 72).) In a brief discussion of clause structure in Sierra Popoluca (a Mixe-Zoque language of Mexico, called Highland Popoluca according to the *Elsevier Encyclopedia of Language and Linguistics* (Second Edition); they present examples such as *imacpa t^{y}aka tahpi* 'he-grabs-it chick hawk, The hawk grabs the chick.' They say: 'In Sierra Popoluca the nucleus of the clause is the verb, and free nouns merely add detail. The nouns are not manifesting true subject and object slots, but *detail* slots.' Their comments applied to languages of Central America in which clauses had an obligatory core consisting of verb stem and person-number affixes. They treated full NPs as adjuncts, outside the core.), Pensalfini (2004, p. 360) proposes that this organization into clause core with case-marked clitic pronouns arises from a restriction on which positions in the clause are able to host encyclopaedic information. The computational system of the language faculty applies to the core of a clause, directly manipulating functional items, which have only formal features, but not combining the functional items with lexical items carrying encyclopaedic referential information.

A final comment on the split NPs by Pensalfini (2004, p. 374) is that in the Native Australian language Jingulu it is also common to find a pronoun with the same reference as an overt nominal, or to find a nominal repeated in a clause, as in (28). Pensalfini remarks that this makes it unlikely that these words were generated together within a single NP and somehow split up at a later stage in the derivation. (28) contains two occurrences of *bikirra*, the second with a focus suffix, and two constituents with demonstrative force, *Jiminiki*, glossed as 'this', and *nyambala*, glossed as 'DEM' for demonstrative. The general point about two occurrences of the same item is clear, but the syntactic organisation of (28), its textual and extra-linguistic contexts and its intonational organization and rhythm are not described at all.

(28) **Jiminiki** **bikirra** **nyambala** kurdarlyurru ka-ju **bikirra-rni**.
this grass DEM (n) green (n) 3sg-*do* grass-FOC
'This grass is green.'

Non-configurationality in Russian NPs

We turn now to data from Russian and the relationship between certain modifiers and the nouns they modify. The relationship is of interest because of the occurrence of 'split NPs', that is, NPs in which the head noun (or what in writing would be the head noun in an NP) is separated from its modifiers by other constituents. We will see that the term 'split NP' is a misnomer, because it assumes that the relevant constituents are initially part of an integrated NP, which becomes split. The Russian data constitute important evidence against this view, important because the 'split NP' construction is not typical of formal written Russian, is found in spontaneous spoken Russian and raises questions about what counts as the head of a NP.

(These and the other relevant data are taken from Zemskaja (1973), Lapteva (1976) and Morozova (1984), together with an analysis of the sample from Kapanadze and Zemskaja (1979). Given the censorious and inflexible attitudes displayed by many educated Russians towards any variety that can be seen to differ from formal written Russian, it is worthwhile reminding ourselves that Zemskaja and Lapteva recorded and transcribed the language spoken by educated Russians in informal and relaxed settings.)

There are three typical cases; in (29), an adjective and a noun are both preceded by a preposition; in (30), adjective and noun are at opposite ends of the clause; in (31), a quantifier/numeral/possessive noun and a noun are in a dependency relationship, but are not adjacent. The related adjective/quantifier and numeral are in bold.

(29) Adjective and noun in a prepositional phrase

živem	v	**novom**	v	**rajone**.
we-live	in	new	in	quarter

'we live in a new quarter.'

(30) Adjective and noun

interesnuju	prinesi	mne	**knigu**.
interesting	bring	to-me	book

'bring me an interesting book.'

(31) Numeral and noun

trista	ja	nasobiral	**značkov**
three-hundred	I	collected	badges

In (29), the adjective *novom* modifies the noun *rajone*, with which it agrees in case, number and gender. In written Russian, we would expect to find *v novom rajone*, with a single preposition assigning locative case to the noun, which in turn assigns locative case to the adjective (according to the traditional account). In (29) there are two occurrences of the preposition. In (30) the adjective *interesnuju* modifies the noun *knigu*, with which it agrees in case, number and gender. *Knigu* is the direct object of *prinesi*, and in written Russian, we would find *prinesi mne interesnuju knigu* or *interesnuju knigu prinesi mne* or *knigu interesnuju prinesi mne*; different word orders are possible in written Russian, but the adjective and noun are always adjacent. In (31) the numeral *trista* assigns genitive case to *značkov*; in written Russian we would find *ja nasobiral značkov trista*, with numeral and noun adjacent.

Non-adjacent adjectives and nouns are not always at opposite ends of clauses nor does the adjective always come first. Consider (32)–(35).

(32)

zdorovennuju	oni	**kanavu**	zdes'	rojut
huge-acc-fem-sg	they	trench-acc-fem-sg	here	dig-3Pl-Imperf

I	ukladyvajut	vot	**eti**	vot	**truby**.
And	lay-3Pl-Imperf	look	this-Pl-Acc	look	pipe-Pl-Acc

'They are digging a huge trench and laying – just look at them – these pipes.'

(33)

nekotorye	daže	do	vos'mi	turov	delajut	**baleriny**.
some	even	to	eight	turns	do-3Pl	ballerina-Nom-Pl

'Some ballerinas even do up to eight turns.'

(34)

Kuricu	na	**bol'šuju**	položi	**tarelku**.
chicken-Acc	on	big-Acc-Fem	put	plate-Acc-Fem

'Put the chicken on the a/the big plate.'

(35)

doma	ne	budu	stroit'	**zimnego**
house-Masc-Gen	not	Aux	build-Inf	winter-Masc Gen

'They're not going to build a winter house.'

The second clause of (32) and the word order in (30) will turn out to be of particular interest in the discussion of how non-adjacent adjective and noun are to be analysed. Here, we simply present the salient structural details. In the first clause of (32), the adjective is in initial position, but its noun is separated from it only by the subject of the clause, *oni* 'they'. In the second clause *eti* 'these' and *truby* 'pipes' are separated by the deictic particle *vot*. In written Russian and in more formal spoken Russian, we would find only *vot eti truby*, with the particle preceding the sequence of demonstrative and noun. The clause-initial constituent in (33) is an adjective, although it is translated into English by a quantifier. The Russian word *nekotorye* agrees with its noun in number, gender and case and must be analysed as an adjective. In (34), the adjective is not in initial position and is separated from its noun by the verb. *Tarelku*, in the accusative case, is the direct object of *položi*. In (35), it is the noun that is in clause-initial position and the adjective in clause-final position.

(36)–(38) are examples of non-adjacent numeral and noun and non-adjacent possessive noun and noun. In (36), the numeral *tri* follows the main verb *prixodili* 'came' and its noun (modified by an adjective) precedes. In (37), the possessive noun in the genitive case, *Igorja*, is in clause-initial position, while the head noun is in clause-final position. The reverse holds in (38), with the possessive noun *Tamary* at the end of the clause and the head noun *podružki* in second position.

(36)

Ital'janočki	**moloden'kie**	prixodili	**tri**	k	nam	v	gosti.
Italian-girls	young	came	three	to	us	into	guests

'Three nice young Italian girls came to stay with us.'

(37)

Igorja	k	nam	sobiralas'	priexat'	**mama**.
Of-Igor	to	us	was-intending	to-come	mother

'Igor's mother was intending to visit us.'

(38)

kogda	**podružki**	priedut	**Tamary**?
when	friends	will-arrive	of-Tamara?

'When are Tamara's friends arriving?'

Non-configurationality and information structure

Variations in word order seldom, if ever, come free, even in spontaneous speech. Lapteva (1976, pp. 213–23) suggests that the different orders are associated with different intonation patterns and different information structure. She distinguishes two post-posing constructions – 'distantnaja postpozicija', and a pre-posing construction. (Terms such as pre- and post-posing carry the presupposition that two items are originally adjacent and then separated or that the construction in which the two items are adjacent is more basic than the other one.) A distant post-posed adjective may be an afterthought or an important component of the message. As an afterthought, it does not carry focal accent ('dynamic stress') and is spoken at a quicker tempo. As an important component of the message, it can carry the focal accent and refers to some property of a given entity that is not objectively new but given in a particular situation. Lapteva remarks that this is typically the case in clauses organized in a sequence of stressed and unstressed constituents in which the rhythm helps the listener to interpret the disjoined adjective and noun. As examples of post-posed adjectives Lapteva gives (39) – an afterthought, and (40) – an important component of the message.

(39)	ja	tože	platok	vzjala	teplyj.
	I	too	shawl-nom-masc	took	warm-nom-masc

(40)	a	zamok-to	vstavila	novyj.
	and	lock-nom-masc -particle	has-put-in	new-nom-masc

'And has she/you put in a new lock?'

Distant pre-posed adjectives, whether clause-initial or clause-internal, are equal to or more important than the noun with respect to information load. Lapteva's example is (41), in which the adjective *čistoj* carries a falling pitch, there is a sharp rise on *net* and another falling pitch on the noun *rubaxi.*

(41)	a	u tebja	čistoj	net	rubaxi?
	And	at you	clean	not	shirt

'But haven't you got a clean shirt?'

The afterthought analysis of examples such as (39) has one disadvantage; it does not fit with the fact that these and the other examples cited by Lapteva were produced, according to the transcription, without a pause, yet the typical afterthought, or at least the stereotypical afterthought, is added after a short silence. Alternatively, an afterthought expression has its own intonation envelope. For instance, the English utterance *get me a pizza a small one* sounds peculiar without a pause (even very short) between *pizza* and *a small one* or without a separate intonation pattern over *a small one*. The same holds for Russian, but Lapteva marks only one out of thirty odd examples as having a pause (Lapteva, 1976, pp. 213–14). In another example, reproduced here as (42), she indicates a clause break by a comma, but a clause-final post-posed adjective immediately precedes the comma. That is, the adjective is intended to be read as part of the first clause both in intonation and in rhythm.

(42) a potom devčonki tak pripustilis' zadnie, tak bežali, užas.
and then girls-pl so quickened-pace rear-pl, so ran, horror
'And then the girls, the ones at the back, quickened their pace so much, ran so fast, that it was terrifying.'

In fact, Lapteva's example in (39) is more revealingly set out as in (43) (following the information in Lapteva (1976, p. 213).

(43) A u menja platok.
at me a-shawl
B ja tože platok vzjala teplyj.
I too a-shawl have-brought warm

That is, *platok* is given. Speaker B picks up the words of Speaker A and adds the information that her shawl is a warm one. *Teplyj* certainly conveys new information, but whether it is an afterthought is not certain. Clearly there is much work to be done on the position of adjectives in spontaneous spoken Russian; the central point for our purposes is that the word-order is not free, but controlled by discourse factors.

Only two of the split NPs have the order noun-X-adjective, where X stands for some constituent(s). That is, most of the split NPs with adjective and noun are not to be explained as afterthoughts. Interestingly, there is only one clear example of an afterthought or at least of problems with the parallel processing of language and the accessing of information in memory.

It is in the conversation extract in (44)

(44) kak raz popal na etot samyj/ na festival'// Venecianskij
particle fell on that very on festival Venetian
'What should he do but end up at that festival - the Venice festival.'

The '//' indicates an intonation contour marking a completed syntactic structure. The adjective *Venecianskij* carries its own intonation contour and constitutes a separate chunk of syntax. The language-processing difficulties are signalled by the use of the dummy word *samyj* (equivalent here to the use of *what's its name* by speakers of English, as in *he went to that em what's its name Venice festival*). *Samyj* is followed by a single oblique marking the intonation pattern 'utterance not finished' and the speaker repeats the preposition *na* along with the appropriate lexical item *festival'*. These are all signs of processing problems, and the intonation signals that the utterance is finished with the word *festival'*. *Venecianskij* really can be interpreted here as an afterthought.

Lapteva's analysis of pre-posed adjectives as carrying a large information load applies to an example of Zemkaja's in which the adjective is separated from the rest of the clause by an intonation break signalling an unfinished piece of syntax. Zemskaja's example is reproduced in (45). The adjective *glazirovannyx* delimits the set of entities that the speaker is interested in; the rest of the utterance specifies what the speaker wishes to know about those entities.

(45)	A	glazirovannyx/	net	u	vas	syrkov?
	And	glazed-gen-pl	not	at	you	cheese-gen-pl

'And what about glazed cheese curds? Have you got any?'

In the light of Lapteva's comments, it is tempting to say that the constructions with non-adjacent noun and adjective are either the result of planning problems, which lead to constituents being added as afterthoughts, or serve a special informational purpose, namely highlighting the adjective. The highlighting is achieved by moving the adjective out of its original position in a NP. None of this explains why spontaneous spoken Russian has them and not written Russian; that is, why the unusual construction with non-adjacent head and modifier is found in the variety that otherwise has much simpler syntax. The answer proposed later in this chapter is that the adjective and noun are linked, as signalled by the inflections, but that the adjective is more accurately seen as an independent NP, the noun constituting another separate NP. That is, in (32), the first clause can be glossed as 'It's a big one they are digging – a ditch'.

Siewerska (1984) discusses a parallel construction in Polish, labelling it 'phrasal discontinuity' rather than 'split NP'. She provides valuable information about its discourse function, being both a linguist and a native speaker. One of her examples is (46), which can be imagined as a reply to the comment 'Apparently they have a beautiful house'.

(46) Nie! **Pekny** maja **ogród**. **Dom** maja **kiepski**.
No! Beautiful they-have garden. House they-have crummy.
'No! It's the their garden that's beautiful. The house is crummy'.

The initial and final adjectives *pekny* and *kiepski* are contrastive. *Pekny* is given, being repeated from the initial comment, and *kiepski* is new and highlighted in clause-final position. That is, as in the Russian examples, the order of adjective and noun is not random, but constitutes a contrastive construction.

This section can usefully be brought to a close with more figures, since Zemskaja and Lapteva do not quantify the occurrences of split NPs. In an extract of conversation containing 2,310 NPs there were 36 split NPs, constituting a mere 1.6 per cent of the total. Prima facie this is a minute proportion of the total number of NPs, which might be thought not worth bothering about. These first impressions are misleading because there are only 285 candidates for splitting, that is 285 NPs consisting of an adjective and noun. That is, 12.6 per cent of the candidates were actually split. This percentage is hardly overwhelming, but it does indicate a construction that has to be taken seriously. To put it in perspective, the number of split NPs was greater than the number of NPs containing a relative clause and half the number of NPs containing a prepositional phrase.

Analysing 'split NPs'

This section deals exclusively with Russian data, partly because JM understands it much better than the Warlbiri or Pitjantjatjara, partly because there is more Russian data available and partly because it is possible, as shown earlier, to glean comments on split NPs and information structure. Nonetheless, JM believes that the following discussion applies equally well to the Native Australian data, which are like the Russian data in representing spontaneous spoken language.

How should 'split NPs' be analysed? The terminology used by Lapteva, post-posing and pre-posing, suggests an analysis in which, say, the adjective (or quantifier/numeral) and noun are initially combined into a single NP, with the adjective subsequently being moved out of the NP to form a separate constituent. Exactly this view is taken by Pereltsvaig (2008), who criticizes the direct extraction of constituents from NPs and proposes instead to copy entire NPs, but interpret only a part of them. She points out that direct extraction violates a number of constraints on movement. It applies to non-constituents, as in (47), to one conjunct in a pair of conjoined constituents, as in (48), and to islands, such as case-marked nouns, which otherwise prevent extraction, as in (49).

(47) Protiv sovetskoj on vystupal vlasti.
Against Soviet-fem-gen he demonstrated power-fem-gen
'He spoke out against Soviet power.'

(48) Ja tvoi vystirala chulki i rubashku.
I your-pl washed stockings and shirt
'I washed your stockings and shirt.'

(49) Po sintaksisu ona byla starshe professora
of syntax she was older professor-gen
'She was older than the professor of syntax.'

Pereltsvaig comments that the moved chunk can be a more complex non-constituent string than in (47) and gives (50) as an example.

(50) ja prosto probovala
I simply tried

vot eti češskie s supinatorami kupit' tufli.
see these Czech with arch-supports to-buy shoes
'I simply tried to buy these Czech shoes with arch-supports.'

What is moved by direct extraction is the chunk *eti češskie s supinatorami* 'these Czech with arch-supports', to which Pereltsvaig presumably assigns a structure along the lines of Det AP PP. (It is not quite clear how Croft would analyse split NPs. He observes (2001, pp. 186–7) that in most cases syntactic contiguity reflects semantic relations but that mismatches can occur. He says (discussing an example from Wardaman, a Native Australian language, but his comments apply to the Polish example in (46)) that the only reason that the elements in bold in (46) are treated as constituents is because of the semantic relation holding between the garden and its property of being beautiful and the house and its property of being crummy. Is this the same approach as Pereltsvaig's or the one set out below? What we can say with certainty is that Croft does not connect the construction with spontaneous spoken language.)

An alternative approach, one that occurs very readily to analysts of the syntax of spontaneous speech, is to treat the adjective (or quantifier or numeral) and noun as independent constituents, which were never combined into a single NP. We saw at the beginning of this chapter that in spontaneous spoken English and Russian (and in the corresponding varieties of other languages)

NPs are very simple, typically consisting of a single constituent such as a pronoun or noun, or of a Determiner and Noun. Depending on the context, such simple NPs may not carry enough information to enable the addressee to identify the speaker's intended referent. More information can be provided, but as in the extracts examined earlier, speakers spread the information over separate clauses or, if they do produce a relatively complex NP, produce it on its own and not as the subject or object of a clause. Analyses that handle the 'split NPs' as integral NPs that have been split up do not accord with the evidence from spontaneous speech, but do fit nicely with Zemskaja's observations cited at the beginning of the chapter to the effect that spoken Russian is non-configurational. This is a good place to point out that the Native Australian languages are spoken-only. A plausible hypothesis is that the combining of demonstratives, quantifiers, adjectives and nouns into NPs happens as groups of language users develop rehearsed or scripted texts, such as narratives, myths and texts for use in public (or private) ceremonies. The rise of complex NPs also happens when written texts appear and are elaborated.

There are already two major analyses of NPs in English. Following the publication of Abney (1987), it is generally accepted that a sequence such as *the quick brown fox* has *the* as its head and is a Determiner Phrase, not a NP. (See for instance, Cann, 1993, but see also the discussion on pp. 50–53.) The discussion below suggests that the determiner-as-head analysis has to be taken seriously in syntax (with the emphasis on syntax, since a distinction has to be drawn between the constituent with the greatest semantic load in an NP, typically the noun, and the constituent that determines the fine syntactic class of the phrase, typically the determiner).

Russian long adjectives: nominal and deictic

The 'split NPs' in Russian have a straightforward explanation: long adjectives are very noun-like and can function as the sole constituent in NPs. A word first about Russian adjectives. They fall into two classes, known as long adjectives and short adjectives; long adjectives are both attributive and predicative, but short adjectives are only predicative.

The short forms of *interesnyj* 'interesting' are exemplified in (51).

(51) a. Odin proekt byl interesen 'One – scheme – was – interesting.'
b. Odna mysl' byla interesna 'One – idea – was – interesting.'
c. Eto opisanie bylo interesno 'This – description – was – interesting.'
d. Eti teorii byli interesny 'These – theories – were – interesting.'

The short adjective forms – *interesen*, *interesna*, *interesno* and *interesny* – have the same gender and number as the subject noun, but have no case inflections. They occur only as the complement of *byt'* 'be'; that is, they never occur inside NPs, nor do they occur as complements of verbs, such as *kazat'sja* 'seem', which require their complement to be in the instrumental case, that is, to have an instrumental case suffix and therefore to be a long adjective.

The long adjective forms are exemplified in (52).

(52) a. interesnyj proekt '(an/the) interesting – project'
b. interesnaja mysl' '(an/the) interesting – idea'
c. interesnoe opisanie '(an/the) interesting – description'
d. interesnye idei '(the) interesting ideas'
e. v interesnom proekte 'in – (the) interesting – project'
f. avtor interesnogo proekta
'(the) author of-(the)-interesting of-(the)-project'

The adjective forms in (52) are called 'long' because they consist of the stem plus an affix: *-yj*, *-ja*, *-oe*, *-ogo*, *-ye* and *-om*. The long forms take the same number, gender and case as the noun they combine with and occur both in NPs, as in (52), and as the complement of verbs, including *byt'* 'be'. (The choice of long or short predicative adjectives is a controversial topic in Russian grammar, but is not relevant for present purposes.)

The key fact is that the long affixes derive historically from deictic pronouns and are still deictic in Modern Russian. The question *Ty kakoe plat'e kupila*? 'You which dress bought?, Which dress did you buy?' can be given a one-word reply: *zelenoe* '(the) green (one)', *šerstjanoe* '(the) woollen (one)'. These one-word replies are also appropriate answers to the question *čto za plat'e ty kupila*? 'What kind of dress did you buy?'. The 'adjective' forms can also function as referring items and as subject, direct object or oblique object. In, for example, a situation where a number of dresses are on display, the speaker can say *Zelenoe dorogo* '(The) green (one) – (is) – too dear' without having previously used the word *plat'e* 'dress'. At this point, we can usefully recall Baker's view of examples such as (16b), (18) and (27), that these languages collapse N and A into a single distributional and morphological class of nominals, case-bearing elements, which appear freely ordered with respect to one another, and the verb. His comment might have been written with respect to spontaneous spoken Russian.

(This analysis based on deixis is indirectly supported by historical changes in Bulgarian, another Slav language. Bulgarian lost the distinction between long and short adjectives; compare *rokljata e zelena* 'the-dress is green' with *zelena roklja* 'a-green dress'. Bulgarian developed a definite article from a deictic. The deictic is realized by a suffix on the first constituent in a given NP, whether that constituent is a noun or adjective; compare *rokljata* 'the dress' and *zelenata roklja* 'the-green dress'. In structure, *zelena* + *ta* is analogous to the Russian *zelena* + *ja* (feminine, to match the Bulgarian adjective) and *zeleno* + *to* is analogous to the Russian long neuter adjective *zeleno* + *je*).

The data give rise to an important question: in the above examples, are the long 'adjectives' adjectives as we understand the category in English examples such as *the green dress*, or are they nouns, with the following noun in apposition? That is, should the structure of, for example, *zelenoe plat'e* '(the) – green – dress' be glossed as 'the green one – dress', where *plat'e* 'dress' provides an intension for the deictic element *-oe*? It will be argued that the answer to these two questions is 'yes'.

Consider now the second clause in (32), repeated below as (53).

(53) I	ukladyvajut	vot	**eti**	vot	**truby**
And	lay-3Pl-Imperf	look	this-Pl-Acc	look	pipe-Pl-Acc

'They are digging a huge trench and laying – just look at them – these pipes'

The demonstrative *eti* 'these' is both preceded by a deictic particle *vot* and separated from its noun by another occurrence of *vot*. (This particle is treated as deictic, because *vot* is in general equivalent to the English 'Look!'.) It is possible to speak or write the corresponding phrase *vot eti truby*, in which *eti* is said to be a demonstrative adjective modifying *truby*. We could see *eti truby* as the source for *eti vot truby* in (32/53), as an NP that is broken up by *vot*. However, an alternative view, which fits better with the pronominal nature of *eti* and with previous examples, is that *eti* and *truby* are separate NPs and that *vot* does not break up an NP, but occurs before each of the independent NPs. In context, the utterance is quite appropriate. The speaker points verbally – and possibly physically – and says *vot eti* 'look – these ones' and then adds information to make absolutely clear the reference of the deictic: *vot truby* 'look – (the) pipes'. (Since nouns in Russian lack a definite article, a single noun can be interpreted as definite or indefinite depending on context and/or syntax.)

In their ability to be the sole constituent of NPs and to function as referring expressions, long adjectives in Russian are not unusual. Demonstratives (such as *eti* in the above paragraph and *tot* 'that one'), quantifiers (such as *vse* 'all' and *każdyj* 'each') and numerals (particularly collective numerals) can all occur as the sole constituent in NPs. They also function as referring expressions, although they are referentially more dependent on the immediate context of utterance than are long adjectives. Since the details of the relevant constructions would take us too far from the discussion of adjectives, the interested reader is left to read the excellent discussion of numerals in Corbett (1993).

Pereltsvaig's examples (47)–(50), repeated below, can be analysed in similar fashion. One drawback is that Pereltsvaig supplies no textual context, although it is undoubtedly the context that determined the constituent order.

(47) Protiv sovetskoj on vystupal vlasti.
Against Soviet-fem-gen he demonstrated power-fem-gen
'He spoke out against Soviet power.'

(48) Ja tvoi vystirala chulki i rubashku.
I your-pl washed stockings and shirt
'I washed your stockings and shirt.'

(49) Po sintaksisu ona byla starshe professora
of syntax she was older professor-gen
'She was older than the professor of syntax.'

(50) ja prosto probovala
I simply tried

vot eti češskie s supinatorami kupit' tufli.
see these Czech with arch-supports to-buy shoes
'I simply tried to buy these Czech shoes with arch-supports.'

(46) can be glossed 'Against the Soviet one he demonstrated – the/their power'; (47) as 'I washed your ones/things – stockings and shirt'; (48) as 'the one of syntax – she was older than the professor', which would look more plausible in the context of a discussion about which professor she was or was not older than. (50) is very naturally interpreted as 'I simply tried, see, these Czech ones with arch supports, to buy the shoes.' In context, the chunk *eti češskie s supinatorami* is a perfectly good NP.

Repeated prepositions in Russian

Finally, we go back to example (29), repeated below as (54).

(54) živem v **novom** v **rajone**.
we-live in new in quarter
'We live in a new quarter.'

What syntactic structure should be assigned to (29/54)? We could say that there is a single prepositional phrase, which happens to have two occurrences of *v*. To explain the two occurrences, a (hitherto unknown) process of preposition spreading could be invoked. The alternative solution is to take the syntactic facts at face value and treat (29/54) as containing two PPs, the first being *v novom* and the second being *v rajone*. *v rajone* is in apposition to *v novom*, and the gloss is 'We live in a new one in a quarter.' Preposition spreading sounds an attractive transformational solution, but raises serious questions. What other languages have preposition spreading – or postposition spreading? Case spreading is a familiar phenomenon, not least in Russian; in a phrase such as *v novom rajone*, the noun and the adjective agree in case, and the traditional view is that the case marking spreads from, or is assigned by, the noun to the adjective. Again recalling Baker's comments, we can see the Russian data as not posing any problem, since nouns and long adjectives are both noun-like. (This is of course a very traditional analysis in the linguistics of Indo-European languages.)

Preposition spreading would not only be very unusual, but would require empty prepositional nodes for the preposition copy to attach to. The use of empty nodes is familiar, but in relation to NPs and the various arrangements of NPs round the central verb. In the Principles and Parameters analysis of active and passive clauses, the verb and all its complement NPs are generated under one node in the initial structure. Higher up the tree there is an empty NP node. Either of the complement NPs can be moved into this empty NP node; if the original subject NP moves, the resulting clause is active; if the original direct object NP moves, the resulting clause is passive.

There is no such rationale for empty preposition nodes. In any case, having empty preposition nodes means having two prepositional phrases, each containing a NP. In other words, a putative preposition-spreading rule leads us to the second analysis proposed below, that *novom* and *rajone* are in two juxtaposed PPs and that they themselves are NPs. A third disadvantage of preposition spreading is that we postulate more complex structure to handle a variety of language in which the syntactic structures are relatively simple. To sum up, the 'split' NP construction and the double-preposition construction provide independent reasons for treating the long adjectives as nouns.

The analysis of 'split NPs' as consisting of separate constituents, which are in apposition, as in the case of the prepositional phrases, or one of which elaborates the reference of another, is in tune with Elson and Pickett's comment quoted on p. 78 that the nouns in Sierra Popoluca clauses merely add detail to the pronominal affixes on the verb (Elson and Pickett, 1967, p. 72). It is also in tune with Lyons' hypothesis on the ontogenesis of referring expressions consisting of deictic determiner and noun. (See Lyons, 1975, reprinted 1991.) We will ignore the part of Lyons' argument based on the generation of referring expressions such as *that dog* and *the dog* in the standard model of transformational grammar, but other parts of the argument are still valid. For instance, Lyons points out that in the English phrases *that dog* and *the dog* the head cannot be *dog* because singular count nouns cannot be used as referring expressions without some kind of determiner or quantifier. Lyons proposes to analyse *dog* as in apposition to *that* or *the.*

Split NPs and reference in spontaneous speech

The relevance of the NP data from spoken Russian (and spoken English) is this. The high incidence of referring expressions with one constituent, particularly personal pronouns, deictic determiners and quantifiers, reflects the use of language in context. Speakers make, usually justifiably, generous assumptions about what their addressees can pick out from the immediate context of utterance. These assumptions lead to the extensive use of referring expressions that are syntactically simple and light in information. If speakers want to supply extra information, they can add a noun – that is, if they are speaking Russian they can add a noun, but if they are speaking English they have to add a combination of definite article and noun. The point is that historically the construction of definite article plus noun arose from a combination of deictic determiner plus noun, the definite article being a reduced deictic determiner. In spontaneous speech, we can still see the type of situation in which a combination of deictic and noun arose and we can see the situational justification for regarding the noun as in apposition to the deictic.

Analysts who deal exclusively or mainly with written language may find the foregoing discussion vague and even tiresome, with its insistence on unintegrated syntax. Why resist an analysis based on direct extraction or movement/copying when that yields incomplete NPs which can be handled in a compositional approach to meaning? Of course, compositionality is relevant to the analysis of spontaneous spoken language; it is just a property of much smaller chunks of syntax than is usual in written language. Even in written language some mechanism is required in addition to composition of meaning, for the simple reason that descriptions of individuals can be built up over several (text) sentences and a given text will contain many references to whatever individuals participate in the situations it describes. DRT is one mechanism that has been developed over the past 30 years to handle references to individuals in sequences of clauses, whether the individuals are given or new. Information about individuals can be thought of as stored in file-cards, to which pieces of information are added as they are supplied in the text. A good example is in (55), from the opening paragraphs of Lee Child's novel *One Shot.*

(55) The man with the rifle drove north. Not fast, not slow. Not drawing attention. Not standing out. He was in a light-coloured minivan that had seen better days. He was alone behind the wheel. He was wearing a light-coloured raincoat and the kind of shapeless light-coloured beanie hat that old guys wear on the golf course when the sun is out or the rain is falling. The hat had a two-tone red band all round it. It was pulled down low.

The reader opens a file for the individual and enters [man] [has rifle]. Five text sentences later the reader adds [is alone in minivan], then [is wearing raincoat (raincoat is light-coloured)] and [is wearing beanie hat], then all the information about the beanie hat, since that is also part of the description of the man. This is a written text, and the information is introduced in dribs and drabs. (See the discussion of text sentences in Chapter 1.)

The file metaphor applies slightly differently, but nonetheless straightforwardly to examples such as (50), reproduced below as (56).

(56)	ja	prosto	probovala				
	I	simply	tried				
	vot	eti	češskie	s	supinatorami	kupit'	tufli.
	see	these	Czech	with	arch-supports	to-buy	shoes

'I simply tried to buy these Czech shoes with arch-supports.'

We do not know if (56) is right at the beginning of a conversation or in the middle. Shoes may have been mentioned already or the speaker may simply have mentioned going shopping. If shoes have already been mentioned, the listener will have opened a file for the set of shoes and may be ready to open sub-files for particular pairs of shoes. If the speaker has merely mentioned shopping, a file will not have been opened. *Eti* has no content, but it functions as a signal to receive upcoming information. The speaker can add 'are Czech' to the file, and as soon as they hear *s supinatorami* 'with arch-supports' they add 'are shoes' to the file without waiting for the speaker to utter *tufli.* (Perelts-vaig gives no information about intonation and rhythm. Is *tufli* to be analysed as an afterthought, perhaps separated by a pause from *kupit'* and outside the body of the clause?)

The examples cited by Zemskaja are relevant to recent attempts to formulate constraints on the positioning of heads and modifiers. Hudson (1990, p. 117) proposes a 'relaxed Adjacency Principle': 'D is adjacent to H [can be counted as adjacent to H] provided that every word between D and H is a subordinate either of H, or of a mutual head of D and H.' Consider (57).

(57)	Kuricu	na **bol'šuju**	položi	**tarelku**
	chicken-Acc	on big-Acc-Fem	put-Imper	plate-Acc-Fem

'put the chicken on the a/the big plate'

D is *bol'šuju* and *tarelku* is H. These can be counted as adjacent if the word that comes between them is a subordinate of *bol'šuju*, a subordinate of *tarelku* or a subordinate of some word on which they are both dependent. These conditions are not met, because the intervening word, *položi*, is the head of the clause (in the long-standing verb-dependency tradition within which Hudson works). That is, *bol'šuju* and *tarelku* are both dependents of *položi*, and *položi* itself does not depend on any other word. We offer the hypothesis that constraints on adjacency and head–modifier relationships can be formulated for written language but that the choppy nature of syntactic structure in spontaneous speech makes it unlikely that general constraints can be established for all languages.

Secondly, there is the question of complexity. An analysis with Scrambling is more complex than one without Scrambling, and we might expect an example analysed by means of Scrambling to be more complex than one analysed without Scrambling. The difficulty is that Russian split NPs occur in spontaneous spoken Russian, which is precisely where syntactic structures are at their simplest because of lack of planning time. From this viewpoint, the application of a more complex analysis to a simple structure is unappealing. Moreover, it ignores the deictic function of long adjectives in Russian and the availability of anaphoric treatments.

How then can grammars handle examples such as (57), *Kuricu na* ***bol'šuju*** *položi* ***tarelku*** 'the-chicken on a/the-big-one place a/the-plate'? *bol'šuju* 'big' and *tarelku* 'plate' are syntactically linked but non-adjacent. The first step towards a solution is to note that the problem is not confined to Russian long adjectives. Pollard and Sag (1994) ask how French speakers know to say *elle est belle*, pointing to a table or a car and using the feminine singular pronoun rather than the masculine singular pronoun *il* and the feminine singular adjective *belle* rather than the masculine singular *beau*. The relevant French nouns have feminine gender – *table* and *voiture* or *bagnole* – but the example contains no overt full nouns.

Pollard and Sag (1994, p. 60), working within a unification constraint-based framework, suggest that the feature structure for nominals includes indices relating to three types of agreement: syntactic agreement, involving syntactic objects such as case values; index agreement, which arises when indices are to be token-identical; pragmatic agreement, which arises when contextual background assumptions are required to be consistent. Furthermore, the indices are not specified as part of syntactic categories but in the internal structure of referential indices. Indices are abstract objects whose discourse function is to keep track of the entities being talked about; for example, in *My neighbour*$_i$ *thinks she*$_i$ *is a genius* the subscript 'i' is a third-person singular feminine index (Pollard and Sag, 1994, pp. 66–7). With respect to the French example given earlier, they propose that the index of the pronoun must coincide with the index of a French common noun denoting the set of entities containing the entity referred to by the pronoun (Pollard and Sag, 1994, p. 79).

All this is relevant to Russian long adjectives in split NPs. The adjectives agree in gender and number with a noun. As discussed earlier, the long adjectives consist of a stem and an ending that historically derives from a deictic, and they still function as deictics in Modern Russian. Taking advantage of the proposals in Pollard and Sag (1994), we can say that the occurrence of pronouns in Russian, including long adjectives, must make reference to the relevant lexical item.

This approach to the problem is particularly pleasing, as it is compatible with the view, outlined in at the end of Chapter 1, that the distinction between competence and language production should not be taken to be clear-cut, especially with regard to the syntactic structure of spontaneous spoken language. With respect to (57), the speaker can be thought of as first fixing on the situation to be talked about and then deciding on what is to be referred to first – in this case a property of a particular entity, the plate. The reference is performed by means of a long adjective, *bol'šuju*, but as Pollard and Sag put it, the reference of *bol'šuju* is mediated by the lexical entry for *tarelku*, which supplies the information that the noun and therefore any pronoun must be feminine. Since there is only one entity and since *tarelku* is not in the class of pluralia tantum nouns, the number is singular.

The 'split' NP constructions in spoken Russian bear on recent work in which minor grammatical items, and not major lexical items, are given the status of heads of constructions. They are relevant because an argument can be made (with respect to both spoken and written Russian) for taking adjectives to be the syntactic heads of adjective–noun sequences. The fact (let us take it to be a fact) that adjectives and nouns in spoken Russian can occur as independent, non-adjacent NPs lends support to the argument that adjectives play just as important a role as nouns in integrated NPs.

While not agreeing with the entire analysis of particular constructions, Hudson (1987) invokes the criteria laid out in Zwicky (1985). The head of a construction is the constituent that carries any inflexions in languages with inflectional morphology (the morphosyntactic locus); the constituent that denotes the kind of entity denoted by the construction (*planted potatoes* denotes a kind of planting rather than a kind of potato and *planted* is the head); the constituent that is subcategorized with respect to its sister constituents in the construction (the subcategorizand); the constituent that determines the morphosyntactic form of some sister (the governor); the constituent that is obligatory and the constituent whose distribution is similar to that of the mother. Hudson rejects one of Zwicky's criteria, concluding that the direction of agreement between constituents is irrelevant. Long adjectives in NPs, 'split' or integrated, meet most of the other criteria. They carry inflexional morphology (as do nouns); in traditional accounts, they are subcategorized with respect to the gender, number and case of the noun; they have similar distribution to nouns, as demonstrated earlier. The semantic criterion has to do with denotation; the head of a construction denotes the kind of entity denoted by the entire construction. This criterion is insightfully applied to verb phrases by Hudson (1987), who analyses *planting potatoes* as denoting a kind of planting rather than a kind of potato. It does not apply unambiguously to combinations of adjective and noun, but the ambiguity itself is significant. The crucial question is this: does a phrase such as *bol'šuju tarelku* 'big plate' denote a kind of big thing or a kind of plate? The answer must be that both denotations are possible depending on context; in rather crude terms, it depends on whether the phrase turns up in a reply to the question *kakaja bol'šaja vešč*? 'what big thing?' or *čto za tarelka*? 'what for a-plate', that is, 'what kind of plate?' That is, in Russian, nouns and long adjectives meet the same criteria and both have an equal right to be considered the head of a 'Noun' Phrase.

We have argued that split NPs, including long adjective and noun, should not be derived by scrambling from a solidary NP but that the two constituents should be generated in situ. What about the combinations in which long adjective and noun are adjacent? Let us remind ourselves first that the long adjectives are deictic, that, for example, the adjective *xorošij* ('good') consists of the stem *xoroš-* and the deictic suffix *-ij*. In grammars of Russian, these suffixes are described as case affixes, but given that they derive historically from deictics and given that the long adjectives are regularly used deictically, it is reasonable to assume that the affixes have not lost their deictic nature. Just as Lyons suggested that the determiner plus noun structure in English and other languages began with nouns being put in apposition to deictics, so we suggest that the Russian adjective–noun construction arose out of nouns being put in apposition to long adjectives, which are deictic. That is, examples such as *xorošij meč* 'a/the-good sword' arose out of a structure that can be glossed as 'good-that-one a/the sword'. The modern Russian phrase is translated into English simply as 'a/the good sword'.

Categorial grammar sheds further light on this analysis. Let us begin with a straightforward example. Categorial grammar treats a VP as a category that requires a NP to yield a sentence; for example, *swam in the loch* is merely a verb phrase, but it can be converted into a sentence by the addition of a NP such as *the children, the monster* and so on. In Montague terms, a VP belongs to the category *t/e*, that is, it requires an element belonging to the category *e* – that is, an element referring to an entity –to produce an element belonging to the category *t*, the category of elements referring to truth values. Sentences are held to refer to truth values, truth values being assigned to propositions.

We are concerned here with the various categories of elements inside elements of category *e*, that is, inside NPs. The starting point is the generally accepted analysis, which takes determiners to apply to single nouns or to combinations of adjective and noun. In *the red cup*, the determiner *the* picks out a specific entity that is in the set of red things and in the set of cups. As already observed, English common count nouns do not become referential until they have a determiner. A singular common count noun can be treated categorially as an element that requires a determiner to become a member of the category *e*. In purely syntactic terms, such a noun allows the addition of a determiner or a numeral or a quantifier, but once the addition has been made no further determiners, numerals or quantifiers can be added.

How do adjectives appear in this perspective? In English, the addition of an adjective to a singular common count noun yields an element still belonging to the category of elements that require a determiner, etc., to become a member of the category *e*. That is, the categorial perspective presents the noun as the head of the adjective–noun structure. The Russian situation is different.

A singular common count noun in Russian, say *čaška* (cup), may be referential or non-referential depending on the syntactic construction. The addition of a long adjective yields an expression that is also referential or non-referential depending on the syntactic construction. The major difference between English and Russian is that while *red* on its own cannot belong to category *e*, the Russian adjective *krasnaja* can belong to category *e* on its own. In fact, like *čaška*, it is referential or non-referential depending on the syntactic construction.

Conclusion

To sum up, the categorial perspective brings out the difference between Russian and English adjectives. The crucial evidence for Russian is the deictic source and nature of the long adjective. On the evidence that adjectives are at least equal in status to nouns in the adjective–noun construction, we propose the adjective as potential head of NPs. The appositional structure referred to earlier has not died out, but is alive and well in modern Russian (and, to pick up the comment made right at the beginning of this section) in Warlbiri and Pitjantjatjara.

4 Constructions

Chapter Outline

Clause constructions as a network

What is a construction? When we analyse a construction, we are interested in the smaller blocks that have been combined to build up a bigger block. We look at what sort of smaller blocks have been used and the order in which they are set out: for example, *crush* + *ed* and not *ed* + *crush*, *into the house* and not *the house into*. We look at how the smaller blocks are linked: by order, as in the examples in the previous sentence, or by some syntactic linkage, such as agreement in number, as in *The girls were swimming* and not **The girls is swimming* (for standard English), or by agreement in person and number, as in Russian *ja slušaju* '*I obey*' versus *on slušajet* 'he obeys' versus *Oni slušajut* 'They obey'. 'Construction' is understood this way in introductory textbooks such as Huddleston (1988, pp. 7–8) and Collins and Hollo (2000, p. 10), but is not mentioned at all in Hudson (1998). It is mentioned in Culicover (2009, p. 33), but Culicover's definition is idiosyncratic and much narrower. He regards a construction as 'a syntactically complex expression whose meaning is not entirely predictable from the meanings of its parts and the way that they are combined in the structure' (Culicover, 2009, p. 33). This places constructions at one end of the spectrum of syntactic units recognized by Croft and Cruse (2004) and Goldberg (1995).

We focus here on constructions in clauses. Three ideas are central. The first is that we can recognize basic simple clauses and more complex clauses and can work out the relationships between them. That is, constructions are not isolated structures, but fit into a general network. The second idea is that different constructions enable speakers and writers to signal what they are doing with a particular utterance and to perform different linguistic acts. (These are known as 'speech acts', but they are performed both in speech and in writing.) They make statements, ask questions and issue commands or requests. They ask different types of question and present situations in different ways. A third idea, which arises from the previous one, is that speakers and writers need different constructions with different functions to create texts – conversations, lectures, sports commentaries, novels, poems, newspaper reports and so on. Different constructions enable speakers and writers to introduce new entities into the content of a conversation, to handle economically already-mentioned entities, to highlight bits of information and to keep track of the people and things in the content of a conversation, story, etc. The existence of different constructions is essential for successful communication.

The idea of a basic construction and paths going out to other constructions can be illustrated with the examples in (1). Possible labels for each construction are in small capitals inside square brackets. The labels are for illustration only. A systematic set of labels would be far more complex than is required for this discussion.

(1) [DECLARATIVE]
  a. Frank bought the piano for Jane. [OBLIQUE OBJECT]
  b. Frank bought Jane the piano. [DOUBLE OBJECT]
  c. The piano was bought for Jane by Frank. [PASSIVE, OBLIQUE OBJECT]

(2) [INTERROGATIVE]
  a. Did Frank buy the piano for Jane? [OBLIQUE OBJECT]
  b. Did Frank buy Jane the piano? [DOUBLE OBJECT]
  c. Was the piano bought for Jane by Frank? [PASSIVE, OBLIQUE OBJECT]

The basic construction in (1a) is related to the other constructions in (1b,c) and also to the interrogative constructions in (2a–c). Paths do not go direct from the basic construction to every other one, say from the construction in (1a) to the constructions in (1b), (2a) and (2c); instead paths go from the basic [DECLARATIVE] construction to the other [DECLARATIVE] constructions and then from each of the [DECLARATIVE] constructions to the corresponding [INTERROGATIVE] one. Thus, a path goes from (1a) to the [DOUBLE OBJECT] construction in (1b) and another path goes from (1b) to the [DOUBLE OBJECT INTERROGATIVE] construction in (2b). Another path goes from the construction in (1a) to the [DECLARATIVE, PASSIVE, OBLIQUE OBJECT] construction in (1c). From (1c) a path goes to the [INTERROGATIVE, PASSIVE, OBLIQUE OBJECT] construction in (2c). The paths are not to be interpreted as rules building one structure out of another as did transformations in the standard model of transformational grammar. Rather, they are like the implicational rules of Generalized Phrase Structure Grammar: if language X has construction Y, then it also has construction Z.

Constructions, speech acts and discourse functions

Different constructions are required for different speech acts. Declarative clauses convey statements, interrogative clauses convey questions and imperative clauses convey commands (in the broadest sense of that word). There are different constructions for different types of question: if the speaker is enquiring whether something happened, a construction is used – *Did the parcel from Jennifer arrive yesterday?*. If the speaker knows that a parcel arrived but is seeking details as to particular aspects of the event, a [WH INTERROGATIVE] construction is used – *Which parcel arrived yesterday?*, *When did the parcel from Jennifer arrive?* and so on. If the speaker is fairly certain that the parcel from Jennifer arrived yesterday but is seeking confirmation from the addressee, a [TAG INTERROGATIVE] construction is used – *The parcel from Jennifer arrived yesterday, didn't it?*

There are different constructions for different discourse purposes. The speaker may wish to present a situation and omit the agent. A [PASSIVE] construction is chosen – *The car was being driven badly.* The speaker may wish to present a patient as controlling a situation. A [MIDDLE] construction is chosen – *This car drives beautifully on twisty roads.* The speaker may wish to contrast one entity with another, for which purpose an [IT CLEFT] is suitable – *It was Juliet's car that broke down (not anybody else's).*

Splitting or lumping: fixing the boundaries between constructions

Any language has a very large number of constructions. In languages with both spoken and written varieties, some constructions are typical of spontaneous speech, others are typical of writing and a third set is used in both. Some constructions will be archaic, others will be current and a third set will be confined to particular genres. And constructions will range from fixed sequences such as *Let well alone* through templates that allow a limited amount of variation, such as *as far as I can see/make out/know (the banks won't lend anybody any money)* to structures that allow unlimited variation, such as declarative clauses. Many constructions consist of one clause, but some consist of two clauses, for instance IT Clefts, WH Clefts and Tag Questions.

(3) a. It was only on Monday that we realized the dog was missing.
b. What we're going to discuss today is renewable energy.
c. You're going to the ball aren't you?

In the IT Cleft in (3a) *that we realized the dog was missing* is one clause; the other clause is *It was only on Monday*. In the WH Cleft in (3b), the two clauses are *What we're going to discuss today* and *What we're going to discuss today is renewable energy*. (If we adopt the neat analysis proposed by Bresnan and Grimshaw (1978), the second clause is *we're going to discuss Ø today*.) In (3c), the speaker makes a statement by means of the declarative clause *You're going to the ball* and asks the question by means of the clause *aren't you?*

An important issue concerning constructions is how finely to split up data from a given language. Introductory textbooks such as Miller (2008) usually mention the existential–presentative construction exemplified by *There's a fox in the garden*. The simple label 'existential construction' signals that the analyst considers there is only one (general) construction. The label 'existential–presentative' signals that the construction has two functions, which are often, but not always, concurrent. Croft and Cruse (2004, p. 241), on the basis of data in Lakoff (1987), propose a set of four existential constructions. Their list is in (4).

(4) a. There's a fox in the garden. CENTRAL EXISTENTIAL
b. There's a man been shot. STRANGE EVENT
c. There is a Santa Clause. ONTOLOGICAL
d. Suddenly there burst into the room an SS officer holding a machine gun. PRESENTATIONAL

(4a) is the most frequent construction. In speech, it is typically introduced by *there's* whether the following noun is singular or plural. One view is that *there is* has been reduced and grammaticalized into a marker. The first NP is typically indefinite, since the construction is used to introduce entities not previously mentioned in an interchange. (4a) contains a locative phrase, *in the garden.* In the central existential construction, such a locative phrase is obligatory, certainly when examples of the construction occur as the first contribution to a text or section of text. The ontological construction in (4c) also has an indefinite NP, but does not contain a locative phrase, presumably because it is used to assert the existence in general of something, whereas the central existential construction is used to assert the existence or presence of something in some place.

(4b) presents an entity and an event, while (4d) presents an event. It so happens that the agent in (4d) is referred to by an indefinite NP because in the putative context this is the first mention of the SS officer. An example such as *Suddenly there burst into the room the two policemen we had noticed in the square* is equally unmarked; the definite NP *the two policemen* is used because it may be assumed that they have been mentioned before. The verbs that occur in this construction are typically verbs of movement or appearance (which can be interpreted as movement from absence to presence): *There appeared big black clouds, There arrived a car at the door, There strolled into view a lady with a little dog, There sailed into the harbour a very elegant yacht* and so on.

The label 'strange event' assigned to (4b) by Croft and Cruse is not entirely appropriate, as events referred to by means of this construction are not necessarily strange (depending on one's expectations of garages and so on): *There's a mechanic working on your car right now, There's several policemen just been sent to control the traffic* and so on. The example with the Perfect *been sent* looks like a resultative; perhaps Croft and Cruse's 'strange event' construction should be split into 'resultative' and 'event'. One noteworthy property of the proposed 'event' construction is that it contains a relative clause. The preceding two examples contain reduced relative clauses but consider (5), noting that (5a) is an example of the central existential construction; it has a locative phrase, *in our street,* and an optional relative clause, *owns two Rottweilers.* (5b) is an example of the proposed existential resultative construction.

(5) a. There's a guy in our street [Ø] owns two Rottweilers.
b. There's a tree [Ø] has fallen on a very expensive car.

If the zeros were replaced by *who* and *which*, these relative pronouns would be the subjects of the relative clauses. In English non-existential constructions only direct object relative pronouns can be omitted, but in spoken English subjects can be omitted from relative clauses in the existential–presentative construction. This is in fact a major property of the construction. The revised list of existential constructions is in (6). The labels have been altered to capture the fact that the constructions are all existential.

(6) a. Existential presenting an entity
There's a fox in the garden.
There's a guy in our street [Ø] owns two Rottweilers.
b. Existential ONTOLOGICAL
There is a Santa Clause.
c. ExistentiaL presenting an event
Suddenly there burst into the room an SS officer holding a machine gun.
d. ExistentiaL presenting an event resultative
There's a man been shot.

A description of English or other languages that treats constructions as theoretical primitives has to establish many different constructions to handle the differences in interpretation and syntax. The same applies to models of grammar such as Construction Grammar. In Halliday's models of the late 1960s and the 1970s, and in Systemic Grammar to which they gave rise, lots of different constructions are recognized, although they are the end point of different sets of choices. For example, a choice of [indicative mood], [finite], [declarative], [active], [ditransitive] and [unmarked] would result in, for example, *We sent Barnabas a book on entomology*. The same choices apart from [marked] instead of [unmarked] would result in *A book on entomology we sent Barnabas* (an order of words that looks peculiar out of context).

Constructions and first language acquisition

The question of how fine to draw distinctions between constructions is relevant to more than just formal models of grammar or descriptive grammars of this or that language. It bears directly on research into children acquiring their native language. The difficulties are nicely illustrated in Crain and Nakayama (1987). They ran an experiment in which children were invited to convert declarative sentences containing subject relative clauses into interrogative sentences. The method used was to get the children to put a question to a puppet character. The spoken instruction given was, for example, *Ask Jabba if [the boy who is watching Mickey Mouse is happy]*. The six sentences used in the experiment are set out in (7).

(7) a. The boy who is unhappy is watching Mickey Mouse.
b. The dog that is sleeping is on the blue bench.
c. The ball that the girl is sitting on is big.
d. The boy who is watching Mickey Mouse is happy.
e. The boy who is being kissed by his mother is happy.
f. The boy who was holding the plate is crying.

In Chapter 12 on first language acquisition, we will pick up two questions. When can it legitimately be claimed that a group of children have mastered a particular construction? When can the results obtained from one group of children be generalized to all children acquiring a particular language as their native one? Here, we question Crain and Nakayama's assertion that the children who took part in their experiment had acquired the wh relative clause construction. The examples in (7) contain two types of wh relative clause. In both, *who* is the subject, but the relative clause in (7e) is passive and the others are active, and the relative clause in (7a) contains a copula construction, *who is unhappy*, while the other active ones are transitive. The 'two types' of wh relative clause referred to here are the active and passive ones, but clearly further distinctions can be drawn with respect to whether the active relative clauses have a copula construction or a non-copula one, and if it is the latter, then again distinctions have to be drawn with respect to whether they are transitive or intransitive.

More importantly, the examples in (7) contain none of the more complex wh relative clauses presented in (12)–(14) in Chapter 5 on grammaticality and Chapter 11 on complexity: No relative clauses with *whom* or *whose*; no relative clauses introduced by a preposition + wh word, as in *the shop in which we bought this carpet*, *the guy to whom you were talking*, not to mention *the man by whose dog we had been chased*; certainly no examples such as *for all of whom this was the best treatment* or *moved to London, in which city he spent the rest of his life* and so on. The children who interpreted the wh clauses correctly in Crain and Nakayama's experiment understood two of the simplest types of wh relative clause constructions. They had not mastered THE wh relative construction, and they had only mastered a fraction of the SET of wh relative clause constructions. As Bavin (2005, p. 389) says, 'How children's spontaneous productions and how their performance on experimental tasks are interpreted is very much dependent on the theoretical assumptions made.'

Constructions and syntactic properties

The Classical Greek conditional construction

Constructions offer a solution to tricky phenomena such as the sequences of tenses in combinations of conditional clause (protasis) and main clause (apodosis). A good example is the Classical Greek conditional construction, as in (8).

(8) a. ei touto epoioun, edikoun
if this they-were-doing, they-were-wrong
b. ei touto epraxen, edikesan an
if this they-had-done, they-would-have-been-wrong

The combination of adverbial clause and main clause appears to involve cross-clause dependencies, although dependencies typically do not cross clause boundaries into adverbial clauses. In (8a), the English copula + adjective structure *were wrong* corresponds to a single verb in Greek, *epoioun*. This verb is in the Imperfect tense, which is what is required by the grammar of classical Greek for a fulfilled condition; the conditional clause contains an Imperfect verb, *epoioun*. (8b) expresses a remote, unfulfilled condition. The conditional clause contains an Aorist tense form, *epraxen*, and the main clause contains an Aorist form and the particle *an*. Such examples, however (both the Classical Greek ones and their English equivalents), are not instances of dependencies crossing from clause to another. The syntactic constraints affect both the main and adverbial clauses, and the dependencies appear to be associated with the entire two-clause construction, rather than flowing from the main clause to the adverbial clause, or even vice versa.

The category-of-state construction in Russian

There has been much discussion by Russianists of examples such as those in (9)–(14).

(9) V gorode bylo teplo, syro i dušno.
In town was warm humid and stuffy
'It was warm, humid and stuffy in town.'

(10) Ivanu bylo gor'ko i dosadno.
Ivan-DAT was bitter and annoyed
'Ivan was grieved and annoyed.'

(11) Mne nužno exat' v Moskvu.
I-DAT necessary to-travel to Moscow
'I have to go to Moscow.'

(12) Jasno, čto Zenit — lučšaja komanda.
Clear that Zenit better team
'It is clear that Zenit is the better team.'

(13) Vsem ponjatna novaja politika.
All-DAT understandable new policy
'Everyone understands the new policy.'

(14) Nam byla slyšna gromkaja muzyka.
We-DAT was audible loud music
'We could hear loud music.'

These examples have certain properties of syntax and morphosyntax that can be neatly handled by attributing them to the construction. (9)–(14) are stative constructions; in particular, (13) and (14) are the Russian analogues of the stative structures noted in Lakoff (1970). The latter form one subtype of stative construction and the other examples belong to a second subtype. Let us call them simply Stative 1 – examples (13) and (14) – and Stative 2. In Stative 1, the initial noun is animate (typically human) and in the dative case. In Stative 2, the initial noun is non-animate and typically denotes a place. It is in the prepositional (locative) case. Both Stative 1 and Stative 2 exclude adverbs of manner such as *bystro* 'quickly', *s èntuziasmom* 'enthusiastically' and *lovko* 'skilfully' and adverbs of instrument such as *molotom* 'with a hammer' and *umom* 'with one's brain/intelligence'. They both allow durative and habitual time adverbs and adverbs of cause: *V gorode teplo ot južnogo vetra* 'In town warm from southerly wind, It's warm in the town because of the southerly wind', *Ivanu gor'ko ot neudači* 'To-Ivan bitter from failure, Ivan is bitterly disappointed by his failure' and so on.

Earlier Russian scholars such as Ščerba (1928) and Vinogradov (1938) asked what word class *teplo, syro, dušno, gor'ko, dosadno, nužno* and *jasno* belonged to. From their morphology they could be adverbs, since Russian adverbs end in *-o* or *-e*, as in the adjective *šumnyj* 'noisy' and the adverb *šumno* 'noisily', or the adjective *lučšij* 'better' and the adverb *lučše* 'better'. They could also be short neuter forms of adjectives. Russian adjectives, like adjectives in many other languages, occur as modifiers of nouns in NPs (attributive adjectives) or complements of *byt'* 'be' in copula clauses (predicative adjectives). Adjectives come in two paradigms, the short forms, consisting of the adjective stem (possibly plus one of three suffixes: *-a* – feminine singular; *-o* – neuter singular; *-i* or *-y* – plural), and the long forms, consisting of the stem plus a 'long' suffix realizing case, number and gender: for example, *umnyj* 'clever', masculine, nominative, singular; *umnogo* masculine, genitive, singular; *umnyx* genitive, plural. The short forms only occur as complements of *byt'* 'be'. The short forms only function as predicative adjectives, but the long forms can occur as either predicative or attributive adjectives.

Finding it impossible to decide what *teplo*, etc., might be, Ščerba introduced another word class, which he labelled 'category of state', a solution which remained controversial but was adopted by some linguists, for example, by Tixonov (1960). More recent grammars such as Švedova (1970) describe examples such as (9)–(14) as various 'structural schemas' belonging to an adverbial class ('narečnyj klass'). The head of these structural schemas is a predicative. The term 'predicative' is a convenient cover term that enables analysts to sidestep the question of word class, and the term 'adverbial' is mysterious, since the construction is realized in all types of clause, main and subordinate.

In fact, syntax provides an answer to the problem. *Teplo, syro, dušno, gor'ko, dosadno* and *jasno* can occur in the comparative form: *ešče bolee dosadno* 'even-more- annoyed', *v gorode bylo teplee* 'in town was warmer' and so on. Adjectives occur in the comparative form and this is sufficient reason to class *teplo*, etc., as adjectives. What about the fact that it is the short *-o* form that typically occurs? Note first that in Stative 1 it is not just the *-o* form that turns up. In (13) and (14), *ponjatna* and *slyšna* are feminine forms, agreeing with the feminine nouns *politika* and *muzyka*. The *-o* forms occur where there is no noun for the adjective to agree with.

Not having a noun to agree with is a permanent property of Stative 2 and is a typical but not necessary property of Stative 1. The type of initial noun, its case and whether it is governed by a preposition are likewise properties of Stative 1 and Stative 2. That is, the various restrictions on types of adverb and cause phrase and the occurrence of the short *-o* forms can be considered properties of a general Stative construction of which the other two are sub-types. Instead of elaborating default rules for which form appears when there is no noun for it to agree with, the occurrence of the *-o* form can be specified as a property of the construction. In an early paper, JM suggested that the *-o* forms were the traditional category of adjective playing a role in a special type of construction and that rather than having one large set of base rules (typical of that stage in the development of generative models) it would be more useful to have different sets of rules for different types of sentence [sic]. (Miller, 1973, pp. 358–9). The inspiration for these comments was the work of Halliday and Anderson (1971), but it is pleasing to see that the concept of construction has its rightful place in at least one major current of thought in contemporary grammar, Construction Grammar and Cognitive Linguistics.

Number agreement and the existential construction

We return to the existential construction and to IT clefts. Henry (2005) examines variation in Belfast English, a variety that is spoken but not written. She focuses on the following examples:

(15) a. There's three books on the table.
b. There is three books on the table.
c. There was three books on the table.

Henry (2005, p. 111) worked with a set of speakers who used the number agreement system of standard English, that is, they used (16a,b) but not (17a,b).

(16) a. The eggs are cracked.
b. The doors were opened.

(17) a. The eggs is cracked.
b. The doors was opened.

The existential construction in (15a–c) revealed intriguing variation in usage. Some of Henry's speakers used only *there's*. Others used *there's* and *there is* but not *there was*, and a third group used *there are* and *there was* but not *there is*. There was further variation depending on whether the speakers used *there was lots of books* or *there were lots of books*, Some speakers always had number agreement in the negative existential construction *There weren't any books*, while others always had agreement in the positive construction *there were books* but did not have agreement in the negative one *there wasn't any books*. Some speakers allow *there seems to be many students in the room* but not **There appears to be many students in the room*.

Henry (2002, p. 267) comments that the central goal of syntactic theory has been to develop a theory of the representation of language in the mind/brain of individual speakers and that this goal is not compatible with the treatment of the existential construction in Chomsky (1995, Chapter 4), where he argues that *there's* is a low-level substitution for *there are* and that the construction without agreement is not productive since it does not occur in the uncontracted form in questions or in the past tense. (Chomsky is wrong: there are many speakers who say *Is there any biscuits left* and also, as Henry shows, *There was three books on the table.* As Henry also shows, there are speakers who have the pattern of usage reported by Chomsky.) Chomsky's account will not do; for many speakers, *there's* is not a substitution for anything, because they do not use *there are.*

Henry's solution (2005, p. 120) is to propose a return to the concept of rules and a research programme that seeks to identify and constrain their nature. Another solution is to pursue the idea of independent constructions with their own patterns and to treat the existential as a construction with specific properties, among them the occurrence of *there's* in every present-tense existential clause regardless of whether the following noun is singular or plural. For other speakers, the specific properties will include the occurrence of both *is* and *was* while for a third set they include the occurrence of *was* but not *is* or *'s*. Another construction-specific property will be the occurrence of *there were books* but *there wasn't any books*, and so on. Number agreement in the existential construction is different from number agreement in the ordinary declarative construction.

The IT Cleft in spoken and written English

The final construction we look at is the English IT cleft. Two general points arise from the account in Quirk and Greenbaum (1985, Sections 18.28 and 18.48) and the critique below: one is that there are major differences between spoken and written English and the other is that the differences are best handled by recognizing different constructions and attributing properties to them. Consider the IT cleft in (18).

(18) It's the girl that I was complaining about.

Quirk and Greenbaum ponder over the clause *that I was complaining about.* On the surface, this looks like a relative clause, as *that* can be replaced by *who* – *It's the girl who I was complaining about* – and *who* can, at a pinch, be replaced by the very formal and stilted *about whom* – *It's the girl about whom I was complaining.* There would appear to be no difference between the final clause in the IT cleft and relative clauses, but Quirk and Greenbaum turn to the examples in (19) and (20).

(19) It was because he was ill (that) we decided to return.

(20) It was in September (that) I first noticed it.

The final clauses in (19) and (20) are *that we decided to return* and *that I first noticed it.* Quirk and Greenbaum (1985, p. 1387) observe that 'such a construction, where there is no noun-phrase antecedent, makes inappropriate the use of the term 'pronoun' for the linking word *that*.' (That comment applies to ordinary relative clauses too. – see p. 27.) They point to the impossibility of replacing *that* by *which* – **It was because he was ill which we decided to return.* The final clause in (19) modifies the adverbial clause of reason *because he was ill* and the final clause in (20) modifies the prepositional phrase *in September.* (The lack of a NP antecedent does not automatically disqualify a sequence as a relative clause, since relative clauses can also have propositional antecedents, as in *He showed us round, which we thought was very nice and beyond the call of duty.* In this example, the antecedent of *which* is the proposition, or event, SHOW ROUND (HE, US).)

As mentioned earlier, in (19) and (20) *that* cannot be replaced by *which.* This runs counter to relative clauses with proposition or event antecedents; they MUST be introduced by *which.* Perhaps the problem lies in the choice of wh word. Time nouns can be modified by relative clauses introduced by *when,* as in (21).

(21) a. I remember the September when it rained the whole month.
b. You've forgotten the holiday when we nearly crashed the car.

Instead of (20), speakers – and writers, depending on the type of text – use the construction in (21), in which the second clause is introduced by *when.*

(20a) It was in September when I first noticed it.

Similarly, prepositional phrases denoting places can be modified by the final clause in an IT cleft and place nouns can be modified by relative clauses introduced by *where,* as in (22).

(22) a. It was in the restaurant that he proposed to her.
b. I remember the restaurant where he proposed to her.

(21) and (22b) are important because they hold the clue as to how speakers of English (emphasis on 'speakers') solve the problem exercising Quirk and Greenbaum. The construction will be discussed below. In contrast, the difficulties posed by (19) are not easily disposed of. Other types of clause can occur in focus position in IT clefts, as in (23). The clauses are however confined to clauses of reason, as in (19), and clauses of time and place, as in (23):

(23) a. It was when they arrived that the mood changed.
b. It was as they were leaving that they noticed the fire.
c. It was after they left that the fire broke out.
d. It was where she held the party that bothered me.

It is the adverbial clauses in focus position that raise analytical problems, not the prepositional phrases and, as will be argued below, the unresolvable problem seems to attach to clauses of reason.

The first set of difficulties proposed by Quirk and Greenbaum, then, can be dealt with. They go on to raise other difficulties, ones related directly to the lack of a distinction between written magnasyntax and the regular structures of spontaneous spoken English. They point out that in relative clauses *that* cannot be omitted unless the antecedent noun is, as it were, also the subject of the relative clause. Compare (24a,b) and (25a,b).

(24) a. *I'll lend you the book kept me awake.
b. I'll lend you the book that kept me awake.

(25) a. I'll lend you the book I hated.
b. I'll lend you the book that I hated.

In (24), *book* is the subject of *kept me awake*, while it is the direct object of *hated* in (25). *That* is omissible in (25) but not in (24). But, as Quirk and Greenbaum remark, *that* can be omitted in IT clefts that appear to be parallel to (24), as in (26).

(26) It was the President himself spoke to me.

How peculiar is (26)?Quirk and Greenbaum themselves provide examples of the existential–presentative construction in which *that* is absent, although *something* is both the antecedent of the final clause *(that) keeps upsetting him* and its subject. An example is in (27).

(27) There's something (that) keeps upsetting him.

Quirk and Greenbaum use the omissibility of *that* in (27) to analyse the sequence *keeps upsetting him* as also not a relative clause. They contrast (27) with (28), which they claim is incorrect.

(28) *I know a man lives in China.

In formal written English, (28) may well be unacceptable. (JM's intuitions are unclear.) In spontaneous spoken English, however, (28) is not just acceptable but is the normal structure. Interestingly, it is like (26) in having an existential–presentative function, and the IT cleft in (26) also has a presentative function. Other existential–presentative structures also allow the complementizer to be omitted, such as (29), uttered in the course of a television programme by a theatre manager, and (30), uttered by a teacher but not recorded on tape.

(29) I had a witch disappeared down a trap (=trapdoor in the stage).

(30) we've got plenty of kids know very little about English.

The existential–presentative structure in (26) is not only the norm in spontaneous spoken English but occurs in written English too. (31) is from a survey of a property prepared for Scottish Coal by the Perth (Scotland) office of a firm of national surveyors. It has two existential–presentative structures; the relevant one is in bold and the relative clause with missing complementizer and missing subject NP is in bold italics.

(31) There is a porch of solid construction which has been rendered, under a pitched slate roof. **There is a sash and case window in the porch *requires repainting.***

The upshot of the earlier discussion is this. Quirk and Greenbaum examine what were traditionally thought of as relative clauses in IT clefts and existential structures and reanalyse them as annex clauses. Their analysis can be countered, albeit subtly, for written English. Their analysis does not apply at all to (spontaneous) spoken English.

There is one more important comment to be made on (spontaneous) spoken English. A new construction is appearing, which bypasses the problem perceived by Quirk and Greenbaum. It is not yet mentioned in grammars of English, but is the regular construction not just in informal conversation but in radio discussions and in television programmes. (When JM mentioned the 'new' construction to a colleague in Melbourne, the latter replied that he had always thought that was what speakers said anyway. JM has clearly noticed the construction late in the day, but at a time when it is spreading. Interestingly, it is not mentioned in Biber et al. (1999).) Examples are given in (32) and (33).

(32) It was in September when I first noticed it.

(33) It was in Edinburgh where we found the picture.

The new structure contains a WH sequence that could be analysed as a relative clause, but a headless relative clause, one with no antecedent. In other words, in (32), *when I first noticed it* is not a relative clause modifying *in September* but a free-standing headless relative clause. The sequence *It was in September* establishes the temporal referent, some point of time in the period of time labelled 'September'. The clause *when I first noticed it* picks up the referent, adds information to it and can be glossed as 'at which time I first noticed it' or even 'that's when I first noticed it'. With the substitution of 'locational' for 'temporal' and *where* for *when* the same analysis can be applied to (33). Not only do Quirk and Greenbaum's objections not apply to (spontaneous) spoken English, but this new structure bypasses their analysis altogether.

Another advantage of constructions emerges from the above account of the properties of IT clefts and the syntactic properties and large variety of relative clauses. Many constructions are used in all text types, from spontaneous speech to formal written documents. Other constructions are typically used in formal writing, for example, the more complex relative clauses. They are not absolutely confined to formal writing, but people who use them in speech are generally viewed as 'speaking like a book'. A third set of constructions is typical of spontaneous speech. (See Miller and Weinert, 2009, for an extended discussion.) An example is the *be sat* and *be stood* construction, which is not non-standard but is widespread in spontaneous speech (see pp. 9–10). The concept of a construction is essential for a well-founded contrastive grammar of spontaneous speech and formal writing (whether of English, French, Turkish, Chinese or any other language with spoken and written varieties). It is also essential for an understanding of different text types; for instance, constructions are at the heart of Biber's corpus-based work on different grammatical 'dimensions' of text.

Lone *if* clauses

Finally, we examine two constructions that demonstrate the advantages of constructions for dealing with syntactic structures typical of spontaneous speech and with their discourse functions. The first structure is the isolated *if* clause, noted in task-related dialogues by Miller and Weinert (2009, pp. 100–1). An example is in (34).

(34) Right if you go right along there until you're at the right hand edge of the granite quarry.

The *if* clause conveys an instruction. The speaker is instructing the listener where to draw a line on their map representing the next stage in a route through a set of landmarks. The usage probably originated in a conditional construction, say, *If you do this, you'll be doing the correct thing* or *If you do this, we can get on with what we need to do.* In some contexts, such as medical ones, it may be possible to invent a plausible apodosis – *if you just roll up your sleeve, I'll take your blood pressure/I'll give you the flu jab* and so on. In other contexts, such as the route-drawing one, a single plausible apodosis is difficult to find. The *if* clauses can be handled as a special construction, allowing for the *if* clause to contain complement or relative clauses or to be modified by adverbial clauses, as in (35). (In Miller and Weinert's dialogue data, 59 out of 90 conditional clauses were on their own and conveyed instructions.)

(35) a. If you just lie back and relax until the anaesthetic is working.
b. If you just bring back the books that you don't need.
c. If you could just tell Fiona that her parcel has come.

The *if* clause can be treated as a special kind of main, imperative clause. The subject in (35a–c) is *you*, but it can be any pronoun and even an NP, as shown by (36a–c).

(36) a. If they could just have a look at your proposal.
b. If I could just talk to your boss.
c. If the guy who repaired the car could just explain to me what the problem was.

Associated with the construction is the discourse information that structures realizing it serve to convey instructions in a polite and informal manner. How a particular speaker chooses between this construction and more direct imperatives depends on location, type of interaction, types of participant and even on factors such as the speaker's physical and psychological state and the behaviour of the other participant(s) in the exchange.

Lone *when* clauses

Cheshire (2005, pp. 90–4) gives an account of lone *when* clauses in her Reading corpus. (37) and (38) are typical extracts from the conversations.

(37)	Nobby	yeah Miss Threadgold she ain't bad
	Rob	yeah she. she went camping with us
	Jenny	yes he told me she'd been camping
	Nobby	when we went camping
	Rob	she's a good laugh
	Jenny	is she
	Nobby	yeah

(38)	Jenny	have you ever been in hospital?
	Valerie	I have
	Christine	oh yeah I have
	Valerie	I got run over by a car
	Christine	I fell off a gate backwards <LAUGHS> and I was unconscious
	Tommy	oi when I – when I went in hospital just for a little while . . .
	Valerie	sshh
	Tommy	cos my sister and my cousin they bent my arm..they twisted it right round

Cheshire analyses most of the lone *when* clauses in her data as 'pivotal in the development of talk' and signalling that the speaker is beginning a story. (The *sshh* uttered by Valerie is addressed to Christine, telling her to let Tommy have his say.) The narrative that followed the clauses was familiar to the other participants (though not to the researcher) because they had taken part in the events or had heard the story before. As with the *if* clauses discussed earlier, the lone *when* clauses can be treated as a special main clause construction. Information about its discourse function can be associated with the construction and also information about its semantics and pragmatics. For instance, it is quite plausible to see this use of *when* as related to the deictic use discussed on pp. 175–190. That is, it can be treated as equivalent to 'the time that (such-and-such happened)' and in discourse terms it can be taken as equivalent to 'You know the time that such-and-such happened,' which is also a good story-opener.

Conclusion

Linguists working in the field of generative grammar thought the development of general constraints, each applying to a number of constructions, was an exciting and worthwhile move. (JM was one of them.) With hindsight, we can see that the move was perhaps not even worthwhile for generative grammar because it obscured for a considerable time the variation in the complexity of speakers' competence. Attention was focused on major theoretical generalizations and actual usage was overlooked. The business of constructions for particular speech acts and discourse moves was downgraded, and the lessons of work on spoken and standard and non-standard varieties remained invisible until the work of Alison Henry pulled together Chomskyan generative grammar and the details of variation in central syntactic structures in Belfast English. Constructions and rules are alive and well.

5 Grammaticality

Chapter Outline

Overview

A central concept in the practice of syntax is grammaticality. The word itself dates from the early days of generative grammar, but it labels an idea that has informed the analysis of language for 2,000 years or more: some sequences of words are correct or grammatical while others are incorrect or ungrammatical. This idea informs reference grammars and textbooks of the grammar of languages for native and non-native speakers and at all levels from elementary to advanced, theoretical work on syntax, including generative grammar and the development of software for the handling of text by computer and the construction of grammar checkers. A number of linguists prefer the term 'acsceptable' to 'grammatical'; the use of the term implicitly recognizes that sequences of words in a given language are acceptable or unacceptable to particular groups of users, that is, it admits variation in language. In practice, many, if not most, accounts of, say, English focus on the standard written variety and on what is acceptable to users of that variety.

Chomsky (1957) declared the goal of generative grammar as generating all and only the correct sentences of a given language. Whether this goal can be achieved is doubtful; even huge reference grammars with very large coverage, such as Quirk and Greenbaum (1985), do not mention all the syntactic constructions in all the varieties of English (not even if we limit ourselves to the set of varieties that is grouped under the label 'standard British English'). Things go from bad to worse when the knowledge of native speakers is taken into account. A major mistake in the Chomskyan approach to first language acquisition is to project on to actual speakers the analyses produced by linguists over many years. The problem was excellently described by Ong, who dealt with vocabulary and proposed the term 'magnavocabulary'. Miller and Weinert (2009) proposed by analogy the term 'magnasyntax', and it may even be necessary to invent a term such as 'magnadiscourse' to cover the kind of variation described by Biber (1988) and Biber et al. (1999).

What is Ong's concept of magnavocabulary? Ong (1982, pp. 103–8) points out that English, like all national written languages, has been worked over for centuries. Ong suggests that the elaboration of modern written English began in the chancery of Henry V in the fifteenth century and has been continued up to the present by dictionary makers, writers developing new genres and new styles, normative grammarians and so on. There are massive collections of printed texts (and nowadays electronic texts and, better late than never, spoken texts). The texts cover centuries of output and thousands of authors (in the broadest sense). The researches by dictionary makers over the last two and half centuries are embodied in modern dictionaries such as the Oxford English Dictionary (OED) and Webster's Third New International Dictionary. The contents of these dictionaries are what Ong calls a magnavocabulary.

This magnavocabulary of English is not the property of any one speaker – the most erudite scholar would be hard put to it to have even a passive command of 20 per cent of the contents of the OED. The OED contains a large amount of Greco-Latinate vocabulary, and it is known from primary and indeed secondary schools that school pupils command very little of it. Gropen et al. (1989) report that in their experiments no Latinate dative verbs were used in the speech of the parents talking to their children, not even verbs such as *donate*, *explain* and *demonstrate*, which seem pretty tame to highly educated speakers of English. The fact is that a small minority of speakers of English control the Greco-Latinate part of its vocabulary, and that part includes just the more common words. A smaller number, specialists in fields such as science, engineering, medicine, the humanities and social sciences, law, divinity and so forth, also control the Greco-Latinate technical terms in their specialism. Anticipating one of the arguments against the Chomskyan theory of first language acquisition, we emphasize that the Greco-Latinate vocabulary is typically learned from written texts, is learned over many years and is taught at school and university.

Miller and Weinert (2009, pp. 376–83) suggest that analogous to magnavocabulary is magnasyntax. Over the centuries, written English has been codified and documented and handbooks of English grammar have been published. These grammars set out the morphology and syntax of written English and include word, clause and phrase constructions from texts produced last century and this century. The latest comprehensive grammar, Quirk et al. (1985), describes constructions that are current in speech and writing, constructions that are current only in formal writing and constructions that are rare even in formal writing. When linguists set themselves the task of writing rules that generate all and only the correct sentences of a language, what they are tackling is this magnasyntax, which is not the syntax of any particular speaker of English or of any particular genre of current English or even of the English of any particular period, but the set of all syntactic constructions recorded in written (and spoken) English since 1800 or 1600, depending on the grammar. This is clear from the arguments in, say, Radford (1988), which draws on a range of quite disparate constructions to establish the constituent structure of NPs; everyday neutral examples such as *your red pencil and his* are side-by-side with highly formal, rare examples such as *honest politician though he is*.

It will already be evident that the concept of grammaticality is extremely complicated, reflecting, for any given language, an alarmingly intricate set of language codes and practices. For English and many other languages (such as Chinese, Japanese, French, Turkish, Greek and so on), the term 'language' covers a very large range of variation: standard and non-standard varieties; within the standard, spoken and written genres from informal conversation about familiar topics in relaxed settings through many other spoken genres to formal writing about complex topics for publication in books, journals, newspapers; to reports for local authorities or national government; to papers for business meetings in commercial, financial, legal and educational institutions and so forth. Moreover, the users of languages such as those mentioned earlier are not only faced with a huge number of different genres synchronically but potentially have to deal with diachronic variation, dealing with texts written in the past as well as with texts written in present time. For example, in secondary school in the 1950s, JM studied textbooks written before the Second World War (his German grammar book and reader were in Gothic script) and the English classes dealt with novels written a century earlier. Agatha Christie's detective novels still sell very well, but many of them are now 60 years old and some are 80 years old and contain a good collection of archaic words and phrases.

As we will see later in the chapter, speakers' intuitions about their native language may be quite fuzzy beyond a certain core of frequently used syntactic patterns and fixed phrases. (The classic example is Labov's one mentioned on p. 9, but Milroy (1987, p. 149) talks of the mismatch between what speakers claim they say and what they actually say in naturally occurring interactions. Milroy refers to the difficulties in accessing the intuitions of linguistically naïve speakers, which she experienced in Belfast and which had also been reported from a range of countries, including the Soviet Union, as it was then, and Australia.) Intuitions about spoken language are either lacking altogether or are notoriously unreliable. Intuitions about the more complex or unusual constructions of formal writing are equally unreliable, or noticeable by their absence.

Any discussion of grammaticality and acceptability must reckon with the role of gatekeepers who keep undesirable words and grammar out of published texts. (See the detailed account in Cameron (1995).) These gatekeepers are copyeditors for publishers, especially publishers of academic monographs and serious literature; teaching staff in universities and schools, especially secondary schools; large commercial organizations such as banks, who have set formats for literature that is sent out to customers; and even organizations such as the Federation of Plumbing Employers of Scotland and Northern Ireland, who issue standard letters to all plumbing firms, guiding them in drawing up estimates, invoices, letters demanding payments that are late, letters of apology and so on. Many written documents are produced by cooperation between two or more people; that is, many speakers and writers do not need to have clear-cut intuitions or indeed any intuitions about certain types of text and the appropriate grammar and vocabulary because the latter information is supplied or their draft texts are checked and revised.

Sampson (2007, pp. 9–10) is exercised by the very low frequency of many grammatical constructions. The low frequencies are not surprising when we remember that large corpuses of data are collections of magnasyntax. (See the discussion of Ong below.) They include all sorts of written texts and nowadays also include transcripts of all sorts of spoken texts. There are constructions that only turn up in certain types of text, and only the regular producers or consumers of a given type of text have its peculiar features at their fingertips. (See, for instance, the text in (24) below.) Many speakers and writers of

English work with a limited range of texts – in some cases very limited, as shown by Philpott's research reported in Chapter 11. They do not necessarily have intuitions about complex pieces of grammar that occur in other text types. And no one speaker has reliable intuitions about all the grammatical constructions that occur in a large database of magnasyntax.

We have not touched on the problems posed by non-standard varieties of English and other languages. Many years ago, when he was at the University of Reading, Trudgill (personal communication) asked his colleagues, all English, to fill in a questionnaire. They were asked to go through a set of sentences, say which were acceptable and which were not, and to specify which of the latter set were possible constructions of English and which could not possibly be constructions of English. One of the examples was along the lines of *These windows need painted* and was judged by all the respondents not even to be a possible structure of English. JM happens to use this structure, which is the normal construction for him and many other speakers of Scottish English. He does not use it in writing, however.

Grammaticality, magnasyntax and constructions of English

Relative clauses

Relative clauses provide an excellent illustration of the range of structures available for what many analysts count as one construction. The view taken here is that there are many different relative clauses, all sharing the property of modifying nouns but ranging from the typically simple structures of spontaneous speech to the very complex structures found only in formal written language. The simplest structures are in (1), and as complementizers they have zero, *that* or *wh*. The relative pronouns *which* in (1c) and *who* in (1d) are the direct objects of their relative clauses. In (1b), *that* is a relativizer, not a pronoun. It is invariable, in contrast with the oppositions between *who* and *whom* and between *who*/*whom* and *which*; and it cannot be preceded by a preposition – **the house in that we live* versus *the house that we live in*. We assume that the structure of *that* relative clauses is, for example, *the house* $_{\text{Rel Cl}}$[*that we live in [Ø]*], that is, that in the relative clause there is a gap corresponding to the NP modified by the relative clause. (1a) is the relative clause construction typical of spontaneous spoken English, lacking both a relativizing conjunction and a relative pronoun.

(1) a. the house we renovated
b. the house that we renovated
c. the house which we renovated
d. the boys who we disliked

Written English has a contrast between *who* and *whom*, and the possessive relative pronoun *whose* still occurs. *Whom* is rare in spontaneous spoken English and *whose* is even rarer. (It does not occur at all in the Miller–Brown conversations, for instance.)

(2) a. the boys whom we disliked
b. the boys whose behaviour was outrageous

In (3), *who* is the subject of the relative clause. ((3) and (5) are from Trudgill (1983).)

(3) He's a man **who** likes his beer.

According to the conventions of formal written English, *who* cannot be omitted in this structure nor can the relativizer *that*: **He's a man [Ø] likes his beer.* In contrast, in spontaneous spoken English, in presentative–existential constructions, the wh pronoun and the relativizer *that* can be omitted, as in (4). (4b,c) are from the Miller–Brown conversations.

(4) a. There's a man in this pub **[Ø]** likes his beer.
b. we had this French girl **[Ø]** came to stay
c. my friend's got a brother **[Ø]** used to be in the school.

Trudgill provides in addition the following non-standard relative clause structures. There are different relativizing conjunctions, *what*, *as* and *at*; in (5d), the relative clause is not part of a presentative–existential construction, but has a missing subject NP. In (5e), the relative clause has an ordinary pronoun, *he*, as its subject, but no relativizing conjunction.

(5) a. He's a man **what** likes his beer.
b. He's a man **as** likes his beer.
c. He's a man **at** likes his beer.
d. He's a man **[ ]** likes his beer.
e. He's a man **[ ] he** likes his beer.

Almost by definition the constructions in (5a–e) do not occur in formal written English or indeed in written English, excluding dialogue in plays and novels. Other constructions that do not occur in formal written English are exemplified in (6a–c) and (7b,c). (6a–c) are naturally occurring examples of relative clauses containing shadow or resumptive pronouns. (7a) and (8a,b') are examples of relative clauses containing prepositions. In spontaneous spoken English, prepositions occur at the end of the relative clause, as in (7a) and (8a,b), or are omitted, as in (7b,c). Structures such as (8a', b') are found in formal written English.

(6) a. the spikes **that** you stick in the ground and throw rings over **them**
b. an address **which** I hadn't stayed **there** for several years.
c. We've just heard about a diversion on the A80, **where** there's road works **there**.

(7) a. the shop I bought it **in**
b. of course there's a rope **that** you can pull the seat back up [ ].
c. I haven't been to a party yet **that** I haven't got home [ ] the same night. (informally recorded – radio discussion)

(8) a. of course there's a rope **that** you can pull the seat back up **with**.
a'. of course there's a rope with which you can pull the seat back up.
b. I haven't been to a party yet **that** I haven't got home **from** the same night.
b'. I haven't been to a party yet from which I haven't got home the same night.

Also typical of formal written English are non-restrictive relative clauses, that is, relative clauses that are used to provide extra, incidental information but not to help the listener pick out what the speaker is referring to. (8') is a typical example. In writing, the relative clause is separated from the modified noun by a comma, and in speech, there is a pause between the modified noun and the relative clause and between the relative clause and whatever material follows it. Non-restrictive relative clauses are rare in spontaneous spoken English, but do occur in written texts that are read aloud.

(8') My sister, **who'**s a lawyer, helped me to sort out the problem.

Instead of non-restrictive relatives, spontaneous spoken English has coordinate structures, as in (9).

(9) The boy I was talking to last night — and he actually works in the yard — was saying it's going to be closed down.

Grammars of English list WH infinitival relatives such as *a house in which to live*. The map-task dialogues and the Miller–Brown conversations contain no wh infinitival relatives, but they do have infinitival relatives without wh pronouns, as in (10) and (11).

(10) eh Laurine - question to tell you - eh if you haven't got the volcano - where do you go if you haven't got the volcano.

(Primary 4 class)

(11) I've got a place to start.

(Primary 6 class)

(10) and (11) exemplify two properties shared by all the infinitival relatives in the data. A number of instances appear idiom-like and are possibly learned and used as entire chunks: *question to tell you* can be analysed thus, especially as it is simply a phrase and not part of a clause. *Question to ask* and *something to tell* are relatively frequent phrases in a primary classroom. Note again the lack of prepositions: we might expect *I've got a place to start at/from*, which fits the context. Other examples with the 'missing' preposition in square brackets are: *It's not the ideal place to go [**to**] for teenage drinking, . . . because there's vandals and it's a horrible place to live [**in**].*

The Miller–Brown conversations contain 52 infinitival relatives. Two adult informants produced six apiece, while one speaker, who produced a large number of restrictive WH relative clauses, produced 5. The remaining 35 were distributed over 15 speakers. In general, infinitival relatives do not seem problematic in the free conversations. They occur regularly but not frequently; they do not contain prepositions; some of them could be analysed as fixed phrases and there are no wh infinitival relatives.

Formal written English has relative clause structures far more complex than are found in spontaneous speech. Consider (12)–(14).

(12) The hospital admitted several patients that month, **for all of whom** chemotherapy was the appropriate treatment.

(13) We read several government reports **the gold lettering on the covers of which** was admired by all the officials.

(14) They moved to London, **in which city** they established a large and successful legal office.

(12), from Quirk and Greenbaum (1985), has a wh pronoun inside a quantifier phrase, *all of whom*, which in turn is inside a prepositional phrase, *for all of whom*. In (13), a famous example from Ross (1967), the wh pronoun is inside a prepositional phrase, *of which*. This phrase is inside a NP, *the covers of which*, and the whole is inside a prepositional phrase, *on the covers of which*. The latter phrase is inside a larger NP, *the gold lettering on the covers of which*. In (14), from Quirk and Greenbaum (1985), the wh pronoun modifies the head noun, *city*, of the phrase *which city*, which is part of the prepositional phrase *in which city*.

At this point, it is time to repeat that the examples in (6a–c) and (7b,c) are not mistakes. They are the norm in spontaneous spoken English and not sporadic. There are parallel structures in other languages of Europe, such as French and Russian. (See Miller and Weinert, 2009, pp. 111–3.) They should be considered as constructions designed for use in the circumstances in which speakers produce and hearers interpret spontaneous spoken English, French, etc. Blackman (1908) presents a view of the constructions that is all too frequent. He dissects examples of the spoken language constructions and argues that even the classic writers of English literature make 'mistakes'. The view taken here is that the examples show that the spoken language structures are not new, but have been in use for two or three hundred years. Blackman's examples of 'incorrect' relative clauses are in (15)–(18).

(15) Who is the poet but lately arrived in Elysium whom I saw Spenser lead in and present him to Vergil.

[Lyttelton's Dialogues of the Dead]

(16) This is the time that the unjust man doth thrive.

[Shakespeare]

(17) Who riseth from a feast with that keene appetite that he sits downe?

[Shakespeare]

(18) He spoke with the same good-humoured ease that he had ever done.

[Jane Austen]

(15) has a shadow pronoun; Blackman requires *whom I saw Spenser lead in and present to Vergil*. The other three all show the non-use of prepositions. Blackman requires *at which the unjust man doth thrive*, *with which he sits down* and *with which he had ever done*.

The set of relative clause structures is completed by ones like (19), from Quirk and Greenbaum (1985), which is archaic even by Blackman's standards.

(19) a continent, on the south-side whereof was a small neck of land

Quirk and Greenbaum say that such structures strike readers as stiff and pedantic, but the structure is no more complex than their examples in (12) and (14). What would bother modern readers is the single word *whereof*; it is not used even in formal written texts – we have to make an exception for legal texts, but the latter are notoriously obscure in their syntax and vocabulary – and its structure, wh word followed by 'preposition', is completely outmoded.

With respect to relative clauses, the notion of grammaticality runs into two sorts of problem. One is that most speakers judge (4a–c), (5) and (6a–c) to be ungrammatical. Some speakers are aware of non-standard relativizers such as *what* and *as*, but most speakers are unaware of the structures in (4a–c), (6a–c) and (7b,c). They are to a greater or lesser extent aware of the conventions of formal written English as taught in school and required in formal writing in secondary and higher education and industry and commerce, by legal firms and so on. Schooling appears to be the source of most people's intuitions about what is grammatical and what is not.

The second problem is that a very large number of speakers have no clear intuitions about structures such as those in (12) and (14). They do not use them and may have difficulty understanding them when faced with written texts. [See Dabrowska (1997) and Chipere (2009) on lack of intuitions and understanding and Heath (1983) on how groups of neighbours combine to interpret complex missives from local authorities, with some of the interpretation coming from the experience of people who have already gone through the same situation. The author has long personal experience of trying to elicit intuitions from students studying generative grammar and concluded that many intuitions are indirectly taught as part of such courses.]

It is not just relative clauses that cause problems for the concept of grammaticality. At one point in his career, the writer taught syntax to a number of postgraduate students, all teachers of ESOL studying for an MA. Since central Auckland was littered with banners announcing *Now renting*, it seemed a good idea to talk about the construction, pointing out that it is a middle and that after a period of retrenchment the middle construction is spreading. One student declared that real examples such as *Nothing drives like a Ford Falcon* and . . . *skylarks soon established throughout the country* were errors and did not want to know about examples of middles from Jane Austen.

Indirect questions

Indirect questions such as (20), from a BBC webpage in 2005, were treated as errors by a research project into the teaching of English as an additional language.

(20) Log on at the BBC World Service AIDS site to **find out how much do you know about condoms**.

The marking protocol in the research project required the structure . . . *to find out how much you know about condoms.* (The example in (20) was not used in the project but was collected by JM.)

Gerund non-finite clauses

Even the humble gerund can provoke dissension. Consider the examples in (21), used by JM in a lecture on non-finite clauses.

(21) a. Fanny regretted talking to Mary.
b. Fanny regretted Edmund talking to Mary.
c. Fanny regretted Edmund's having agreed to take part in the play.

(21a,b) were recognized and accepted by the various sets of students who heard the lecture. (21c) was not recognized, and indeed some students wondered if the writer was playing a trick on them and asked if the construction really existed. Not only does it exist, but there are many users of formal written English who would declare it the correct one.

How reliable are intuitions about grammaticality?

Generative grammar deals with magnasyntax. The data taken into account ranges from (devised) spoken data (including non-standard structures, which some analysts handle systematically and some do not) through data that is neutral between spoken and written to data that is literary and even archaic. We will not develop this theme here since it is presented in more detail in the following sections, but it is important to point out that generativists do not see themselves as dealing with magnasyntax. A central role in generative work has always been played by the intuitions of individual speakers, but a major difficulty is that the speakers whose intuitions have been consulted are typically professional linguists, or postgraduates studying linguistics, or undergraduate students. These are all classes of people who work constantly with complex written language, who are used to playing language games and whose intuitions are based on written language. It is also the case, as mentioned earlier, that the skill of judging grammaticality is, to some extent, possibly even a large extent, taught to students of linguistics.

Suppose someone objects (as did a colleague of JM's) that a native speaker can and does judge examples like *honest politician though he is*... to be grammatical. How strong is this objection? It is true that some native speakers of English, those with a good command of the written language, will recognize the construction and interpret the example, but it is an open question whether other native speakers would do the same. (See the discussion of Perera's work on children's reading and writing and the work by Philpott on the workforce in a British factory (pp. 241–242 and pp. 230–232)). Even if they did, what interpretation could be placed on their judgement: that they reckoned on balance that the construction was 'correct'?; that they managed to interpret the example from the occurrence of *though*?; that they simply made a guess? Most presentations of grammaticality judgements in the generative literature include no discussion of how the judgements were collected; whether the examples were presented in different orders; whether they were incorporated in a text or presented singly; whether the grammatical judgement test was preceded by other tests requiring the subjects, say, to fill in gaps, to complete sentence fragments, or to take the five words *is*, *politician*, *though*, *honest* and *he* and arrange them into a clause.

There is a third problem in the collecting of grammaticality judgements: speakers' reactions are affected by linguistic and non-linguistic context. Bard et al. (1996) is instructive. They address the problem of eliciting acceptability judgements, drawing a careful distinction between grammaticality and acceptability and extending their net to take in relative grammaticality and relative acceptability. They emphasize the need to collect judgements from different groups of subjects, to validate results by cross-modal matching and to collect judgements from the same group of subjects on different occasions, changing the order of the elicitation items. Finally, the results are subjected to statistical tests of significance. Very little, if any, of the published work in generative grammar meets these criteria; the only exception is the body of work in the Principles and Parameters framework on the acquisition of language by children. A final interesting point in relation to Bard et al. (1996) is that although they used different groups of subjects, the latter were either undergraduates or 'experienced linguists'; that is, all the subjects were people with a good command of written language.

Do these problems with grammaticality mean that we should abandon the concept? Sampson argues that the concept of 'ungrammatical' or 'ill-formed' word sequences is a delusion, 'based on a false conception of the kind of thing a human language is' (Sampson, 2007, p. 1). Sampson was brought to think about grammaticality by coming across a sentence in John Mortimer's novel *Dunster*.

(22) . . . Dunster seemed to achieve, in the centre of this frenzied universe, an absence of anxiety which I had never known. But then, as I have made it clear to you, I worry.

What Sampson finds peculiar, as does JM, is the sequence *as I have made it clear to you*. Sampson, and JM, would have written *as I have made clear to you*. Sampson (2007, p. 6) states that it is difficult to find specific word sequences that one can confidently predict to be unusable; Sampson (2007, p. 11) also states that it is impossible to specify the boundary between those word sequences that are destined never to have a use and those that have not found a use so far but will do so at some time in the future (whether we are discussing the language of a community or that of an individual speaker).

Grammaticality judgements and variation in language

It is not in fact necessary to throw out the notion of grammaticality, but it is essential to recognize the problem of variation in language, the lack of a single clear dividing line between word sequences that are grammatical and word sequences that are not and the fact that even for one given speaker of English (or any other language) a particular sequence might be of uncertain status.

Matthews (1979, pp. 26–31) discusses the verbs in (23). The writer has added the contemporary verbs in (23g,h).

(23) a. They cabled that the ship had arrived in Auckland.
b. They radio'd that the ship had arrived in Auckland.
c. They telegrammed that the ship had arrived in Auckland.
d. They lettered that the ship had arrived in Auckland.
e. They messaged that the ship had arrived in Auckland.
f. They phoned that the ship had arrived in Auckland.
g. They e-mailed that the ship had arrived in Auckland.
h. They Skyped that the ship had arrived in Auckland.

Matthews found acceptable the sequence of verb plus complement clause in (23a,b,f), but was clear in his own mind that (23d) is unacceptable. He thought (23e) peculiar, but had come across an example in an (unspecified) American news magazine. He found (23c) more acceptable than (23d), but questioned whether we would actually say it. Given changes in technology over the past 30 years, Mattews' judgement cannot be tested, since telegrams, at least in the United Kingdom, have fallen into disuse. And this change has given rise to another case of variation and language change. In the United Kingdom, speakers older than, say, 50 might have the verb *telegram* in their passive vocabulary, but speakers under 20 will not come across the word except in novels set before 1990 or so. In 1979, Matthews did not mention the verbs *e-mail* and *Skype*; they did not exist because those types of communication did not exist. JM finds (23g) acceptable, but is not at ease with (23h). On the other hand, 45 years ago, JM was not entirely at ease with the sequence *hopefully* plus clause – *Hopefully, we can ignore this question* – but now uses it as a matter of course.

The problem of grammaticality affects the middle construction mentioned before. Postgraduate students with whom the writer has discussed the middle in eight lecture courses between 2003 and 2007 accepted examples such as *The text now reads smoothly*, *The apartments are selling well* and *The wool knitted up beautifully*. They were undecided as to the status of examples such as *It won't crush in your sports bag* (in a television advertisement for a make of shirt) and found unacceptable examples such as *The winery is lacking 1963 and 1964 Wynns Coonawara Estate Cabernet Sauvignon, which bottled as Wynns Claret* (in a newspaper article) and *It will take years for the Mersey to clean* (from a BBC TV news report).

In any society, each group of specialists has its own technical language. ('Specialists' is intended to cover every sort of group from footballers through knitters, plumbers, gardeners and so on to medics, lawyers and the many groups of academics.) Texts produced by members of specialist groups usually contain sequences of words that outsiders find surprising, possibly unacceptable and often opaque. Consider the text in (24).

> (24) The sides of the slated roof at the eaves were bedded up with mortar tifting by the slater so that the end slates against the upstand of the skew sloped away from it to divert water in windy weather from being blown against the stone and into the building. The junction between the skew and the slates was finished with a triangular fillet or flashing made of lime and sand which did not tend to shrink or crack.
>
> Naismith, 1985, pp. 97–8

The sequence *were bedded up with mortar tifting by the slater so that the end slates against the upstand of the skew sloped away from it* requires a diagram or model for the reader who has no knowledge of architecture and in particular the architecture of Scottish rural buildings. JM finds unusual the sequence *divert water in windy weather from being blown against the stone and into the building.* The sequence *divert water into a ditch* is normal, but *divert water from being blown . . . into the building* borders on the unacceptable (for JM).

Grammaticality and language change

A further complication is that grammaticality is partly a social phenomenon, which of course does not mean that there are no objective linguistic correlations. There is a central core of structures shared by standard spoken and written English: the sequence of words in the verb group – Modal verb + Perfect Auxiliary + Progressive Auxiliary + V-*ing*, the order of words in the common NP structures – Determiner + Adjective + Noun + Relative Clause; the commonly occurring types of adverbial clause – time (*when*), condition (*if*); the *get* and *be* passives, though usually the short passive is what occurs in spontaneous spoken English while written texts contain both short and long passives; the simple relative clauses as in (1a–d).

The structures just mentioned are merely a sample of core constructions – but what count as core? For Chomsky, core constructions are those that obey certain general constraints; here, core constructions are taken to be those that occur in databases of spontaneous spoken English, preferably informal conversation in relaxed circumstances between speakers who know each other well. ('Ungrammatical' sequences are important in the teaching of English (and French, Russian, etc.) as a second language. Swan (2005, pp. xxvi–xxix) lists 130 common mistakes. JM finds all the examples unacceptable. Swan also lists 25 further mistakes that even advanced students can make; JM does not agree with all of them. For instance, the sequence *return back* is rebarbative to those who are aware of Latin etymologies, but such aware people are a small minority in Britain these days and combinations like *reverse back*, *project out* and *reduce down* are common. Speakers have changed their usage and the combinations allowed by the code have changed too.)

As we move away from this core, more and more variation appears and the intuitions of particular speakers about grammaticality might be just as strong and confidently stated as intuitions about core constructions, but may not be supported by evidence from very large corpuses. Consider *rob* and *steal.*

For many speakers, the pair ROB and STEAL are clearly distinguished; you steal valuables by taking them away illegally, but you rob the owner of the valuables (Trask, 2001, p. 250). ROB is now being used by many speakers for the action applied to the valuables, as in the sentence *They'll probably end up going to jail or something or probably* ***robbing stuff*** (BA dissertation, Lancaster University, 2002).

Trask's entry on ROB and STEAL indicates that what he presents as a new usage is frequent enough to catch the attention of conservative speakers. In fact, this is an old usage that has survived in speech and in non-standard English. In Johnson's *Dictionary*, the third definition for ROB is 'to take away unlawfully'. Examples are *fashion a carriage to rob love from any* (Shakespeare) and *Double sacrilege . . . to rob the relick and deface the shrine* (Dryden). This example highlights the ambiguity of the term 'grammatical'. For some, perhaps many, speakers, possibly younger speakers of English, *rob valuables from someone* is normal usage. It may represent a continuation of the original construction, but it may be a modern development, quite independent of earlier usage. What was declared grammatical for standard English is *rob someone of their valuables*, whether this represents a usage that had sprung up naturally among a particular group of speakers or whether it represents a usage resulting from deliberate elaboration of the language by self-appointed arbiters of 'good' grammar.

Consider too the set of verbs denoting the action of covering a surface with something or some things. There is an established alternation for verbs such as *spread*, *smear* and *spray*: *The child smeared chocolate over her face* versus *The child smeared her face with chocolate*; *I spread jam on the bread* versus *I spread the bread with jam*, *They sprayed the path with weedkiller* versus *They sprayed weedkiller on the path*. Some verbs denote actions affecting the thing(s) set out on the surface, while other verbs denote the surface that is covered: *cover* applies to the surface – *cover a wall with green paint* but not **cover green paint on a wall*. Some of these specialized verbs now occur in both constructions. The writer's usage is represented in *The trees scattered leaves on the lawn* (cf. *Leaves were scattered on the lawn* and *There was a scattering of leaves on the lawn*.) But the following sentence occurred in a written text and suggests the construction *scatter the lawn with leaves*.

(25) My fields are scattered deep with chestnut leaves.
Fidelma Cook, 'French leave'.
The Herald, 17 October 2009, p. 4

A general verb denoting the action affecting the thing(s) moved on to a surface is *apply*. My usage is *apply paint to a door* but not *apply a door with paint*. But note the following example, curiously from the same newspaper though not the same contributor. It suggests the construction *apply soil with herbicides and pesticides*.

(26) A compost heap or box in an organically managed garden is a magnet for worms. What they dislike is wet, acidic soil which has been regularly applied with herbicides and pesticides.

Dave Allan, 'Binning mentality'. *The Herald*, 17 October 2009, p. 37

Different people react differently to such examples. Some do not notice them at all and may go on to use the structures or may already use them. Others will regard Cook and Allan as having committed grammatical errors. JM immediately noticed the sentences as peculiar (at least, peculiar given his usage), but one can recognize that languages change and that English is changing without feeling compelled to follow the new usage or to condemn Cook and Allan. JM, in good linguistic fashion, will be keeping a lookout for other examples of the construction in general and of the construction with *scatter* and *apply*.

Grammaticality and linguistic power

The social concept of grammaticality is often bound up with struggles for linguistic, cultural and political power. The struggles take place in small and large arenas; the one I am about to discuss happened in a university setting. University X has an ethics committee, and every piece of research that involves work with subjects has to be approved, even limited MA projects. The Ethics Committee, or its convener, declared itself dissatisfied with the grammar of many of the applications that were submitted for approval and announced that applications written in unsatisfactory language would be returned for revision. Unfortunately, the 2003 version of the Committee's regulations contained the following pieces of text. The main piece I want to look at is (27d), but the others are instructive.

(27) a. By whom and how, will information about the research be given to participants? (e.g. in writing, verbally . . .)

b. The period data is to be kept will be commensurate to the scale of its research.

c. Is Gene Therapy Advisory Committee on Assisted Human Reproduction (NACHDSE) approval required?
d. It is expected that access to the Consent Forms be restricted to the researcher and/or the Principal Investigator. If you intend otherwise, please explain.
e. It is required that Consent Forms be stored separately from data and kept for six years.

The comma after *how* in (27a) is very unusual and its purpose quite mysterious. The sequence *will be commensurate to the scale of its research* is not acceptable, since *commensurate*, in British English at least, requires *with*. In (27c), the sequence *Gene Therapy Advisory Committee on Assisted Human Reproduction (NACHDSE) approval* is overly complex and difficult to interpret. (27e) matches JM's usage, but the usage is becoming archaic and many would write *It is required that Consent Forms are stored separately*.

On a first reading (27d) seemed peculiar. A second reading pointed to the combination of *It is expected* and *be restricted* as the source of the peculiarity. Wondering whether his reaction was misguided, JM checked Quirk and Greenbaum (1973). On p. 361, they list the volitional verbs *command, demand, insist, order, propose, recommend,* and *suggest* and the volitional adjectives *adamant, keen* and *insistent*. They say that the volitional verbs require the subjunctive and that the volitional adjectives, which express some command indirectly, usually take the subjunctive in American English but *should* in British English. They give the examples in (28).

(28) a. I demand that he **leave** the meeting.
b. The editor insisted that this comment **be** taken out.
c. We proposed that the new Department **deal** only with postgraduate students.
d. The doctor was adamant that the person **leave** the surgery.
e. The doctor was adamant that she **prescribed** the correct medication.

(28d,e) highlight the difference between indirect commands and statements. (28d) conveys the proposition that the doctor asked the person to leave and would not change his or her mind. In (28e), the proposition conveyed is that the doctor was certain, and said so very firmly, that she had prescribed correctly.

(27e), then, is grammatical (it matches JM's usage!) and follows the account in Quirk and Greenbaum; *require* is a volitional verb. A quick check on Google of 180 instances of the sequence *is expected* produced 2 examples with the subjunctive and 178 with *was* or *should*. That is, (27d) turned out to be ungrammatical in terms of both the usage that JM follows and the data turned up by Google.

What is the explanation for (27d)? It could be a case of hypercorrection, the writer of the document being aware of the construction Verb + *that* + Clause with subjunctive verb form. Semantics and pragmatics might have led the writer to the construction. *Expect* in its basic meaning and in many contexts is not a volitional verb: *I expect they will arrive about six*, *We expect her to take at least the silver medal* and so on. Where the speaker is in a position of authority, *expect* can be used to signal a very indirect command: *I expect you to be here at 6 am* (spoken by police inspector to new constable), and in (27d) *expect* is not just a statement of expectation but is part of an indirect command. Nonetheless, *expect* does not normally combine with a clause containing a verb in the subjunctive. The moral of the tale is that pinning down exactly what is grammatical and what is not can be very tricky, and even highly educated writers can go astray.

Limitations on speakers' grammatical knowledge and intuitions

We close this discussion of grammaticality with a last example from Sampson (2007). It illustrates the limits on any one speaker's knowledge of their native language, the fact that different speakers may have different interpretations of a particular construction or chunk of spoken discourse and the need to consult databases such as reference grammars, dictionaries and corpuses. It also raises the question of what counts as a change in a given language. The point at issue is the conversational response *whatever*, as in the following dialogue (invented by JM).

(28) A I don't think that firm is the right one for the job.
B But they've installed lots of wind-turbines and are recommended by Mike and Philippa.
A Whatever.

Sampson (2007, p. 5) thought the response *whatever* was a way of saying something like 'You are such a loser that you mustn't expect me to put effort into giving you a considered answer.' Another gloss, which Sampson came across in a piece on language by a journalist, is 'You are correct, but I am unwilling to admit it explicitly.' The glosses do not coincide, but they have a family resemblance in expressing scorn towards the conversational partner while avoiding overt disagreement with the partner. Context is crucial. In the above dialogue, *whatever* does not express scorn or avoid overt disagreement, but signals A's unwillingness to say explicitly that B has a good point and that A might be wrong. In other contexts, it might carry the meanings mentioned by Sampson. The Cambridge Advanced Learner's Dictionary (2008, p. 1654) offers the example in (29), which seems to be spoken by parent to offspring – a teenager comes to mind.

(29) A Bryce, could you do what I ask you to once in a while?
B Whatever.

Swan (2005, p. 614) gives the example in (30). He comments that *whatever* means 'I don't care' or 'I'm not interested' and can sound rude.

(30) A What would you like to do? We could go and see a film, or go swimming.
B Whatever.

Sampson does not regard this use of *whatever* as a change in the English language but as the exploitation of a possibility that had been latent in the English language before anyone thought to use it. Swan (2005, p. 614) gives examples in which *whatever* has an interpretation close to the original one of 'anything at all': *If you play football or tennis or whatever, it does take up a lot of time. Whenever* can be used in the same way: *We can go there tomorrow or Friday or whenever.* Earlier this morning a radio discussion of why children should read stories offered examples of *whoever* and *whatever*: *If Mum, or Dad or a babysitter or whoever reads the children stories, that's good* and *If they read Harry Potter or Enid Blyton or whatever . . . Whatever* and *whenever* can be used as single-word responses that do not signal contempt and indifference, but leave the choice to the other person.

(31) A When can you come and help us with the painting?
B Whenever.

(32) A Will I cook potatoes or rice?
B Whatever? (I happily eat both.)

It is easy to see how, given the right context, *whatever* could have acquired the various affective meanings mentioned at the beginning of this discussion. Do these usages represent a change in the English language? We follow Sampson in distinguishing between the English language as a code and the users of the code. The code that JM had until recently allowed him to utter examples such as *Whatever you do, don't buy that house without having a complete survey done* and *You can consult whatever books you like.* Sequences such as *Mum, or Dad or a babysitter or whoever, Harry Potter or Enid Blyton or whatever* and *tomorrow or Friday or whenever* are new pieces of code for JM. Thirty years ago he would have used *and so on* or *etcetera.* That is, *whatever* has changed from being just part of a semi-fixed phrase, *whatever you do*, or a determiner, *whatever books you like*; it has become a substitute for *and so on* and *etcetera.* It has also acquired the function of a response roughly equivalent to *anything you like, I don't mind.*

A reasonable assumption is that the last development was for *whatever* to acquire the discourse particle function noted by Sampson and others. To sum up, we agree with Sampson that the recent usages of *whatever* were latent in its original meaning. We nuance his account by suggesting that the usages did not arise all together but in stages, a view that is supported by corpus data. It is also not clear why changes in usage should not count as changes in the English language, unless Sampson is confining the latter to changes in the code as opposed to the use made of the code. But even if we accept the latter approach, the evolution of *whatever* still counts as a change in the code. It has become a substitute for *etcetera* and *and so on* in the sequences in which these occur, and it has acquired a new extended distribution (at least, Zellig Harris would have handled it as such) as a response in discourse.

The above difficulties in analysing data are used by Sampson as a platform for attacking a fundamental aim of Chomsky's work, namely 'to separate the *grammatical* sequences which are the sentences of [a language] L from the *ungrammatical* sequences which are not sentences of L and to study the structure of the grammatical sequences' (Chomsky, 1957, p. 13). This aim has held constant through the various models of Chomskyan generative grammar; Sampson points out that some Chomskyans take a more extreme view. Carnie (2002, pp. 10–11) claims that to get at what we know about our languages we first have to know what sentences are not well-formed. The examples discussed by Sampson and the other examples presented earlier make it clear that the aim is unrealizable. This does not mean that no ungrammatical sequences can be recognized but, to pick up an earlier point, that beyond a certain core the distinction is either applicable with great difficulty or cannot be applied at all. (The issues were discussed in Matthews (1979); he arrived at the same general conclusion.)

To conclude the discussion, we return to Sampson (2007, p. 11) and his assertion that it is impossible to set a boundary between word sequences that will never have a use and those which currently have no use but will acquire a use at some future time. This is very true, but in what way is it relevant to the concept of grammaticality? The last quirk in this concept, in addition to the problems set out at the beginning of the chapter, is that grammaticality not only varies over sets of speakers of 'one and the same language' (a phrase that opens up more issues), but varies over time and within the lifetime of individual speakers. The *hopefully* construction became grammatical for many speakers some 40 years ago (when JM began using it), but remained ungrammatical for many other speakers. The revival of the middle construction and the use of *access* as a transitive verb are only two of many bits of English code that have become grammatical for JM over the past 25 years. We should not infer from these changes that grammaticality is based entirely on sand. JM is aware from his experience of copyeditors over the past 40 years that his intuitions about grammaticality match theirs. That is, as far as written English is concerned, JM belongs to a partly real and partly imagined community of educated users of British English. There is stability in a given language but also much variation, synchronic and diachronic; it is inevitably reflected in intuitions about what is grammatical and what is not.

6 Usage-based Models

Chapter Outline

The usage-based approach

The terms 'usage-based' and 'corpus linguistics' have been in vogue for some years. Having carried out his research on spontaneous spoken language on various corpuses of data, JM is well aware how valuable a good corpus is. Nonetheless, the term 'corpus linguistics' is meretricious. A corpus is simply a collection of data to be searched. Corpuses can be parsed and annotated, and they can be coded for all sorts of information; corpus searches can be carried out with skill and flair, or unimaginatively and unproductively. None of these activities involves linguistics. Linguistics comes into play when corpus data is to be analysed, say for syntactic structure or reference tracking or sense relations.

The collection of spoken or written data by means of audio recordings (or perhaps audio + video recordings) is essential work in many fields. It supplies linguists with naturally occurring data and enables them to study the language of small children, conversations between speakers of all ages, non-standard and standard varieties and so on. Such recordings enable linguists to observe what speakers do rather than what they say they do. Of course, research cannot rely solely on audio recordings of naturally occurring speech or on corpuses of written texts. The investigation of particular areas of grammar, say tense and aspect, or complement clauses, requires a combination of corpus data and data elicited via different tasks, getting subjects to fill in gaps in sentences, or to complete sentences, or to choose between two or more possible sentence completions, and so on. The investigation of non-standard varieties does require audio recordings, given what was said in the previous chapter about the unreliable intuitions of speakers of non-standard varieties and the general unreliability of intuitions about spoken language. (Not that speakers of non-standard varieties are somehow less able than speakers of standard varieties, but overt and accessible intuitions about grammar are acquired in the classroom and it is standard varieties that are used in schools.)

Usage-based models are, rightly, seen as an antidote to theorizing about speakers' competence based on the intuitions of linguists analysing magnasyntax. Barlow and Kemmer (2000, p. viiii) point out that usage-based research allows analysts to develop hypotheses about linguistic structure on the basis of observed utterances, without making claims about mental structure and operation. Usage-based models are nonetheless of great interest to analysts investigating actual speakers. A speaker's linguistic system is, in this perspective, grounded in 'usage events', instances of a speaker's producing and understanding language. General patterns are gradually built up by speakers from specific utterances with specific lexical items produced in specific contexts. Units or patterns which are more frequent become more 'entrenched', that is, stored as cognitive routines which enable the units and patterns to be rapidly processed. The speaker's linguistic ability is seen as constituted by regularities in the mental processing of language, and the sharp distinction between competence and performance central to much generative grammar is, in the usage-based approach, seen as unhelpful. Processing is an intrinsic part of the linguistic knowledge system, which cannot be treated separately from it.

Tense and aspect in English

In this chapter, we will not be challenging the aforementioned tenets of the usage-based approach to the analysis of language nor will we be exploring the relationship between processing and linguistic knowledge. We focus instead on demonstrating how analyses based on standard written English and devised examples of spoken standard English diverge significantly from analyses based on usage, looking in particular at tense and aspect in English. (The discussion indirectly puts in a word for the very traditional skill, which requires much practice, of paying attention both to how speakers communicate a message and to the content of the message. Any results obtained by this method need to be replicated by other researchers, and they do not give information about the frequency of one construction in contrast with another one. Nevertheless, collecting data on the hoof provides up-to-date evidence of changes in usage, which are particularly valuable with respect to spoken usage. The researcher simply needs to remember that one swallow doesn't make a summer.)

It is striking how the two types of analysis diverge, especially with respect to the ongoing changes in the English tense–aspect system. The core of the English tense–aspect system is the contrast between the Simple and Progressive forms and between Past and Present, as illustrated in (1).

(1)	**Simple**	**Progressive**
Past	a. *Shona bought flats.*	b. *Shona was buying flats.*
Present	c. *Shona buys flats.*	d. *Shona is buying flats.*
	e. *White phosphorus ignites instantaneously.*	

In addition, there is the Perfect, as in (2), and the two constructions by which speakers can refer to future time, as in (3).

(2) Shona has bought flats.

(3) a. Shona will buy flats.
b. Shona is going to buy flats.

The traditional analysis is that both the Simple and the Progressive forms can denote single events or habitual/repeated events and that the Simple Present can also denote generic events. As in Michaelis (2006, pp. 220–3), (1a) and (1b), understood as referring to single events, will be called 'episodic clauses'. (Michaelis calls them 'sentences', but see the discussion of 'sentence' and 'clause' in Chapter 2.) When they are interpreted as referring to habitual or repeated events (cf. *During her twenty years in London Shona bought flats but not houses* – perhaps Shona was investing a large inheritance, and *At that stage of her life Shona was buying flats*), they will be called 'habitual clauses'. (1e) will be called a 'gnomic clause'. Habitual clauses such as (1c) assign properties to particular individuals; gnomic clauses such as (1e) have a contingency interpretation: if some stuff is white phosphorus, then it will ignite instantaneously.

Leech's model

We begin the discussion of English tense and aspect and spontaneous spoken language with the account in Leech (1971). This account is particularly helpful because Leech treats English tense and aspect in the European structuralist fashion as a system of binary oppositions, each member of each opposition having its particular reading or set of readings. The system is as follows (see Leech, 1971, viii), the only change being in the labels, which have been altered slightly to bring out the oppositions more clearly.

(4)

non-Progressive	**Progressive**
Simple Present	**Prog Present**
he sees	*he is seeing*
NON-PERFECT	
Simple Past	**Prog Past**
he saw	*he was seeing*
('simple') Present Perfect	**Prog Present Perfect**
he has seen	*he has been seeing*
PERFECT	
('simple') Past Perfect	**Prog Past Perfect**
he had seen	*he had been seeing*

The fundamental contrast in (4) is between Perfect and non-Perfect. Within each term of the contrast, there is a further contrast between non-Progressive and Progressive, and each of these can be past or non-past. (We follow Dahl's notation. Tenses or aspects in a particular language have labels with an initial capital letter – the Progressive in English and the Imperfective in Russian – and labels for a cross-language category are in capitals – the realization of the PERFECTIVE in Russian and Latin.)

Non-Progressive is realized by the Simple Present and Simple Past. To the Simple Present, Leech assigns the meaning 'unrestrictive use', as in *War solves no problems* and *Honest is the best policy*, 'instantaneous use', as in *We accept your offer* and *Napier passes the ball to Attwater, who heads it straight into the goal*, 'states and events' as in *I shall remember that moment until I die* and 'habitual use', as in *I buy my shirts at Harrods.* Leech comments (1971, p. 5) that the Habitual Present represents a series of individual events, which as a whole make up a state stretching back into the past and forward into the future. This is one component of Leech's analysis which is shared with that of Michaelis (2006), albeit the latter sees the Present Tense as coercing any type of situation aspect into the state type, whereas Leech does not assign any such property to Present Tense but sees habituals as denoting complex states regardless of tense.

Two other parts of Leech's account bear on our analysis. He describes as imaginary the use of the Simple Present in narrative, in the description of routes in travel books and in instructions in instruction booklets. By 'imaginary' he means that persons describing the set of events see them as happening as they speak, in their mind's eye.

Leech's account of the Present Perfect does not use the terms in the classification in (5), but the major distinctions he draws correspond to the major interpretations of the Perfect now recognized by analysts. These interpretations are exemplified in (5).

(5) a. **experiential/indefinite past** Have you ever drunk rakija?
b. **resultative** I have written up my thesis.
c. **recent past** The Minister has (just) arrived.
d. **persistent situation** I've been waiting for an hour.

Ongoing changes in the English tense–aspect system

The elegant and pleasing contrasts in (4) and (5) match the use of the tenses and aspects in formal written English, especially in texts inspected by editors. They do not match the usages to be found in the spontaneous spoken English on which the following discussion is based, and we will argue that they do not stand up to scrutiny. The key points in the argument are as follows:

- The Simple Present and the Simple Past are parting company; in particular, the Simple Present can be seen as very much the odd one out in the system.
- There are clear signs that the Progressive is spreading to more and more contexts and that it has begun the process of becoming an imperfective.
- The Perfect is unstable. There are users who combine it with definite past time adverbs, using it as if it were a preterite. Other users prefer the Simple Past instead of the Perfect, with the possible exception of the Result Perfect. (See Miller (2000).)
- Accounts of tense and aspect in English usually do not include the Resultative constructions that occur regularly in spoken English.

The Simple Present and Simple Past

The Simple Present and the Simple Past are kept apart by a major distinction in interpretation. From the perspective of magnasyntax, Simple Past verbs can have episodic, habitual or generic interpretations. (But Michaelis (2006, p. 233) suggests that sentences with past-tense verbs may not be prototypical generics because the situation reported is not on-going at the time of speech. For her, an example such as *The Catholic mass was recited in Latin* is a marginal generic.) From the perspective of magnasyntax, Simple Present verbs have an episodic interpretation (see Leech's 'instantaneous use' stated earlier), a generic use (see Leech's 'unrestrictive use' stated earlier) and a habitual use.

Another analysis is indicated by data from two sources, experimentally elicited judgements and corpus data. Out of context, Simple Past examples are typically interpreted as denoting a single event, whereas Simple Present examples are typically interpreted as denoting repeated or habitual events. The Simple Present typically has a habitual or generic interpretation; it can denote a single event, but only in special text types such as stage directions and sports commentaries or in a special narrative style.

JM's attention was first drawn to differences in the use of the Simple Present and Simple Past while he was working on the Miller–Brown Corpus of Scottish English conversations in 1979–80. The idea that they had different typical interpretations was supported by intuitions collected from many classes of students in the 1980s. As part of lectures on tense and aspect given by JM in the 1980s, students were asked to carry out various tasks. For instance, they were given a list of sentences such as *We visited London* and *We visit London* and asked to add an adverbial phrase or clause. The first example always elicited additions such as *last year* or *when we were on holiday last summer* and the second elicited additions such as *every summer* or *whenever we go to see our cousins.*

Further support comes from two 2,000-word extracts from the Wellington Corpus of Spoken New Zealand English, from now on WSC (Wellington Spoken Corpus), and two 2,000-word extracts from the Miller–Brown Corpus of spoken Scottish English. The WSC extracts are from a radio phone-in discussion programme and a rugby commentary, and the Miller–Brown extracts are conversation, one a narrative and the other a discussion. The tokens of Simple Present and Simple Past verb forms were coded, collected and sorted into those denoting states and those denoting events. Examples of tokens denoting states are in (6).

(6) a. now i **know** of a person who's got TWO TEENAGERS plus herself.
b. i just **feel** that he is actually doing it just for his for his uh client.
c. i'm glad you **share** a sense of outrage.
d. that's what i **want** to hear.
e. how does that knee **look**.

The Simple forms denoting events were then split into those occurring in main clauses and those occurring in subordinate clauses, as in (7).

(7) i would like to you to ask them if you can if you EVER **get** on to them.

The forms occurring in main clauses were divided into those that occurred in the actual dialogue or monologue and those that occurred in the meta-commentary in the WSC data, where the coding includes 'paralinguistic anthropophonics', for example, 'laughs', 'drawls', 'inhales', 'snuffles' and so on. Finally, the former were sorted with respect to whether they denoted single (possibly instantaneous) completed events or repeated/habitual events, or were examples of narrative use, or discourse organizers, sequences such as *you see, you know, I mean, as I say* and so on. The results of the analysis and sorting are presented in (8).

(8)

		State	Hab/rep	single	narr	discourse
NZspc	SPr	11	0	78	0	2
	SPst	6	0	21	0	2
NZrp	SPr	8	21	0	1	7
	SPst	3	0	26	0	0
SCnarr	SPr	9	13	0	0	1
	SPst	10	6	74	0	0
SCdisc	SPr	27	16	0	0	28
	SPst	3	0	4	0	0

NZspc = 'New Zealand sports commentary', *NZrp* = 'New Zealand radio phone-in programme', *Scnarr* = 'Scottish English narrative', *Scdisc* = 'Scottish English discussion'. *Hab/rep* = 'habitual/repeated', single = 'single completed event', *narr* = 'narrative', *discourse* = 'discourse organizers'.

The figures support the view that sports commentaries are different from the other three text types. None of the Simple Present forms in the sports commentary denote habitual or repeated actions, but 78 denote single completed events of the sort in (7).

(9) a. <WSC#MUC002:0095:JM>
Lynagh gives it on to Horan
<WSC#MUC002:0100:JM>
Lynagh doubles around back into Campese who's come in

b. <WSC#MUC002:0120:JM>
Innes gets it kicks away

c. <WSC#MUC002:1280:JM>
they're trying to drop him to the ground but Crowley does VERY well to stay on his feet gets the ball to Bachop and Bachop kicks <laughs>away to touch

In the other text types, none of the Simple Present forms denote single completed events. Instead, they all denote repeated or habitual events, with the exception of (10), which looks more generic than habitual. (Can inanimate entities have habits?) It is uttered in response to the question *What's Galliano?*

(10) It comes in a long bottle with a twig in the centre of it
mbc 1, conversation 2, <c3>

In (8), *it* refers to Galliano, which is a proper name when referring to the company that makes the liqueur but a mass noun when referring to the type of liqueur. The latter interpretation is the relevant one in this context. That is, (8) has a contingency interpretation like (1e): if some liquid is Galliano, it comes in a long bottle with a twig in the centre of it.

In the New Zealand radio phone-in programme and the Scottish English narrative and discussion, most of the Simple Present verbs refer to habitual or repeated actions. The exception is the discussion, in which a very large number of Simple Present verbs refer to states: for example, *I wonder, I recognize the building, I think, I regret, I reckon that . . . , ( ) so happens that (I'm a member of the kirk just locally here), I suppose, I remember, I still maintain . . . lots of cinemas would have still been open* and so on.

There are156 tokens of Simple Past verbs. 125, or 86%, refer to single completed events. 22 refer to states and 6 refer to habitual or repeated actions. If the sports commentary is put on one side, we find that no Simple Present forms refer to single completed events and only six Simple Past forms refer to habitual/repeated events, figures that support the suggestion that it no longer makes sense to view the Simple Present and the Simple Past as constituting one member of an opposition whose other member is the Progressive.

What analysis would make sense? Jespersen (1961b, p. 17) insists that it is wrong to treat habitual and gnomic clauses (he doesn't use these terms) as timeless; if speakers use the present tense, he says, it is because their examples are valid now – or were valid at the time of speech or writing. This comment accords with the approach adopted here (and in Cognitive Linguistics), whereby all distinctions in morphology and syntax are meaningful. What we have said earlier about the Simple Present parting company with the Simple Past does not mean that the contrast between past and present tense is to be disregarded. Quirk and Greenbaum (1985, pp. 179–81) use terms such as 'timeless statements' and 'kind of "timeless present"', but their diagram shows that they analyse habitual and gnomic clauses as holding in a stretch of time that includes the moment of speech – 'now' in their diagram.

The analysis adopted here is based on Leech's idea of imaginary uses (Leech, 1971, p. 13). We suggest that with the exception of the instantaneous event interpretation, the Simple Present has become a kind of irrealis. Simple Presents in sports commentaries are uttered by speakers describing events as they happen, as in (7a–c). They are eminently realis and represent the classic opposition of Simple and Progressive forms, otherwise observed only in the past tense or after *will* and *shall*. Simple Present forms with habitual or gnomic interpretations are irrealis to the extent that the speaker who uses them is not referring to a particular instance of some type of event happening at the moment of speech. For the latter, the Progressive is required, witness the contrasts in (11)–(13).

(11) She makes her own dresses, in fact she's making one right now.
(12) They go to Brussels twice a year, in fact they're driving there at the moment.
(13) Water boils at 100°C. The water in this kettle is boiling so it must have reached 100°C.

An assertion of a habitual or gnomic proposition may be followed by a denial that the proposition is about to be translated into an action or process.

(14) They go to Brussels twice a year, but they might not go there this autumn because their son will be in Beirut.

The validity of the proposition that they go to Brussels twice a year is not affected by the lack of an autumn visit; this is possible because of the irrealis nature of habitual clauses.

Leech (1971, p. 13) mentions various uses that are hard to classify. His examples are in (15)–(17).

(15) To reach Chugwell, we *make* our way up to the River Ede, then skirt the slopes of Windy Beacon . . . [travelogue].
(16) You *take* the first turning on the left . . . then you *cross* a bridge and *bear* right . . . [directions].
(17) You *test* an air leak by disconnecting the delivery pipe at the carburettor and pumping petrol into a container.

These can all be treated as generics. They do not refer to actually occurring events, and they have contingency readings as required by Michaelis (2006):

'If we are trying to reach Chugwell, then we follow this route,' 'If you are going to X, then you proceed thus' and 'If you think there is an air-leak, you do the following.' Quirk et al. (1985, p. 180) give examples of demonstrations, as in (18). These can be handled as a special case of generics (rather than a type of commentary); *I* can be replaced by *you* or *one* and they have a contingency reading: 'If you want to make this dish, you carry out the following steps' or 'If one wants to make this dish . . . '.

(18) I *pick* up the fruit with a skewer, *dip* it into the batter, and *lower* it into the hot fat.

Quirk et al. give an example of what they call a self-commentary, reproduced in (19), and examples of performatives, as in (20).

(19) I enclose (herewith) a form of application.

(20) a. I advise you to withdraw.
b. I apologize.
c. We thank you for your recent inquiry.

(19) and (20) illustrate the difficulties of working with magnasyntax. (19) does not refer to an ongoing action, not ongoing by the time the letter is read by the recipient and not ongoing when the words are written. JM used to compose letters of reference or enquiry that began with clauses such as 'I write in support of the application by X' or 'I write in connection with your letter of the 14th January.' He has now abandoned these formulae in favour of clauses such as 'I am writing in support . . . '. The crucial property of performatives is that the uttering of a performative clause constitutes the performance of an act and not a reference to an act. Much of the later work on performatives lost sight of the fact that there are public ceremonial acts – for example, sentencing in a court of law, marrying and baptizing in church and launching a ship – which do require particular forms of words and other not so public acts, such as apologizing, advising and thanking, which do not require the use of Simple Present verbs. A study of how suggestions are made in business meetings found that the verb 'suggest' did not occur once (Sode-Woodhead, 2001). (19) and (20) are examples of archaic usages that are now highly formulaic (and may be falling into disuse) and not relevant to the core of the English verb system.

The final use of the Simple Present is what Quirk et al. (1985, p. 181) call the 'simple present referring to the past', but they also mention the labels 'historic present' and 'fictional present'. Following the criterion that grammatical differences are to be taken seriously, we assume that speakers who choose this usage do so because they are presenting situations as being in present time. An example is in (21).

(21) There's this man sitting in a bar. A wee guy comes in with a crocodile on a leash.

Leech (1971, p. 12) describes the fictional present as a device for dramatic heightening, putting the reader in the place of someone actually witnessing the events as they happen. He attributes this usage to 'more serious writing', but dramatic heightening is equally a property of 'popular narrative'. The example of more serious writing that Leech provides is taken from *Bleak House*. See (22).

(22) Mr Tulkinghorn *takes* out his papers, *asks* permission to place them on a golden talisman of a table at my Lady's elbow, *puts* on his spectacles, and *begins* to read by the light of a shaded lamp.

Bleak House is an interesting novel with respect to the use of the Simple Present. The events are narrated by two people. One is Dickens, in his role as omniscient narrator. That role enables him to present the events as though they were being witnessed by readers, and this effect is a clue that the historic or fictional present can be related to the Instantaneous Present. Both have to do with events being described as they happen, and both involve a mixture of Simple Present and Progressive. The other narrator is one of the leading characters, Esther Summerson. Her portion of the narrative purports to be from her diary and is written in the past tense, with lots of Simple Pasts. Being a character in the novel and writing up the events from her perspective, Esther Summerson cannot pretend to omniscience and cannot use the Simple Present.

Summary: The system of oppositions and uses set out by Leech (1971) is based on magnasyntax. An examination of usage in different types of spontaneous spoken English reveals a split between the Simple Past and the Simple Present. The uses of the Simple Present can be put into three groups. One group consists of performatives and self-commentaries, which, in their morphosyntax, represent archaic usages and an earlier stage in the historical development of the English verb system. A second group consists of Simple Present forms presenting single completed events as happening instantaneously. This group includes the use of the Simple Present in sports commentaries, jokes and narratives (popular or literary). The third group includes the habitual and generic meanings and includes the use of the Simple Present in habitual clauses, gnomic clauses, travelogues, directions and user manuals.

The Simple Present: contrasts with Russian, Chinese and Turkish

The usages reported earlier show that there is an aspectual opposition only in past tense verb forms. Conceptually, this is not surprising; we know whether events and processes in past time ran their course and reached their final boundary, but events and processes in present time are observed as they take place. Once an event or process has reached its final boundary, it is in the past and another event or process begins. In English, the Simple Present is either confined to particular genres or has a habitual-generic interpretation, which, as Leech (1971, p. 5) points out, can be seen as taking a series of single completed events and presenting it as a state. In other languages, the problem of present-tense forms denoting completed events has been resolved in other ways. In Russian, verb forms that had present tense and perfective aspect have come to be used to refer to future events and processes. In a number of languages, such as Chinese, verbs marked for perfective aspect can only be understood as referring to past events.

Turkish offers an interesting parallel to the English Simple Present and its uses. Lewis (1978, pp. 115–22) discusses what he calls the aorist tense. He explains that 'aorist' has been borrowed from grammars of Greek and means 'unbounded' and that the Turkish term is *geniş zaman* 'broad tense', which signals continuing activity. However the Turkish aorist is to be analysed, it is not a tense. The Turkish verb has a complex structure consisting of a stem to which affixes are added. There are particular slots for particular sets of affixes. As can be seen from (23), the tense affixes occur in the penultimate slot. The square brackets in bold between Slot 1 and Slot 2 signal the omission of several slots, for reflexive, reciprocal, causative and passive affixes (not to mention double causatives and double passives). The structure in (23) also omits a slot for the potential affixes.

(23) The structure of Turkish verbs

Slot 1	**[ ]**	Slot 2	Slot 3	Slot 4	Slot 5
Verb stem		negation	Aorist Future Imperfective	tense	person/number

The Imperfective affix is *-iyor*. It is a classic imperfective, as it is added to stative and dynamic verb stems – *yaz-iyor-um* 'I am writing' and *sev-iyor-um* 'I like' – and is used for reference to a single ongoing event and to a habitual event, as in (24).

(24) Turkish

her	*sabah*	*dōrt*	*saat*	*yazıyorum.*
each	morning	four	hours	I-write

'I write for four hours each morning.'

Slot 4, for tense, is filled either by Ø for Present Tense or by *-di* for Past Tense. (There are four Past Tense affixes, the choice being determined by vowel harmony.) For example, *yaz-iyor-um* 'I am writing' versus *yaz-iyor-du-m* 'I was writing.' The affixes that go into Slot 3 are difficult to classify but tenses they are not. As we have already seen, *-iyor* is an aspectual suffix. The suffix labelled 'future', *-acak*, has a strong modal content. As Lewis puts it (Lewis, 1978, p. 112), this suffix expresses not only what is going to happen, but what the speaker wants to happen. It expresses predictions, and in combination with the Past Tense suffixes it has to be interpreted as expressing intention, as in (25). From a broader perspective, *-acak* looks very modal.

(25) Turkish
bunu yap-acak-tı-m.
this . . . do-future-past-1SG
'I was intending to do this.'

The aorist has a strong irrealis component, in the sense that, like the habitual-generic Simple Present, aorist verbs are not used to refer to specific actions. The aorist *yaz-ar-ım* 'write-aorist-1SG' cannot be substituted for *yazıyorum* in (22). As Lewis (1978, p. 117) puts it, *yazarım* would be incongruous with the precise expression of time in (22); it has to be translated along the lines of 'I am a writer' (and 'I wasn't necessarily writing anything earlier today, or yesterday or indeed for the whole of the past year').

The Turkish aorist has other resemblances to the Simple Present. It is used in stage directions – *Esma gir-er-Ø, otur-ur-Ø*. 'Esma enter-aorist-3SG, sit down-aor-3SG, Esma enters and sits down' – and in proverbs – *it ür- ür - Ø, kervan geç-er- Ø* 'dog bark-aor-3SG, caravan leave-aor-3SG, The dogs howl, the caravan moves on'. The Turkish Aorist looks like a marker of irrealis mood. Obviously, it is very bad methodology to take an analysis that is supported by good morphosyntactic, semantic and pragmatic criteria in one language and apply it to another language. Nonetheless, given the irrealis component of the English Simple Present noted earlier, we can at least speculate whether the Simple Present, in its habitual-generic and related uses, is changing into a marker of irrealis mood. We leave it as speculation.

The Progressive

The standard analyses of the English verb have the Simple and the Progressive in opposition. Just as an examination of real usage shows that the Simple Present and the Simple Past are moving apart, so it shows changes in the Progressive. The classic Progressive is used to present single actions or processes as they are ongoing and is supposedly excluded from stative verbs. While it is true that the most stative of stative verbs, KNOW, does exclude the Progressive (see, for example, Quirk et al., 1985, p. 198), at least at the time of writing, many stative verbs do allow it, as Quirk et al. (1985, pp. 199–208) make clear. The Progressive also appears to be spreading into habitual clauses – Quirk et al. (1985, pp. 199–200) give examples – and into gnomic clauses. From a typological–historical perspective, these uses of the Progressive are not surprising, since the change of Progressives into Imperfectives is common and since Imperfective verbs are used to refer to single ongoing events, to habitual events and to generic events. Of course, the classic pattern of use of the English Progressive will survive for some time yet, particularly in formal written texts scrutinized by editors, but the new pattern is visible in speech and in informal writing.

Early English originally had a simple present and a simple past (Elsness 1997). Appearing in the fourteenth century, the progressive came into regular use in subordinate clauses by the eighteenth century and by the late twentieth century, in British English, had become very frequent in main clauses, especially in speech. Smitterberg (2000) demonstrates that the Progressive became more frequent in the genres of Letters, Drama, Fiction and History but less frequent in the genre of Science. The databases of Mair and Leech (2006, p. 323) show the Progressive becoming generally more frequent but also spreading into new parts of the verb system such as the Passive. Collins and Peters (2008, p. 346) observe the same phenomenon in Australian English and New Zealand English. Here, we focus on main clauses and the spread of the progressive to all lexical or situation aspects.

We commented earlier that the Progressive occurs with stative verbs. 'Can occur' is less misleading, as there is no suggestion that stative verbs typically or even regularly take the Progressive. Rather, instances of stative verbs in the Progressive turn up and there are examples which Quirk and Greenbaum declare unacceptable, such as (26a) and the real (written) example (26b). (27a,b) are further examples of stative constructions in the Progressive.

(26) a. *I **am understanding** that the offer has been accepted.
Quirk and Greenbaum, 1985, p. 203

b. I am sorry to have to worry you again with . . . X's resubmission. However Department Y **is still not really understanding** what it is that X needs to do.
University of Auckland, 2004,
e-mail from a committee convener

(27) a. 'And there is an older generation who **are seeing** NCEA as lowering the standards . . . '
NZ Listener, 9–15 June 2007, p. 23

b. She lives in a house which **is dating** back 200 years.
BBC photography programme, Sunday,
17 June 2007, 9–9.30 pm

c. it may be that internal linguistic factors . . . **are governing** the choice between have to and have got to . . .
Tagliamonte 2004:43

d. people **weren't** even **believing** the true stories.
Australian ICE, S1A-026(B):64

(26) and (27a) offer two classic stative verbs, UNDERSTAND and SEE, in the progressive. (27b,c) are examples of stative constructions even if the verbs are not classically stative and (27c) is also generic. (Remember Leech's comment quoted above to the effect that habituals denote series of events and each series is a kind of state.) It is worthwhile noting that (26) was part of a formal e-mail written by an academic senior in status and age and that (27c) is from an academic text. Academic texts are scrutinized by referees and performance errors are unlikely.

(28a,b) occurred in final degree examination scripts. In examinations, students have little time for planning and editing and produce constructions typical of speech or informal writing but unusual in formal writing. (28a,b) are generic, but have stative verbs in the progressive – PRECEDE and DEPEND. (29) has a progressive in a clause denoting a repeated event: the students repeatedly forget the new numbers.

(28) a. The first vowel in [complaints] is short as it **is preceeding** [sic] the nasal bilabial /m/.

Final degree examination script,
University of Lancaster, June 2002

b. Naturally a child **is depending** on his parents, or other adults to provide an environment where he can learn new words.

Final Honours examination script,
Edinburgh, June 1983

(29) The code is often changed and students **are forgetting** the new number.

Minutes of Staff-Honours Students Liaison Committee Meeting,
University of Edinburgh, February 1998, (Written by a 4th year student)

(28a,b) may reflect a choice of perspective. In examinations, students discuss examples given in the question paper and write down their analysis as it proceeds. They may use the progressive to metaphorically put their readers in the middle of on-going events. If correct, this explanation does not contradict the comments on the increasing frequency of the progressive but provides one of its causes.

Simple Past and Perfect

Analysis of spontaneous spoken and informal written English reveals a third mismatch between the usage of many speakers and the accounts given in reference grammars. Accounts of the Simple Past and the Present Perfect are mismatched; missing is any analysis of the various resultative constructions built round an *-ed* participle. Leech's description of the Perfect, summarized in the examples in (3) earlier, is an elegant and accurate statement of the use of the Perfect by many speakers and, especially, writers of standard British English. Leech's description is now almost 40 years old [but see also Dahl (1999) and Michaelis (1994)]; not only are linguistic habits moving on, but it looks as though many users of standard and non-standard British English had and have different habits. We find examples of the Perfect combining with specific Past Time adverbs; examples of Simple Pasts in combination with adverbs such as *yet*, *ever*, and *just* where we might expect to find Perfects; and various resultative constructions which are not included in the major reference grammars. [The use of the Simple Past plus adverbs is the standard pattern in American English, but is generally assumed not to be typical of British English. Quirk et al. (1985, p. 193) say that in American English there is a tendency to use, for example, *Did you ever go to Florence, I just came back* and *Did the children come home yet?*]

The data to be presented suggest that the classic Perfect unmodified by adverbs exists only in a very restrictive variety of standard English and that in spoken English the different Perfect constructions distinguished by adverbs have always been the typical pattern. The data also indicate a complex pattern of grammaticalization: the possessive–resultative construction with relatively specific meaning evolves into the Perfect with a more general and more abstract interpretation; the Perfect in turn splits into different constructions, each with a more specific meaning than the Perfect and marked by an appropriate adverb; the original possessive–resultative construction not only persists but itself undergoes change that increases the morphosyntactic distance between it and the Perfect; and various other resultative constructions develop. Grammars of (standard) English maintain that the Perfect excludes definite past time adverbs, as in (30). [See Klein (1992).]

(30) *She's left for Rome yesterday/this morning.

The fact is that combinations of the Perfect and specific past time adverbs occur in written English as well as in spontaneous spoken English. The example in (31) was in an uncensored written text, while (32) was in a newspaper text – with the intensive use of computers newspapers are no longer edited as rigorously as they once were.

(31) The invoice **has been sent off** to Finance for payment **before I went off on holiday.**

Letter from staff in university finance department

(32) BEI's success is all the more welcome as Britain **has lost ground 10 years ago** with the Saudis' decision to opt for American frequencies of 60 hertz rather than the British 50 hertz -giving the American manufacturers a head start.

The Times

Examples from spontaneous speech are in (33) and (34).

(33) I've **talked to the player this morning** and he isn't leaving the club.

TV interview

(34) Some of us **have been to New York years ago** to see how they do it

Simon Hughes, Liberal Democrat MP,
BBC News at Ten interview, January 2002

(33) and (34) are not innovations. Elsness (1997, p. 250) cites similar examples from Shakespeare, Pepys and dialogue in Galsworthy. Denison (1993, p. 352) asserts that in Middle English the Present Perfect and the Simple Past were used interchangeably with definite past time adverbs. Comrie (1985, p. 33) comments that 'with considerable dialectal and idiolectal variation' some speakers of English combine specific past time adverbs with the Perfect and points out that adverbs referring to recent points or periods of time – *recently, this morning*, etc. – regularly combine with the Perfect.

The above examples look less peculiar when we remind ourselves that the constraint on the combination of Perfect and specific past time adverbs applies only in relation to actual moments of speech or writing. These can be thought of as primary deictic centres. Events narrated by means of the Perfect may relate not to the moment of speech but to some other time, as in the narrative in (35). These Perfects do combine with specific past time adverbs, such as the ones in bold in (35).

(35) At 1 o'clock on the afternoon of 29th May 2009 a passenger is sitting in the departure lounge. He **has checked in around 12.30, has gone through security around 12.45**, and is waiting for his colleague.

The deictic centre for (35) is secondary, that is, it is not the time at which the text was written. Secondary deixis also allows specific past time adverbs to combine with Perfect infinitives, which, being non-finite, are not anchored to a fixed moment of speech. Examples are in (36) and (37).

(36) It's annoying to arrive at the station at 10.30 only to find that the train **has left at 10.15 and not 10.50**.

(37) **To have arrived at 2 pm on Tuesday** was a miracle [is a miracle/will be a miracle]

We turn now to examples of the Recent Past, Experiential and Result Perfects. (38)–(40) are British English examples of Simple Pasts + *just* referring to the Recent Past. (Around 1972/73, JM's four- and three-year old children began to talk explicitly about immediate past time. They used the Simple Past plus *just*, not the Perfect. Since neither child went to nursery school, they must have picked up the construction from their parents, though neither parent was aware of using it.)

(38) Er, as Charlie **just pointed out**, it is of great concern.

Discussion at Trades Union Congress,
recorded in the British National Corpus

(39) Sorry, Jane's not in. She **just went out** (=has just gone out).

Noted informally in conversation

(40) my father bought a round of drinks after the meal there wasnae one for me you see and one of the men happened to comment he says 'Bob' he says 'you **forgot** the boy' 'No' he says 'I **didnae forget** the boy.'

Macaulay, 1991 p. 197–8

This usage is widespread throughout varieties of English. It is the norm in North American English. A search through the Australian component of ICE in the Macquarie Corpus (S1A, private dialogue) revealed an equal number of Simple Pasts and Perfects combining with *just.* A number of the examples of Simple Pasts could only be judged in bigger contexts, which are omitted here. The New Zealand component has not been searched in the same way, but one suggestive example, in (41), comes from an advertisement for the *New Zealand Herald* seen on the back of a bus in Auckland in 2007. The example is suggestive because, certainly in the United Kingdom and New Zealand, contemporary advertisements based on dialogue try to reflect up-to-date spoken usage.

(41) Did you hear what just happened?

The use of *ever* with the Perfect or Simple Past is more complex and what are presented below are British English examples of the Experiential meaning expressed by the Simple Past plus *ever*, in (42)–(44).

(42) A it's a great place - have you ever been to the commonwealth pool
B no really i'm no a very good swimmer
A what what eh no you said you enjoyed fishin **were you ever interested in football**
B no we go to the shootin

Miller–Brown Corpus, 1 – conversation 8, m17

(43) **Did you ever try** to give up smoking?

Advert on ITV, UK, 2003

(44) who's brenda **did I meet her?** [in context = ' . . . have I met her?']

Miller–Brown Corpus, 2, conversation 12, m6

Resultative and Perfect

Spontaneous spoken standard English has a number of constructions other than the Perfect which are used to convey resultative meaning. They all involve the past participle (passive), which was originally resultative [see Haspelmath

(1993)]. One of the regularly used constructions is the one that is taken to be the source of the English Perfect, as exemplified in (45). (45a) is a devised example, but (45b–d) are from the Wellington Corpus of Spoken New Zealand English. (45b) is from a sports commentary; (45c) is from conversation. (46) has a coordinate resultative structure and was produced by a surgeon talking in a radio interview about new technology in Accident and Emergency departments. (47a,b) show how the originally possessive construction has had its possessive nature reinforced by the introduction of *have got*. (47a) is a devised example, but (47b) is from the same source as (45b,c).

(45) a. I **have** the letter **written**.
b. bachop **has his backs lined out to the right** to this side of the field
<WSC#MUC002:1075:JM>
c. and he does **have a car parked not far away**
<WSC#DPC003:1045:FG>

(46) You have access to a vein gained and cardiac analysis done within one minute.

(47) a. I've got the letter written.
b. i said **they've got those well labelled** for this
<WSC#DPC002:0710:MK>

In (47b), the speaker is referring to a bottle of pills. (48a–c) are examples of an existential–presentative construction with a resultative participle. The construction is used to introduce a situation treated as new information. The situation has to do with the result of a previous event.

(48) a. there's something fallen down the sink.
b. there's a cat trapped up the tree.
c. there's one person injured in the explosion.

In the existential–presentative construction, *there's* is pronounced with the reduced vowel. The Wellington Corpus of Spoken New Zealand English contains at least one example of an existential–presentative with the full deictic and a passive/resultative participle. See (48d), from a sports commentary.

(48) d. there's **the ball won** by the australians
<WSC#MUC002:0005:JM>

(48d) contains a definite NP, *the ball*, whereas typical existential–presentatives contain indefinite NPs. What is being presented is not the ball, which has been mentioned many times in the course of the match, but the situation 'the ball having been won by the Australians.'

Consider now the construction in (49a–c).

(49) a. That's the letters written and posted.

Kennedy, 1994

b. That's him consulted.

TV comedy show 'Harry Enfield and Chums'

c. Here's the tyre repaired and good as new.

Conversation in garage

What is the structure of (49a,b)? They are instances of a copula construction: *that* is connected by the copula *'s* with NPs containing a resultative participle, *the letters written and posted* and *him consulted.* In this respect, they are parallel in structure to reverse WH clefts such as *That's what you need to do.* (Note that 'reverse' captures the fact that such clefts are the reverse of *What you need to do is go on a long holiday*, in which the WH phrase is in sentence-initial position.) Reverse WH clefts are used to reinforce a point and to bring a section of dialogue to a close – see the overview of previous work and the analyses of naturally occurring examples in Weinert and Miller (1996). Examples such as (49a,b) are TH clefts, but have the same discourse function as reverse WH clefts.

(49a–c) could in principle be replaced by the basic Perfect construction – *I've written and posted the letters, I've consulted him* and *The tyre has been repaired and is as good as new.* The replacements, however, introduce an explicit or implicit Agent in a non-cleft construction, thereby changing what is highlighted and reducing the salience of the current result. It is worthwhile stating explicitly that the construction is not unique to Scottish English. (49b) is from a television comedy programme from southern England and the construction is in regular use in Colchester in Essex. (Dave Britain, University of Essex, pc.)

Scottish English (and doubtless other varieties of English) has another resultative construction in addition to those in (45)–(49). The resultative participles in those examples modify Patient nouns (which are not necessarily direct objects). In the resultative construction exemplified in (50)–(55), the participle modifies the Agent or subject noun. The subject noun may refer to an Agent, as in (50b,c) – and in (50a), depending on the analysis of SEE. The participle also modifies an Agent subject noun in (51)–(53). (It is important to note that these examples are not analogous to the *fallen leaves* and *undescended testicles* examples discussed in Bresnan (1982, pp. 29 and 30), which involve participles modifying Themes – to use Bresnan's terminology.)

(50) a. but that's me **seen** it (= I've seen it now)

Macaulay, 1991

b. that's you **finished** (= 'You have finished (the task))

Map Task Dialogues;
see Weinert and Miller (1996)

c. that's Ian **arrived**. [informally recorded in conversation]

(51) and –eh when I was waiting on the milk eh-the farmer came oot and he says '**That you left the school noo Andrew?**' says I '**It is**' he says 'You'll be looking for a job'

Macaulay, 1991

(52) **j50** once she goes to haddington it'll no be so bad i mean she's moving to haddington in june
m51 even haddington joyce is far enough you know
j51 i know martin but at least it's not all wee windy roads to it ['windy' = winding]
m52 no you can get on the a1
j52 you're on the main road to haddington
m53 i think you can stay on the main road
j53 aye the musselburgh road and you're there through macmerry and that way and then you're at haddington aren't you
m54 aye that's right haddington's the next one even so joyce it's still a waste to go where does she go after that
j54 **that3's her finished** i think after haddington she goes to college again for a few weeks

Miller–Brown Corpus, conversation 27

That's her finished in (52) is a TH cleft and the interpretation is not that she has been finished off but that she will have finished her period of training once she completes her stint at Haddington. In (51), *That you left the school* is a reduced interrogative TH cleft. The full structure is *Is that you left the school*, as shown by the reply *It is.*

(53) now I'm trying to encourage Sally – you get on in life if you would just do that little bit more you know erm even though you've only got one more sentence to do – why not just do it? Even if it's 20–34 minutes past – instead of 30 minutes – Sally is the kind of person that will say '**that's me done** it' and then stop and she'll go off . . .

Conversation recorded by Gillian Foy (2000)

(54) and (55) offer examples of the resultative construction in the past tense, the equivalent of Pluperfects.

(54) the bus come at twenty-five minutes to six in the morning and he started at seven o'clock twenty-five to six now see if he didnae get that bus that was him **he wasnae oot** (=he hadn't got out of the house) he needed to get the first one in the morning going doon the pit or **that's him slept in**

Macaulay (1991)

(55) he just lay doon on the settee and turned over and **that was him gone** (= he had gone)

Macaulay (1991)

Conclusion

The above account demonstrates the value of the usage-based approach. The Simple Present of English is no longer just the Present-Tense correspondent of the Simple Past and most of its uses are irrealis. The Progressive, as indicated by (26)–(29) is acquiring the characteristics of an Imperfective. The opposition between Simple Past and Perfect is not clear-cut, and the role of *just*, *ever*, and *yet* in signalling the various sub-types of Perfect may turn out to be rather significant. The source construction for the Perfect, the transitive Resultative, has not only survived but strengthened, and the resultative participles are regularly used in a number of Resultative constructions. What we see is a tense–aspect system in the process of change but also different, though overlapping, tense–aspect systems for formal written English and spontaneous spoken English. The latter system may be of long standing, like so many other patterns in non-standard grammar. Regrettably, we cannot apply the usage-based approach retrospectively, merely catch a glimpse or two via dialogue in novels.

Grammar and Semantics: The *Get* Passive

7

Chapter Outline

Introduction

The connection between grammar and semantics is fascinating and central to any language. Case marking, contrasts of mood and modality, tense and aspect, person, number, gender and voice convey essential information about situations and the speaker's attitude to situations.

It is the subject of major investigations and has always been central in explanations offered by teachers of a given language to learners with a different native language. Non-native learners of any language typically find these grammatico-semantic systems the most difficult parts to master; many years after he entered the elementary Russian class at university, JM still gets little surprises.

Explanations of a particular case or aspectual usage in Russian, to take JM's experience, were all the more welcome if they made semantic or pragmatic sense. The approach taken here is that all grammatical formatives must be assumed to be meaningful. It may not always be possible to defend that assumption for particular formatives, say the English preposition *of*, but that must be the initial assumption. That assumption applies to case suffixes, prepositions, tense and aspect markers, modal verbs and so on. It is also assumed that all constructional changes bring a semantic change. For example, Fillmore (1968) drew attention to the locative inversion constructions as in *The gardener planted the garden with daffodils* and *The gardener planted daffodils in the garden.* The first example can only be interpreted as 'the gardener planted daffodils everywhere in the garden'; the interpretation of the second one leaves it open as to whether the entire garden had daffodils in it or just a part of the garden.

JM's treatment of grammar and semantics coincides with that of Cognitive Grammar, especially the work by, for example, Langacker (1991), but it derives directly from the work on localism (see Anderson, 1971 and Lyons, 1977b) in Edinburgh in the late 1960s and early 1970s. Another methodological principle is that where the same form, bound or free, occurs in a variety of constructions, the same basic meaning should be assigned to all instances of it. This principle applies to case inflections, which are bound, but also to forms that function as full lexical items and as auxiliary constituents. (See the discussion of *get* below.) An extension of this principle is that if the same construction, the same sequence of forms, occurs with two apparently different meanings, a synchronic relation should be established, where possible, between the meanings. (Of course, it will not always be possible to apply the principle, given the vagaries of historical change and large variation in linguistic practices and codes among the speakers of what is considered one language, but the goal is to apply a particular analysis wherever there is sufficient evidence for it.)

A second principle is that if in a number of languages one form expresses the same set of meanings – that is, one form per language but a different form for each language – and if the set of meanings includes a spatial one, the spatial meaning is taken as basic and the other meanings derived from it, or from a meaning that can be derived from the spatial one. Examples are the by now well-known parallels between locational and possessive constructions and between locational and progressive constructions. For the former, consider the Finnish examples in (1a–c)

(1) a. Pöydällä on kirja.
table-on is a-book 'There is a book is on the table.'

b. Minulla on kirja.
I-on is book 'I have a book.'

c. Hänellä oli kauniit hampaat.
She-on are beautiful teeth 'She has beautiful teeth.'

The suffix *-lla*/*-llä* expresses 'location on the surface of'. This suffix occurs in (1a), which has a spatial locational meaning, and in (1b,c), which have possessive meanings. All three Finnish clauses have the same syntax, including word order and case suffixes: a noun in the adessive case + a form of the Finnish verb equivalent to *be*, agreeing in person and number with the following noun in the nominative case + a noun in the nominative case. Given these facts, all three clauses are assigned the same locational semantic structure, with possession as a secondary interpretation that is possible for all three clauses but is particularly strong where the noun in the adessive case denotes an animate being and the noun in the nominative case denotes typical possessions of human beings. Finnish is only one of many languages in which locational and possessive constructions have the same syntax and morphology.

Anderson (1973) collected examples from a wide range of languages of progressive constructions that are identical with locational ones. A language not cited by him is Maori, exemplified in (2). (The examples are from Winifred Bauer, pc.)

(2) a. i tana taha
at her side
b. i te waiata ratou.
At the singing they 'They were singing.'

The localist approach to the semantics of grammar is essentially the same approach applied by Jackendoff (1976) and central to his work on lexical–conceptual structures. The idea that movement, source, path and so on are relevant to different domains, with the same prepositions, case suffixes, verbs of movement and location and so on, is one avatar of the localist idea. Localism has been central to Langacker's work since the publication of his 1982 paper on space grammar, a forerunner of cognitive grammar. The localist approach will be illustrated further in the discussion of the *get* passive below. Nothing further will be said here, as readers can consult Anderson (2007) for case and Langacker (1987, 1991) and Jackendoff (1976).

To bring out the importance of the link between grammar and semantics, to highlight the centrality of grammatical criteria in semantic analysis and to emphasize that every grammatical morpheme has meaning, we will examine four topics: the *get* passive, wh words and constructions, parts of speech and thematic or participant roles.

How frequent is the *get* passive?

This account of the English *get* passive encompasses grammar, semantics, pragmatics, and indeed usage. Biber et al. (1999, p. 481) comment that the *get* passive is generally rare and restricted primarily to conversation. This is quite true, given that during the entire twentieth century the use of *get* was forcefully discouraged in schools. What is obscured by the data in Biber et al. is that for the vast majority of speakers conversation is the sort of spoken language they are most exposed to and produce most of the time. Many users of English do not read or write large quantities of written text; many users who do produce written text do so in the context of quasi-conversations by e-mail or Skype.

The *get* passive is rare in a corpus that encompasses a large range of written and spoken text types, but is much more frequent in the most common spoken genre. Miller and Weinert (2009, pp. 88–9), working on Scottish English, analysed passives in the Map Task Dialogues. The figures are in Table 7.1. They also examined a small subset of conversations in the Miller–Brown Corpus and found 18 *be* passives and 11 *get* passives. Suzanne Romaine, working on Scottish English in the mid-1970s, recorded a 10-year-old girl talking about her home and friends, her school life and the television programmes she watched. The girl used 66 passives, of which 60 contained *get.*

For the purposes of this book, JM analysed the transcriptions of conversations 11–20 in the Miller–Brown Corpus, approximately 19,000 words, and conversations 71–80, approximately 28,000 words. In the Australian component of ICE, he examined conversations 1–30 in database S1A, private unscripted dialogue of 60,000 words. He also looked at the Map Task Dialogues. (See the Introduction.) **Table 7.1**

Table 7.1 *be* and *get* passives in spontaneous speech

	BE Dynamic	BE Static	GET
MTD	4	5	9
mbc2	11		24
AusICE	22	46	22
mbc8	20	18	10

AusICE = Australian component of ICE
mbc2 = Miller–Brown Corpus, section 2, conversations 11–20
mbc8 = Miller–Brown Corpus, section 8, conversations 71–80
MTD = Map Task Dialogues

The Map Task Dialogues contain a very small number of passives overall. The two subsets of conversations, mbc2 and mbc8, differ in the number of *get* passives: 24 in mbc2 but only 10 in mbc8. The conversations were held in similar conditions but in different schools. The major socio-linguistic difference is that while all the contributors were speakers of Scottish English, those recorded in mbc2 were nearer the Scots pole of the Scottish English continuum and those recorded in mbc8 were nearer the Standard English pole. (For further discussion and details, see Miller, 2003.) Five of the ten *get* passives in mbc8 were produced by one speaker, a 16-year-old girl, and two speakers produced no *get* passives. All the speakers in mbc2 produced at least one *get* passive. The Australian English data were recorded in various informal settings and from speakers ranging in age from 19/20 to 30. The dynamic *be* passives and *get* passives were equal in frequency. By its very meaning, *get* is excluded from static passives.

Biber et al. (1999, p. 481) state that only a few verbs are common with the *get* passive, even in conversation: only *get married* has more than 20 instances per one million words and only *get hit/involved/left/stuck* have more than 5 instances per one million words. It is worth commenting that a very large range of verbs occurs in the *get* passive, even if few of them occur frequently: AusICE yields, for example, *get caught/cut out/mixed up (with someone)/jarred/disqualified/accepted/rebuilt/bitten.* Mbc 8 has, for example, *get confirmed* (in the religious sense)/*baptized/elected/smashed in/turned back.*

The interpretation of the *get* passive

Huddleston and Pullum (2002) – that is, Gregory Ward, Betty Birner and Rodney Huddleston, who wrote Chapter 16 on the passive – give an account of the *get* passive, which in one respect is puzzling. Following Lakoff (1971) and Givon and Yang (1994), they say that *get* passives are more conducive to an agentive interpretation of the subject (Huddleston and Pullum, 2002, p. 1442).) By this they mean that *get* passives induce an interpretation that the participant referred to by the subject NP, although playing the role of Patient, is responsible for the event happening. They suggest that *get* is the natural choice in *Jill deliberately got arrested* (i.e. Jill engineered her arrest) and in examples such as (3).

(3) a. She managed to get transferred to the finance department.
b. Go and get checked out at the medical centre.

c. Getting elected president of the student union took a lot of time and effort.
d. He did a silly thing: he got caught downloading pornography on their computer.

Like Carter and McCarthy (1999), they regard *get* passives as characteristic of clauses involving adversity or benefit. In the data from CANCODE examined by Carter and McCarthy, many of the *get* passives denote events that have an adverse effect on the person referred to by the subject NP. This is true also of the *get* passives in mbc2, mbc8 and AusICE – see the above selection of verbs from *get* passives. By the same token, some *be* passives also denote adverse events and some *get* passives do not denote adverse events.

Along the same lines, Lakoff (1971), followed by Givon and Yang (1994), appeals to the invented examples in (4). In (4a), the adverb supposedly denotes a quality of Mary's action, but not in (4b).

(4) a. Mary got shot intentionally/on purpose.
b. Mary was shot intentionally/on purpose.

Lakoff also asserts that *get* passives allow the inference that the speaker's emotions are engaged. For example, she says, a *get* passive would be most unlikely to occur in the sort of neutral statement that newsreaders make. This is difficult to judge, as newsreaders read from a script on autocue and the writers of such scripts produce very conservative written language. *Get* passives are typically absent from such texts. The engagement of emotions did get support from Gee (1974), who used the invented examples in (5).

(5) a. Our grant was cancelled (?darn it!).
b. Our grant got cancelled (darn it!).

Some colleagues and students at the University of Edinburgh (Scots, English and American) suggested that (5a) is neutral but that (5b) is appropriate if the event is unexpected. One reading of (6b), they said, might be 'The house got painted by accident,' while Lakoff (1971) proposes 'The house finally got painted.'

(6) a. The house was painted last week.
b. The house got painted last week.

Both Lakoff and Gee consider the *be* passive feeble and colourless, the *get* passive vivid and energetic. The contention here is that this difference can be traced to the fact that the *get* passive is dynamic and built round a verb of movement. If *be* has any concrete meaning, it is just location, and in fact it is so grammaticalized that it probably does not even denote location. The various additional components of meaning mentioned above can be handled as context-dependent interpretations made possible by the dynamic nature of *get*.

Having developed the above points about the interpretation of the *get* passive, Ward et al. assert that *be* and *get* are dummy verbs that carry no identifiable meaning of their own but merely serve to mark the passive voice and to carry the preterite tense inflection (Huddleston and Pulllum, 2002, p. 1443). Is there a contradiction here? Presumably what is meant is that the *get* passive construction as a whole carries the interpretation of responsibility or adverse effect but that the actual verb *get* on its own has no identifiable meaning.

The central point in the analysis adopted here is that *get* does have an identifiable meaning. Before we move on to that topic, we can usefully look at the constructional meaning illustrated in (4a). None of the *get* passives from AusICE, mbc2 or mbc8 can be interpreted as carrying this interpretation. The examples that do carry this interpretation all involve a causative–reflexive construction, as in (7).

(7) a. He **got** himself cut up and that a bit along the leg and this and his trousers.
[The reference is to a motor cycle accident caused by the injured person driving too fast.]
AusICE, S1A-011(B):277

b. She really loves firstname15 and she wants to stay with him now that she's **got** him back and she's worried about what will happen with firstname3 when he comes here and
S1A-083(B):391

She's **got**ten herself into it
S1A-083(A):415

c. So I I've **got** myself into a nice little fix and like I didn't discourage him either which was
S1A-093(A):179

d. is there not any way you can **get** yourself inveigled into a permanent post with the department
Miller–Brown Corpus, conversation 31

e. . . . I mean his pal sort of sits back and eggs him on and of course he **gets** himself landed into it
Miller–Brown Corpus, conversation 56

Givon (1990, p. 620ff) claims that in the situation denoted by (8a) the rival group acted deliberately, whereas in (8b) the picket acted deliberately.

(8) a. The supporters were deliberately provoked by a rival group.
b. The picket got knocked down deliberately by the security guard.

JM's intuitions do not match Givon's; (8b) would have to be rephrased as *The picket got himself/herself knocked down deliberately by the security guard.* Givon claims that *get* passives with *accidentally* are incorrect, but implicitly recognizes that such examples occur when he declares that examples such as *The picket got knocked down accidentally* are 'sub-standard'. There may be a difference in usage between British and American English or it may be that Givon's intuitions are misleading.

Get: a meaningless verb or a verb of movement?

Does *get* in the *get* passive really have no identifiable meaning? Miller (1985, pp. 170–90) argues that the *get* passive is based on *get* as a verb of movement, an analysis that is argued along slightly different lines by Gronemeyer (1999). The argument is based on synchronic and diachronic evidence. The synchronic evidence is that the *get* passive denotes changes of state: *got rejected* denotes a process of transition from a state of not being rejected to one of being rejected. *Got angry* likewise denotes a transition from a state of not being angry to a state of being angry, and in many languages transitions from one state to another are expressed by verbs that also express movement. In English, *get* is a verb of movement par excellence. It combines with directional complements as in (9) and with all the directional particles: for example, *get down off the wall, get up onto the roof, get out, get past without being seen*, and so on.

(9) a. We got to Stirling.
b. The thieves got into the building.
c. They got out of the building by the fire escape.
d. The runners got round the circuit in less than three hours.

Get also denotes caused movement, as in (10), and caused change of state, as in (11).

(10) a. We got the box into the car.
b. The driver got the car as far as the garage

c. It was quite incredible the way we got the case of beers over the fence
Aus ICE S1A-031(B):175

(11) a. She's got to **get** it organised before she goes to hospital for her knee
Aus ICE S1A-016(A):25

b. what you might have done was **get eh get it insured** or something like that
Miller–Brown Corpus, conversation 20

c. so you **got** your grant all fixed up and everything
Miller–Brown Corpus, conversation 14

d. it might take you a week to **get** an alert concurred
Glasgow business meeting

e. as long as she **gets** her work done her be- her school work

f. a mini's easy to manoeuvre i mean you can **get** it parked easier
Miller–Brown Corpuscorpus, conversation 12

The examples in (10) denote events in which something moves from one place to another: from outside the car to inside the car – (10a), from not at the garage to at the garage – (10b) and from one side of the fence to the other – (10c). The examples in (11) denote movement from one state to another: from not being organized to being organized – (11a), from being uninsured to being insured – (11b), from being not fixed up to being fixed up – (11c), from not being agreed or concurred to being concurred – (11d), from not being done to being done – (11e) and from not being parked to being parked – (11f). To sum up the import of examples (9)–(11), there are conceptual parallels between change of location and change of state and between caused changes of location and caused changes of state. (See too Jackendoff, 1976, 1990). The *get* passive denotes changes of state and *get* occurs in the constructions in (9)–(11) and in the dynamic or *get passive.*

We turn now to the diachronic evidence supporting the analysis of the *get* passive as based on a verb of movement. The diachronic evidence is in two parts. One concerns the long-term history of the English dynamic passive, which seems to have been based on a succession of verbs of movement, and the other concerns *get*, which is first recorded as a verb of obtaining but which, by the first appearance of the *get* passive, had been a verb of movement for three hundred years.

The account in Miller (1985, pp. 188–9) is based on citations of *get* in the OED. The earliest, dated 1200, is equivalent to 'obtain'. The next earliest citation is a hundred years later, but it and the following four citations all denote movement: 1300 – 'arrive at', 'get out', 'get away'; 1340 – 'get up';

1513 – 'betake oneself'; 1530 – 'bring someone into or out of a position or state'. The status of earliest recorded GET passive in the written language used to be given to a citation from 1652, *A certain Spanish pretending Alchymist . . . got acquainted with foure rich Spanish merchants.* Gronemeyer (1999, p. 29), citing in support a personal communication from Denison, suggests that the earliest reliable example of a *get* passive is from 1693: *I am resolv'd to get introduced to Mrs Annabella.* (Powell, *A Very Good Wife.* II.i, p. 10, from the ARCHER Corpus.) Whichever citation is taken as the earliest instance of a GET Passive, the important point is that by the time the GET passive had been in use long enough to appear in writing its use as a verb of movement had been established for more than three hundred years.

Gronemeyer (1999) provides paths of change for *get.* As the starting point of the paths, she has the 'obtain' construction, which she represents as [ingressive + 'have']. One path leads via [stative possession] to [obligation]. A second path leads via [movement] to [inchoative] to [passive]. A third path leads via [movement] to [causative], where it splits into a path to [permission] and a path to [ingressive]. Thus, in Gronemeyer's account, all the *get* constructions evolve via [movement] apart from [stative possession] and [obligation], but even they evolve directly from the earliest construction, which has [ingressive] as part of its meaning. (At least, it has 'ingressive aspect' as part of its meaning. One can only assume that 'ingressive' as a component of the obtain construction has the same interpretation as the end point [ingressive] on one of the paths. Gronemeyer (1999, p. 11) comments that the localist analysis in Miller (1985) makes it difficult for him to explain the basic possession construction. Gronemeyer's analysis is itself a classic localist one, the localist analysis of obtaining events being in terms of an about-to-be possessed or received entity moving to a possessor. The stumbling block for Miller's account was how a verb denoting movement to a possessor, typically human, came to denote the movement of (typically animate) entities from one location to another. It is not clear that Gronemeyer herself succeeds in explaining this shift, but the point does not affect the analysis of the *get* passive as having evolved from a movement construction (and as having movement as a central component of its meaning).

Where did the *get* passive come from?

Gronemeyer (1999, p. 37) holds that semantic changes are dependent on syntactic innovations for a meaning construction to be established and generalized.

Contextually ambiguous examples allow language learners to make a novel analysis of semantic–syntactic correspondences, which leads to a shift in meaning. Miller (1985) offers a different take on the development of the *get* passive, arguing from the fact that from the earliest recorded texts the English dynamic passive has been based on verbs of movement. His alternative view is that semantic changes were not implicated in the appearance of the *get* passive but that it represented a new expression of an old conceptual structure.

Old English had three passives: one with *beon* 'be, become', one with *wesan* 'be, become' and one with *weorðan* 'become, arise, happen'. (The glosses are from Holthausen, 1963). As Traugott puts it (1972, pp. 82–3): '*beo* is used to express . . . intermittent generality while *wes-* expresses permanent generality or present action, and *weorþ-* stresses the activity and the event. Sometimes the sense of becoming is still so strong in *weorþ-* + PP that it seems to approximate to our use of *get* as in *It got stolen* versus *It was stolen*.' *Weorðan* gradually disappeared and was replaced by other verbs. According to Mustanoja (1960, pp. 618–19), 'the fact that *wurðe* was used as a highly colourless auxiliary in passive periphrases probably weakened its position in the other functions and created the need for new verbs to express the idea of 'becoming' in a more forceful way. This . . . resulted in the appearance of several verbs (*become*, *grow*, *wax*, etc.) to express the idea of *weorðan*.' Nowadays Mustanoja's hypothesis would be expressed in terms of *weorðan* being completely grammaticalized, losing contact with its original concrete meaning (which seems to have been 'movement' – see below) and being replaced by a verb which did have a concrete denotation.

In examples such as *The sky grew black*, *The leaves turned yellow*, *The king fell ill* and *The noise became unbearable*, *grew*, *turned* and *fell*, which can express movement from one place to another, express movement from one state to another. *Become* nowadays expresses only change of state, but at the period when it replaced *weorðan* and appeared in the dynamic passive, it did express movement from one place to another. Bosworth and Toller give the following examples from Old English: *In ða ceastre becuman meahte* 'thou mightest come into the city'; *Hannibal to ðam lande becom* 'Hannibal came to that land.' *Becuman* could also express slightly more abstract movement: *Him ðaes grim lean becom* 'This grim retribution happened to them'. *Becuman* is also said to express the meaning of 'becoming', but the only example in which the modern English translation contains *become* is *syððan niht becom* 'after it had become night'. This is also translated as 'after night had come', which fits the Old

English lexis and grammar. There are no examples of *becuman* expressing movement from one state to another.

Weorðan also expressed concrete movement. Bosworth and Toller give *ðonne he betwux us and hire wyrþ* 'Then it (the moon) came between us and it (the sun); *gif hi on ðam wuda weorðaþ* 'if they get into the wood'. (R. Le Page in a personal communication suggested that a more faithful translation is 'If they come to be in the wood,' since *wuda* is in the dative case, which expresses location. On either translation and interpretation *weorðan* denotes movement from one place to another, from outside the wood to inside the wood.)

Weorðan seems to have lost its association with concrete movement earlier than *becuman*, which in Middle English texts still has this association. Kurath and Kurath (1963) gloss this meaning of *bicomen* as 'get or attain (to a certain state)' and 'become something', the earliest example of *bicomen* with this denotation being dated 1255.

The change in the dynamic passive can be summarized thus. *Weorðan*, which originally denoted concrete movement but lost that denotation, was replaced in Middle English by *bicomen*, which still denoted concrete movement. *Bicomen* itself eventually ceased to denote concrete movement and, though it did not disappear, acquired substitute verbs in constructions of becoming. These were verbs such as *turn*, *go* and *fall*, which also denoted movement from one location or position to another. Another replacement was *get*, which has become the principal auxiliary for the dynamic passive.

The above data support the idea that the English dynamic passive has from the earliest recorded examples been based on the concept of movement into a state. The earliest construction had the verb of movement *weorðan* at its centre; its successor had the verb of movement *bicomen*; and the latest construction has the verb of movement *get*, but also *become*.

Grammar and Semantics: *wh* words

8

Chapter Outline

Wh words as deictics

The analysis of *wh* pronouns in English bears on the relationship between syntax and semantics (or pragmatics), the question of what structure to assign to the chunk *what you need* in a sentence such as *Tell me what you need*? and the chunk *which you prefer* in *Decide which you prefer and return the other rug*. How is it that *wh* pronouns occur in chunks like *what you need* and also in interrogative clauses – *What are you ordering?*, *Which is cheaper?* and so on – in WH clefts – *What she did was sell her house* – and in fixed phrases such as *Tell you what: you stay here and I'll bring the car round*? What property of *wh* pronouns enables them to function in these different constructions? The discussion of the English *wh* pronouns leads into the more general topic of indefinite and interrogative pronouns and the role of semantics and pragmatics in interpreting the historical data.

We propose here that the crucial property of *wh* pronouns is that they are deictics, that chunks like *what you need* and *which you prefer* are NPs and that indefinite *wh* pronouns are historically prior to interrogative *wh* pronouns. The analysis fits with the account of free relatives in Bresnan and Grimshaw (1978) but not with the account in Huddleston and Pullum (2002). The analysis also goes against the account in Haspelmath (1997) on the grounds that

Haspelmath does not offer a convincing semantic–pragmatic reason for his postulated move from interrogative to indefinite, but there is a solid semantic–pragmatic explanation for the move from indefinite to interrogative (Lyons, 1977b).

Why treat the *wh* pronouns as indefinite deictics? Consider first the example in (1), from a phone-in programme broadcast in Australia.

(1) it's quite a heavy book uh **like** it probably I call it my bible it's probably as heavy as a bible as well **but I tell you what** any time I need to know anything it's got everything about every fruit and herb and vegetable in it

Macquarie Corpus, Austgram3 CommEast

The speaker says *I tell you what.* The speaker knows what he is about to say but the listener does not, and this is the sense in which the *wh* pronouns are indefinite, specific for the speaker but non-specific for the listener. *What* in (1) points forward to the proposition that the book under discussion has a lot of information about horticulture. It is this pointing function that makes *wh* pronouns deictic.

Of course the example in (1) is of a template that allows a very limited number of changes: *Know what*? Or *I tell you what surprises you* as in (2).

(2) I tell you **what** surprises you eh as I say I remember seeing Arthur Street from the university when I went back

Miller–Brown Corpus, mbc 1

What surprises you points forward to the information that the Arthur Street area seemed very small, but the speaker remembers that in his youth there were hundreds of people living there. We start with this template because the analysis is straightforward, but *wh* pronouns occur with the same function in WH clefts, as in (3).

(3) **what** i want to do with you though is probably now her last poem and it's chilling

WSC#MUS001:0420:FG>

(4) **what** you do is marinade them for three or four hours

(5) but **what** raelene was saying um — they've had trouble with staff turnover

<WSC#DPC002:0185:DS>

In (3) *what* points to *her last poem*, in (4) *what you do* points to the proposition conveyed by *marinade them for three or four hours*, in (5) *what raelene was saying* points to *they've had trouble with staff turnover*. The deictic target could be the proposition expressed by these words (the most likely interpretation) or the words themselves presented by the speaker could be Raelene's own.

In (1)–(5), the *wh* chunk is specific for the speaker but non-specific for the listener, but in other examples the *wh* chunk is specific for both. In (6), for example, the *wh* chunks *what they're doing now like* and *what they've done with the dumbiedykes just recently like* point back to a topic that came up in the conversation just 5 minutes earlier; that is, they are specific for both speaker and listener. (*The Dumbiedykes* is an area of Edinburgh.) The *wh* chunk re-establishes the topic, knocking down the old buildings and erecting new ones, and once re-established it can be referred to by *that* – *they should have done that years ago*.

(6) but i still reckon **what** they're doing now like **what** they've done with the dumbiedykes just recently like they should have done that years ago

Miller–Brown Corpus, conversation 1

Wh complement clauses

Consider (7)–(9).

(7) **what** IS important is that you understand <,,> um **how** things WORK and **WHERE** YOU CAN FIND out **what** you want to know **when** you want to know it

WSC#MUS002:0080:TT

(8) it's a good idea eh i think it's abused but eh they don't seem to have a very good eh what's the word reputation in america singles bars from **what** i could gather (uh huh)

Miller–Brown Corpus, conversation 2

(9) <x s6> oh yeah yeah uh huh as i say i can't remember **when** they built the museum it may have been demolished at that time to make way for the scottish museum

Miller–Brown Corpus, conversation 1

(7) has four *wh* complement clauses: the subject is ***what** IS important*, the direct objects of *understand* are *how things WORK* and *WHERE YOU CAN FIND out **what** you want to know*, and the direct object of *find out* is *what you want to know*. The referents of the first three *wh* complements have specific reference for the speaker but not for the listeners. The referent of the fourth complement is non-specific for speaker and listeners. The fact that *wh*

complements function as subjects or objects is a good indication that they are nominal, but (8) provides evidence that they are actually NPs, since the complement *what I could gather* is preceded by the preposition *from*.

Huddleston and Pullum (2002, p. 1036) call the *wh* pronouns 'fused relatives'. They point out that a phrase such as *abandoning what we hold most dear* can be paraphrased as *abandoning that which we hold most dear*. They propose a syntactic structure in which *what we hold most dear* is an NP with *what* as its head, modified by the clause *we hold most dear*. The clause has an empty object NP slot following *hold*. So far, this syntactic structure is the one proposed by Bresnan and Grimshaw (1978), but Huddleston and Pullum adjust the structure so that *what* is a daughter of the NP node and a daughter of the node 'Modifier: Clause' dominating *we hold most dear*. This revised arrangement of constituents captures their view (first proposed in Huddleston, 1984, and Huddleston, 1988, pp. 158–9) that in the above *wh* structures *what* results from a fusion of *that* and *which*. In the *that which* version *that* is dominated by the head NP node and *which* is dominated by the node 'Modifier: Clause'.

Jespersen (1961a, p. 54) commented that Onions (1904) and Sonnenschein (1921) proposed to derive the *wh* forms in *I know what you want* and *Tell me who got the job* by ellipsis, from, say, *I know that what/which you want* and *Tell me him/her who got the job*. He also comments (Jespersen, 1961a, p. 55) that Sweet (1892) called these *wh* words 'condensed relative pronouns' because '*what* unites the grammatical functions of the two words *something* and *which*'. Jespersen asks, without further discussion, whether the *wh* words should be seen as a condensation of *that* and *which*.

One disadvantage of Huddleston and Pullum's analysis is that the *wh* pronouns are not just equivalent to *that which*. In (7), *how* is equivalent to *the way/manner in which* and *where* to *the place in which*. In (9), *when* is equivalent to *the time at which* or *the time during which*. And in (10), *why* is equivalent to *the reason for which*.

(10) And yet even as that novice, still in the process of getting your head round the often microscopic subtleties of **what to many enthusiasts is almost a religion**, it's not overly difficult to appreciate **why that should be so**. They are, after all, both Porsche 911s.

Chris Horton, 'Defenders of the Faith', *911 & Porsche World*, July 2009, p. 84.

Another strand in Huddleston and Pullum's analysis of 'fused relatives' is that the ones introduced by *what* are NPs, but those based on *where* and *when*, as in (11), are PPs.

(11) a. Put it back *where you found it*.
b. He still calls his parents *whenever he is in trouble*.

Now it is correct that *where you found it* can be paraphrased by *in the place you found it* or *in the place in which you found it* and so on, but paraphrases are not a criterion for choosing this or that syntactic structure. The paraphrase might suggest that *where you found it* and *in the place in which you found it* should be linked to the same semantic structure, but the only distributional property is that *Put it back* can be followed by a PP, *Put it back in the cupboard*, or by a *wh* clause as in (11a). Applying the analysis of *wh* pronouns as deictics, we propose that *where* is a deictic that is used for pointing to locations. Whether *where* chunks function as subjects such as in *Where she met him is a mystery* or as direct objects such as in *I don't know where she met him* or as oblique objects such as in *You were asking about where she met him*, they point to locations, and this is what makes them a suitable third argument for *put* in clauses such as *She put it where nobody could see it.*

Whenever and *when* in adverbial clauses

The *wh* chunk in (11b) is an adverbial clause of time and the problem here is whether to analyse *whenever* as a complementizer/subordinating conjunction followed by the core of the clause, *he is in trouble*, or as a deictic *wh* pronoun modified by a relative clause. *Whenever* certainly denotes a set of times, just as *when* in *When we left, we were sad* denotes a time, but that is not a strong argument for treating it as a *wh* pronoun. Many prepositions denote locations, such as *behind* in *behind the house*, but that does not make them nouns, and the fact that *transmit* and *transmission* (in one of its senses) both denote an action does not make analysts abandon the view that *transmit* is a verb and *transmission* a noun.

One Turkish equivalent of adverbial *when* clauses provides an instructive contrast. In Turkish, various nominals are derived from verbs. One set of forms consists of a verb stem plus the suffix *-dik* (*-diğ* between vowels) and with the vowels i, ı, u or ü depending on the vowel of the verb stem. For instance, the verb stem *oku-* 'read' gives *okuduk-*, to which can be added possessive suffixes, plural suffixes and case suffixes. *Okuduğum* can be roughly glossed as 'my reading', *okuduğumlar* as 'the things I am reading' and *okuduğumlarda* as 'in the things I am reading'.

These nominal forms can modify nouns, as in *Okuduğum kitab* 'my-reading book, the book which I am reading'. Turkish has a possessive construction, which in the third person consists of a possessor noun in the genitive case and a noun denoting the possessed. The latter noun has a possessive suffix: thus, *Fatma* (woman's name) *Fatmanın kitabı* 'Fatma-of book-her, 'Fatma's book'. The possessive construction can contain the nominal forms derived from verbs, as in *Fatmanın okuduğu* 'Fatma-of reading-her, 'Fatma's reading'. This possessive construction can modify a noun, yielding the Turkish equivalent of an English relative clause: *Fatmanın okuduğu kitab* 'Fatma-of reading-her book, the book that Fatma is reading', or *Okuduğum kitab* 'reading-my book, the book I am reading'.

Consider now the Turkish noun *zaman* 'time'. It takes demonstratives, *o zaman* 'that time', and a plural suffix, *zamanlar* 'times'. It can be modified by one of the aforementioned nominal forms, as in *okuduğum zaman 'reading-my time'*. This is the equivalent of an English *when* adverbial clause and is translated as 'when I was reading'. (12) shows a combination of this 'adverbial clause' and a main clause.

(12) Okuduğum kitabı zaman, ona cevap verdim.
reading-my book time him-to answer give-past-I
'When I read the book I gave him an answer'.

In the Turkish construction, *zaman* looks very noun-like and *okuduğum kitabı* looks very like a 'relative clause'. That is, there is solid syntactic and morphosyntactic evidence in Turkish for treating *zaman* as a noun in (12), and this evidence highlights just how little such evidence there is for treating *whenever* or *when* as a *wh* pronoun in English adverbial clauses of time.

Main clauses introduced by *when*

There are four more *wh* constructions in English whose analysis contributes to the deictic perspective. The first is the construction in (13), which is very common in spontaneous spoken narrative but regarded by many users of British English as unacceptable in writing. (That observation is based on an examination of corrections made to homework exercises by teachers of English in secondary schools in Edinburgh.)

(13) Fiona was admiring the garden **when** Magnus came out of the house.

The *when* clause, *when Magnus came out of the house*, looks like an adverbial clause of time, but as we will see later, there are reasons for treating it as a main clause. The deictic nature of *when* is quite clear in (13). The sentence describes a situation in which two events happen; the background event is Fiona standing admiring the garden and the main or foregrounded event is Magnus coming out of the house. The time of the foregrounded event, to be conceived of as a point, is contained within the time of the background event, to be conceived of as a line representing a period of time. In (13), that is to say, *when* points to a time that has been established in the discourse, the time of the background event; we can assume that this time is specific for speaker and listener.

(13) may not affect the preceding discussion of adverbial clauses of time and the complementizer, because the clause *when Magnus came out of the house* is probably better analysed as a main clause. There is syntactic evidence for such an analysis, since the prepositional phrase *out of the house* can be moved to the front of the clause: *Fiona was watering the plants* **when** *out of the house came Magnus.* Prepositional phrases can only be fronted in main clauses, or at least in clauses which are weakly subordinate in their syntax. If (13) is changed so that the *when* clause precedes the main clause, as in (14), *out of the house* cannot be fronted. (14a) is acceptable, (14b) is not.

(14) a. When Magnus came out of the house, Fiona was watering the plants.
b. *When out of the house came Magnus, Fiona was watering the plants.

There is also semantic evidence for treating the *when* chunk in (13) as a main clause. (14a) is the canonical combination of subordinate adverbial clause of time and main clause. The main clause expresses the main or foregrounded event, *Fiona was watering the plants*, the one that moves the narrative along, while the adverbial clause of time expresses the secondary or background event, *Magnus came out of the house.* In (13), the two events have swapped status; the secondary event is *Fiona was watering the plants* and it is expressed by the main clause, while the main event is *Magnus came out of the house*, which is expressed by the adverbial clause. The different informational status of the clauses is a strong indication that (13) is not just (14a) with the clauses in a different order.

Wh relative clauses

The second construction is the *wh* relative clause, as in (15).

(15) a. the meeting which I attended
b. the boy who liked chess
c. the writer whose novels I am reading
d. the island where the kings are buried
e. that day when everything went wrong

A central idea in all formal models of syntax is that a given relative pronoun is co-indexed with the NP (or noun, depending on the model) modified by the relative clause. Thus, in (15a) *which* is co-indexed with *the meeting*, in (15c) *whose* is co-indexed with *the writer* and so on. To consider the *wh* relative pronouns deictic, pointing to the referent of the preceding NP, is simply to make explicit something that is implicit in the generative analyses.

The deictic view fits with other facts of English syntax and with the general development of relative clauses in Indo-European. One fact of English syntax is that *which* relative clauses can modify propositions or situations, as in (16).

(16) a. if the pupils wanted a christmas tree **which** they obviously did it's irrelevant i mean he could be a buddhist for all i care

Miller–Brown Corpus, conversation 29

b. but the attitude towards work in courses and everything's serious you know **which** is in some ways half the battle about going to universities

Miller–Brown Corpus, conversation 15

c. well we've both seen elton john in concert twice **which** at the time we thought was great

Miller–Brown Corpus, conversation 12

None of the *which* clauses in (16a–c) can be co-indexed with NPs or treated as pointing to the referents of NPs. In (16b), *which* does pick up the referent of the NP *the attitude towards work*, but it also refers to the situation denoted by the clause *everything's serious*. In (16a) *which* refers to the situation denoted by *the pupils wanted a christmas tree* and in (16c) to the situation 'seeing Elton John in concert'. One way of handling these examples is to adopt a discourse representation analysis in which entities of various sorts, including situations, are established as entities which can then be referred to. The analysis of the *wh* pronouns as deictics connects the examples in (16) to a wider network of deictic uses.

A second fact of English syntax is that *which* occurs in examples such as (17) and (18), where it functions as a general conjunction.

(17) you can leave at Christmas if your birthday's in December to February which I think is wrong like my birthday's March and I have to stay on to May **which** when I'm 16 in March I could be looking for a job

Miller–Brown Corpus, conversation 4

(18) He had heard it given for a truth that according as the world went round, **which** round it did revolve undoubted, even the best of gentlemen must take his turn of standing with his head upside down . . .

Charles Dickens, *Little Dorrit*, Book 2, Chapter 27

(17) contains two occurrences of *which*. The first one, *which I think is wrong*, is in a relative clause modifying a proposition – 'You can leave at Christmas if your birthday's in December to February'. The second one, *which when I'm 16 in March I could be looking for a job*, is not a relative pronoun. It does not belong to any clause, but is followed by an adverbial clause of time *when I'm 16 in March*, combining with a main clause *I could be looking for a job*. The function of *which* is to signal a general link between the material that precedes it and the material following.

This construction is not new in English. It is attested in Dickens' novels – see (18), from *Little Dorrit*, published over the period 1855–57. Mr Wegg in *Our Mutual Friend* has a strong line in this *which* construction, and it was regularly used in cartoons in *Punch* as a stereotypical feature of uneducated language. The deictic analysis of *which* enables us to provide a pleasing parallel historical account of *which* and *that*. Both derive from pronouns in Early English and both change into conjunctions, this change being typical throughout Indo-European and other language families. *That* became a subordinating conjunction, losing all its pronominal features. *Which* became a discourse connective, in which role it preserves its deictic properties, except that instead of pointing to the referent of a preceding NP it points to a larger portion of text. For example, in (17), it connects two chunks of discourse, the one running from *you can leave* to *stay on to May* and *when I'm 16 in March I could be looking for a job*. As a discourse connective, it can be seen as a weak subordinating conjunction, a property that comes out in the interpretation 'what I am about to say follows on from what I have just been saying'. The relevance of the comment about the date of the speaker's sixteenth birthday can only be worked out from the first part of the speaker's statement.

Wh interrogatives

The third construction to be examined in this section is the *wh* interrogative, exemplified in (19). See the account on pp. 186–190.

(19) a. What did she say?
b. Which one did he choose?
c. Who got the job?

IT clefts

One more construction needs to be mentioned, the IT-cleft with unclear syntax discussed in Chapter 4, pp. 110–114. The examples are repeated below as (20).

(20) a. It was in September that I first noticed it.
b. It was in Paris that we met.
c. It was because he was ill that we decided to return.

In (20a) the clause *that I first noticed it* modifies the phrase *in September*, in (20b) the clause *that we met* modifies the phrase *in Paris* and in (20c) the clause *that we decided to return* modifies the clause *because he was ill.* The difficulty is that relative clauses do not normally modify prepositional phrases. They can modify clauses (or propositions expressed by clauses), but only *wh* relative clauses, as in *She left her property to Katarina, which was very surprising.* (20a–c) are different because they exclude *wh* relative clauses, as shown in (21).

(21) a. *It was in September which I first noticed it.
b. *It was in Paris which we met.
c. *It was because he was ill which we decided to return.

As pointed out in the earlier account, (21a,b) do not present any difficulty for analysts of spoken English for the simple reason that speakers use a different construction, as in (22).

(22) a. It was in September when I first noticed it.
b. It was in Paris where we met.

The *wh* sequences seem to be complement clauses, not relative clauses. They can be assigned a structure with an empty constituent, which could be a prepositional phrase, say *at that time* or *in that place*, or a *th* deictic, *then* or *there.* (22a,b) each contain two clauses, the second one being inside an NP, as shown in (23).

(23) **Clause 1** (It was in September)
Clause 2 $_{NP}$ ($_{N}$(when) $_{Clause\ 2}$ (I first noticed it then))

When points to a time, specific in this case, and *then* points to the same time. On this analysis, the combination of clauses is unintegrated, the two clauses simply being juxtaposed. There is a related construction in which they are more integrated. See (24).

(24) When I first noticed it was in September.

In the heyday of transformational grammar, (22a) could have been derived from (24) by extraposition, the transformation that related sentences such as *To avoid catching swine flu is very difficult* and *It is very difficult to avoid catching swine flu.* The transformation moved a finite complement clause or an infinitive to the end of a sentence and inserted *it* into the NP slot left empty by the movement. For spoken English this is not an appropriate treatment because speakers producing utterances off the cuff avoid complex subject NPs. (Miller and Weinert (2009) found that in their samples of spontaneous spoken English 70 per cent of the NPs consisted of pronoun or noun or determiner + noun. Only 6 per cent consisted of the sequence (determiner) + adjective + noun. An analysis of Russian conversation produced similar figures: 37per cent for NPs consisting of pronoun or noun or determiner + noun – but many zero subject NPs, which were not counted, and only 5.5per cent for Ns consisting of the sequence (determiner) + adjective + noun. Other types of NP had even smaller percentages.) To take the more complex structure as basic and transform it into the more frequent structure might be analytically more economical and elegant, but would ignore central facts of spoken English. An explicit account of (22a,b) will probably be based on some model of discourse representation. (The preceding discussion has said nothing about (20c), *It was because he was ill that we decided to return.* Since it is not relevant to the analysis of *wh* words, we leave the construction unexplored.)

We close this section with examples (25)–(28) showing that the construction in (22a,b) is spreading to scripted spoken English such as news broadcasts to newspapers and to public notices.

(25) It was five years ago when Nelson Mandela realised his prison number could be put to another use.

BBC, News at 10, 1 December 2007

(26) He was born in 1918 in India, the son of a regimental sergeant major, but it was in 1931 in England when he discovered a taste for performance.

The Independent, 28 February 2002

(27) In the beginning skating was used as a means of transportation, it wasn't until the last century when skating became viewed as recreational.

Notice in Stratford Museum, Stratford, Ontario,Canada, October 1999

(28) It's here where we have the highest chance of frosts.

BBC TV weather forecast, February 2002

Indefinite and interrogative pronouns

Are we to treat as identical the *wh* pronouns and adjectives in interrogative constructions such as *Which friend phoned?*, in WH clefts such as *What he'll do is resign*, in complements such as *I asked when she was leaving*, in relative clauses such as *the street where she lives* and in the fixed phrases *tell you what* and *know what?* The answer is yes and the argument for the answer is in two parts, the first dealing with the basic grammatical facts from English, then from Indo-European and other language families, the second providing a semantic–pragmatic explanation for the connection.

We need give no more than an outline of the basic grammatical facts, since they are presented in detail and cogently discussed in Haspelmath (1997). The English facts are that the *wh* pronouns derive from the Early English *hwa* '*who*', *hwæt* '*what*' and *hwylc* '*which*' (of many). Quirk and Wrenn (1957, p. 39) say 'the interrogatives could be used indefinitely', equivalent to *anyone* and *anything*. In their non-specific interpretation, the *hw*/*wh* forms were extended by the addition of *ever*, as in *whatever you do, you can't win* and *whoever said that is an idiot*. In Indo-European, generally the forms of interrogative and indefinite pronouns and adverbs are related. Lyons (1977, p. 758) mentions French, Classical Greek, Latin and Russian. Haspelmath (1997) supplies detailed evidence from two samples, one of forty languages, including a large sample of Indo-European languages but also Turkic languages, Hausa, Swahili, Chinese, Japanese, Korean and Quechua, and one of a hundred languages, including ones from the Caucasus, South and Central America, Australia, Africa and the Pacific. In the latter sample, 64 languages have, in Haspelmath's words, indefinites based on interrogatives.

The difficulty with Haspelmath's wording is that while he argues convincingly that non-specific and irrealis are next to question and conditional on an implicational scale, he does not give any semantic–pragmatic explanation of why he takes the direction to be from interrogative to indefinite. He does say why he favours that direction (1997, pp. 174–6). He distinguishes between bare interrogatives and complex interrogatives created by the grammaticalization of various source constructions. Examples are English *wherever* (< *where you ever go/live/*, etc.), French *n'importe qui* (< *n'importe qui vient* 'not important who comes, It's not important who comes'), Turkish *kimse* (< *kim* 'who' + *se* 'if'). He has no examples of complex indefinite pronouns being reduced to bare interrogatives. In all of his language families ('All' or 'most'? Haspelmath says '. . . in language family after language family . . .' .), bare interrogative pronouns are resistant to etymological analysis and appear to be among the slowest changing elements in any language. The bare interrogative pronouns in Indo-European, he maintains, derive from bare pronoun forms that are interrogatives as far back as they can be traced.

The reconstructed original root is ****kwi-/*kwo-***, which is nicely reflected in the modern Slavic languages. The basic root is *ku-*, where *u* represents a jer, an extra short (back) vowel. In Old Church Slavic, the root *ku-* occurs in the interrogative adjective *ku-ij* 'which one', in which *-ij* is a deictic suffix. (Old Church Slavic or Old Church Slavonic is the South Slavic language of a set of Bulgarian, Macedonian and Moraviian manuscripts dating from the tenth and eleventh centuries.)

It occurs in the interrogative pronoun *ku-to*, in which *to* is also a deictic. (Data from Schmalstieg, 1983.) *Ij* is the source of the Slavic personal pronouns and *to* is a demonstrative. *Ku-* occurs in *ku- žde 'each, every'*. In Modern Bulgarian, the interrogative pronoun for humans is *koj*, derived from *ku-ij*, the relative pronoun is *koj* + *to* (masc), *koja* + *to* (fem) and *koe* + *to* (neuter).

The earliest examples of the Indo-European root ****kwi-/*kwo-*** are in Hittite texts dating from the seventeenth to sixteenth centuries BCE. Held, Schmalstieg and Gertz (1987, pp. 32–4) list the demonstrative pronoun 'that' as, for example, *a-pa-(a-) aš* 'that nominative singular' and *a-pu-(u-) un* 'that accusative singular'. They list the demonstrative pronoun 'this' as the roots *ka*, *ku* and *ki* plus suffixes expressing case and number, for example, *ka-a-aš* 'this nominative singular' and *ku-u-un* 'this accusative singular'. What they call the relative–interrogative pronoun (i.e. a pronoun that occurs in relative clauses and in *wh* interrogative clauses) consists of the root *ku-* plus suffixes expressing case and number, for example, *ku-iš* (nominative singular). This pronoun could also be used as an indefinite, but there was a complex indefinite pronoun consisting of the relative interrogative pronoun plus the particles (to use Held et al.'s term) *-ki*, *-ka* or *-ku*. These particles are identical in form with the roots of the demonstrative pronoun 'this'; it looks as though there is a parallel between Hittite and Russian. The Russian interrogative pronoun 'who' is *kto*, which derives from the root *ku*, discussed in the preceding paragraph, and the demonstrative *to*. One of the indefinite pronouns in Modern Russian is *kto-to*, that is, *kto* plus, in historical terms, another instance of *to*. (This type of derivation of interrogatives from indefinites is not mentioned by Haspelmath.) This is the specific indefinite pronoun – someone called and I can tell you about them – in contrast with the non-specific indefinite pronoun *kto-nibud'*. The latter can be glossed as 'someone, but I can't tell you anything about them'.

What could count as a convincing semantic–pragmatic explanation of an indefinite pronoun acquiring an interrogative function? Lyons (1977b, pp. 758–62) proposes an elegant analysis based on the concept of presupposition. The starting point of the analysis is shared with many other accounts, including that by Halliday (1967a), who relates the yes–no and *wh* interrogatives to information treated by speakers as given or new. For present purposes, since presupposition as a logical relation opposed to entailment is controversial in some quarters, we will interpret it as what speakers take for granted. Consider the questions in (29).

(29) a. Did someone open the door?/Did anyone open the door?
b. Who opened the door?
c. What did the boys open?

The speaker uttering (29a) takes nothing for granted about the event, but wants to know if the door was opened. *Yes* or *no* would be sufficient answers, but in the case of *yes*, politeness and Gricean constraints would impel many addressees to supply the name of the person opening the door. The speaker uttering (29b) takes it for granted that the door was opened and asks the addressee to supply the name of the person who carried out the act. The speaker uttering (29c) takes it for granted that the boys opened something and asks the addressee to say what was opened.

The speakers' presuppositions – what they take for granted – can be expressed by means of sentences containing the modern English indefinite pronouns *someone* or *something*, as in (30).

(30) a. Someone opened the door.
b. The boys opened something.

Lyons points out that an example such as (30a) can be uttered with two intonation patterns, one that marks an utterance of (30a) as a statement and one that marks it as a question. (In fact, in informal spoken English, the question utterance is most likely to be *someone opened the door*?, with no auxiliary *did*.) The question can be understood as a yes–no question – 'Did this event happen?' – or as a *wh* question – 'I know the door was opened; tell me who did it'. The type of question could be clearly signalled by variation in stress as well as intonation. Lyons observes that 'the relationship between the statement and the two kinds of questions is rarely, if ever, systematically made solely in the non-verbal component of languages'. Nonetheless, in principle, marking the difference does not require different syntactic structures. This then is the route by which indefinite pronouns come to be used as interrogatives: 'I know that some person, for me as yet non-specific, opened the door. Please specify that someone'.

Lyons (1977b, pp. 760–1) also suggests a route by which indefinite pronouns can come to function as relative pronouns. The speaker who declares *The man who broke the bank at Monte Carlo is a mathematician* is asserting that a particular person is a mathematician and taking for granted/presupposing that someone did indeed break the bank at Monte Carlo and that the someone is a man. Lyons proposes what he calls Quasi-English, in which the presuppositions are embodied in a clause which can modify a noun – *someone broke the bank at Monte Carlo* – and which is inserted into NPs to yield *The* [*someone broke the bank at Monte Carlo*] *man is a mathematician*. This is the path by which indefinite pronouns come to function as relative pronouns.

Lyons closes his discussion by stating that, 'unfortunately' the *wh* relative pronouns of English are more closely related historically to interrogative than to indefinite declarative clauses. It is not clear whether Lyons is referring to their historical source or to the syntax of the clause types, but in any case we do not have to accept his statement unless someone provides a plausible semantic–pragmatic route from interrogative pronouns to relative pronouns as well as to indefinite pronouns. Moreover, the direction of change proposed by Haspelmath turns out to be based on evidence from earlier stages of Indo-European languages that is not as robust as it seems at first sight. The Hittite and the Slavic (especially East and West Slavic) evidence points to an indefinite interpretation for the ***kwi-/*kwo-*** root. And there is the difficulty that while it is tempting to take the earliest attested texts as a starting point for Indo-European, they are nothing of the kind. It is just that we cannot get hold of earlier written texts or earlier speakers. Even on the assumption that the ***kwi-/*kwo-*** root was initially interrogative, it might well have developed from an earlier indefinite. Haspelmath observes that across languages interrogative pronouns are very resistant to change, but indefinite pronouns are subject to rapid change. It is quite possible that the early interrogatives represented extensions of indefinite pronouns, which then changed or were replaced by alternative forms.

Conclusion

To recap: English *wh* pronouns are central to WH clefts, WH complement clauses, relative clauses, *wh* interrogatives and one adjustable template, *tell you what, know what* and so on. The above discussion is an attempt to answer the question why they occur in these different constructions and whether the *wh* pronouns have a particular property that is exploited in the constructions. The first key component of the account is that the pronouns are indefinite deictics, which can have specific or non-specific reference depending on the context. What the deictics refer to can be animate beings, inanimate things, times, places, propositions and events. The second key component is a good semantic explanation of why indefinite deictics can acquire the functions of interrogative pronouns and relative pronouns. The analysis rests on the assumption that arrangements of forms and changes of form are not semantically arbitrary. Haspelmath's implicational scale in which the juxtaposition of two functions is important provides no reason why there should be a progression from one function to the other. Lyons' account does.

Grammar and Semantics: Parts of Speech

9

Chapter Outline

Parts of speech and denotation

The third topic in this overview of semantics and grammar is parts of speech or word classes. A widely received view among linguists since the publication of Bloomfield (1933) has been not only that parts of speech cannot be defined or established in terms of meaning but also that there is no reliable connection at all between a given part of speech and meaning. Bloomfield's example was *oats* and *wheat*: why should one be plural and the other singular when they both denoted types of grain? (Perhaps, the answer lies in how the grains are used and what the cereals look like when they are ready for use. Wheat comes in a mass of flour, whereas oats come in readily distinguishable grains or flakes. *Pease* was reinterpreted as a plural, probably because the individual peas in a peapod are very obvious and countable. The peas that nowadays come out of tins are very obvious individual units.) Bloomfield's extreme view has been tempered in two ways. Better and more subtle theories of denotation and speech acts have enabled more subtle handling of parts of speech, although with the proviso that the parts of speech for a given language first have to be established on formal criteria. An extreme view at the other end of the spectrum has been set out by Croft (2007), and that is that formal, distributional criteria don't work but that speech acts constitute the indispensable foundation.

Miller (1985, pp. 206–19) provided an account of parts of speech in which connections with meaning were central. It involved a combination of distributional criteria, the concept of prototypes, Lyons' work on first, second- and third-order entities (Lyons 1977b, pp. 438–450) and speech acts. First-order entities are physical objects. They have relatively constant perceptual properties, they are located in three-dimensional space (or are perceived as so located, as when small children look at pictures) and they are publicly observable and describable. Prototypical nouns, that is, noun forms that meet all the distributional criteria for noun-hood, denote first-order entities such as tables, books, teddies, dolls, baths, water, nappies, different kinds of food, milk, juice apples, dogs, trees and so on. These are the sorts of entities that parents talk about with small children and which small children talk about in the early stages of language acquisition. The connection between nouns, distributional properties and concrete entities is straightforward and quickly established.

Second-order entities are events, processes and states of affairs. They are located in time and may have perceptible (and even significant) duration in time. Events and processes are denoted by verbs. A key property is the fact that a single event or process is typically of short duration. Adjectives denote states, which are typically, if not permanent, at least of longer duration than events and processes. And of course events and processes are dynamic, involving change over time and the expenditure of energy (in the broadest sense), while states are homogeneous and do not involve the expenditure of energy.

Third-order entities are abstract objects such as propositions, which are outside space and time – and outside the experience of small children beginning to use language. First-order entities are said to exist or to be (as in *There exists a peculiar fish* and *There is an X in the kitchen*) and second-order entities are said to happen or take place (as in *The collision happened around 1 am* and *The wedding took place last month*). Propositions do not exist or occur, but are held or entertained by humans.

Adjectives are traditionally said to denote the properties of things, while adverbs denote the properties of events, processes and states of affairs. But if things are thought of as bundles of properties, what is the distinction between a property and a thing? The idea of different orders of entities can only be made to work if we go back to Miller and Johnson-Laird's work on how humans succeed in perceiving objects among the flux of visual and auditory stimuli. They argue that a notion of 'permanent object' is fundamental to human perception and that the object comes first and properties are sorted out later. The perceptual mechanism is able to differentiate an object from the background against which it appears. The same object that at one moment is a perceptual figure may become part of the background in the next, but people assume that it continues to exist in a stable form even when they are not looking at it. The simplest perception of a concrete object seems to depend on a prior concept of object permanence. Miller and Johnson-Laird make the important point that people can recognize an object they have seen before even when they are subject to a novel set of stimuli. The perceptual mechanism creates a coherent psychological entity in response to various sets of perceptions (Miller and Johnson-Laird, 1976, pp. 39–40).

The above argument means that the distinction between entities and properties is not just naïve folk philosophy (though one might wonder whether it is accidental that the distinction between objects and entities is applied in all our everyday talk of people, things and events), but is an essential part of theories of perception.

The perception of a change or pattern of changes as an event is more subjective than the perception of a set of stimuli as an object. Our talk about events, say Miller and Johnson-Laird (1976, p. 90) is even more dependent on conceptualization. They suggest that some pattern of change may be regarded as an event simply because that is how we talk about it, not because we perceive it that way. And even more abstract concepts are entertained by humans, concepts that are crucial to everyday understanding and cooperation: these are concepts such as 'intention', 'feeling' and 'thought'. (See the discussion of reference and truth and problems with the common sense view of objects in Jackendoff, 2002, pp. 300–32.) One advantage of localism is that it provides an explanation for patterns of grammar and meaning, not just within one language but across many languages, and offers semantic–conceptual structures that allow children to break into meaning via the most concrete object and relations, moving out from that platform into more abstract and complex relations. The relations between concrete objects are transferred to abstract domains (see, for example, Jackendoff, 1990, 2002, pp. 356–369), and the ways of talking about concrete objects and relations are also transferred.

A central tenet of localism, and also of cognitive grammar, whether of the Langacker or Lakoff variety (see Langacker (1991) and Lakoff (1987)) is that human language does not relate directly to the objective world 'out there'. Rather, it relates to the conceptual world constructed inside people's heads. As Jackendoff (2002, p. 308) puts it, the perceptual world is not totally out of synch with the 'real' world, since organisms have to act and cooperate reliably in the 'real' world. But the perceptual world *is* reality for us, although percepts are 'trapped in the brain'. In spite of percepts being 'formal structures instantiated in neurons', the perceptual systems give us the sense of 'being out there'. Jackendoff sets out a clear and eminently convincing case for that approach to language and the conceptual world and demonstrates that many referential acts cannot be understood without it. Here, the advantages of the approach will be demonstrated in the next chapter, in a discussion of participant/thematic roles and case marking.

Returning to parts of speech, we can sum up the state of play thus. It is possible to differentiate parts of speech by denotation, provided we begin with prototypical nouns denoting concrete first-order entities; prototypical verbs, denoting more easily perceived and conceptualized events such walking, running, jumping, sitting, eating, lifting (and for small children, patting dogs, stroking cats, looking at pictures, pointing at objects, pressing light switches and so on); prototypical adjectives denoting the more perceptible properties of entities, such as size, colour, texture, smell, tactile properties, type of movement, type of noise made and so on); prototypical adverbs, denoting the more perceptible properties of actions, processes and events, such as speed, amount of noise, and so on. The perceptual and conceptual systems must be what enable speakers of one language to break into another one with very different grammar. Nouns in Chinese have different distributional properties from nouns in English, but educated native speakers of English understand something about a form that is described as a noun or a verb in Chinese. Very young bilingual children do not have words such as 'noun' and 'verb' in their vocabulary, but understand which sequences of forms in their two languages apply to a given situation, object, action, process or property.

Parts of speech and speech acts

Our analysis has to be more complex than that since it is not adequate to have nouns with denotation w, verbs with denotation x, adjectives with denotation y, and adverbs with denotation z. This neat scheme is disturbed by the versatility of nouns, which can denote concrete first-order entities, second-order entities such as actions and processes, and properties of all kinds. Consider the denotation of *amazement* in (1).

(1) *amazement*

action of amazing	His amazement of the crowds with his acrobatics
property of someone	the amazement of the crowds at his acrobatics
the property of some action	*amazingly skilful*

There are forms such as *look* that denote actions or things.

(2) He looked at the intruder.
His look stopped the intruder in his tracks.
He has a worrying look.

The fact is that in English (and other languages) nouns denote any kind of entity, while verbs, adjectives and adverbs are restricted to one kind of entity (counting actions, processes and states as all second-order entities). This more nuanced view still leaves us with clear-cut differences in denotation if we consider only nouns denoting first-order entities, but it would be pleasing if we could find some semantic property that differentiated all four major parts of speech. There is one, at least, there is a pragmatic property, the type of speech act performed with a particular part of speech. (The following discussion is based on Miller (1985, pp. 215–40). A very similar, apparently independent, proposal is set out in Croft (2007, p. 421).) 'Speech act' here does not refer to making statements, asking questions, apologizing, promising and so on but to rather more grammatical acts: referring, predicating and modifying. Searle (1969) describes reference and predication as propositional acts. The idea of reference as an act performed by speakers and writers was adopted by Lyons (1977b) and incorporated in an opposition with denotation: denotation and lexemes belong to the language system; reference is an act performed by speakers and writers and is part of language behaviour. (Strictly speaking, it is NPs that refer, or that can be used to refer, to entities, but they can support this function only because they contain nouns.)

The idea that predication is an act is prevalent in traditional grammar. It is puzzling that in spite of the ubiquity of the formula of someone saying something about some person or thing, or predicating a property of some person or thing, discussions of speech acts do not include predication. Perhaps the difficulty, as Searle (1969, p. 123) says, is that predication never comes neutrally but always in one illocutionary mode or another. 'Predication is not a separate act. It is a slice from the total illocutionary act; just as indicating the illocutionary force is not a separate act, but another slice from the illocutionary act.'

Whether a speaker is making a statement, asking a question or issuing a command is clearly and conspicuously signalled by the grammars of natural languages (or by the pitch patterns). Natural languages also have ways of signalling what part of a clause carries reference and what part carries predication. In English, this is signalled by determiners and plural suffixes in NPs; in other languages, it may be signalled by order of constituents in a particular construction or it may be signalled by special markers. The most well-known example of the last type is probably Nootka, which used to be regularly cited as an example of a language without separate classes of noun and verb. Now while it is true that Nootka stems do not carry suffixes or other markers signalling that they are nouns or verbs, the clauses cited in Hockett (1958, p. 225) contain markers signalling which word carries the reference and which the predication. Harris (1946) comments that in much work on syntax labels such as 'noun', 'verb' and 'adjective' are used interchangeably for the positions in a syntactic structure and for the forms that occur in a given position. We will see from the Nootka examples that labels such as 'noun' and 'verb' could be applied to particular positions in the structures even if the stems occur in either position without any change in shape. Consider (3) and (4).

(3) a. qo•?asma• ?i•h?i.
He-is-a-man the-large, 'The large one is a man.'
b. ?i•hma• qo•?as?i.
he-is-large the-man, 'The man is large.'

In the above examples, *ma•* marks the predication or word carrying the predication and *?i* marks the word carrying the reference. The same applies in (4).

(4) a. mamo•kma• qo•?as?i.
he-is-working the-man, 'The man is working.'
b. qo•?asma• mamo•k?i.
he-is-a-man the-working, 'The worker is a man.'

Hockett (1958, p. 225) describes Nootka as having all-round players and Latin as having specialist players. It is true that whole words in Latin are specialist players, but the roots look more like all-round players: the stem *am* 'love' occurs in *amat* 'he/she loves' and *amor* 'love' (noun). In *amat* the *a* marks a verb stem to which a person-number ending can be added, here *–t*. In *amor*, the *–or* marks the stem as a noun, one to which a case-number-gender suffix can be added. The nominative singular suffix is Ø for this class of nouns. In Latin, then, the word carrying the reference and the word carrying the predication are marked by means of suffixes; in Nootka, the stems are not marked but the slots are marked – though in the examples cited by Hockett *?i* and *ma•* could be treated as marking the stems.

In the Classical Greek copula construction constituent order indicates when adjectives carry a predication. Examples are in (5).

(5) a. Hē kalē gunē
The beautiful woman
b. Hē gunē hē kalē
The woman the beautiful, 'the beautiful woman'
c. Hē gunē kalē.
The woman beautiful, 'The woman is beautiful.'
d. Kalē hē gunē.
Beautiful the woman, 'The woman is beautiful.'

Adjectives directly following a noun or preceding the definite article are predicative; in other positions they are attributive, or, to use the speech act terminology, modifying. What the Nootka, Latin and Greek examples show is that the speech acts of reference, predication and modification are signalled by position in a construction even if there is no marking in stems and words, and they are also clearly signalled by stem changes. The combination of differences in denotation (particularly in relation to the vocabulary and the limited world of very young children) and speech act provide strong evidence that differences between parts of speech are motivated by semantics and pragmatics.

10 Grammar and Semantics: Thematic Roles

Chapter Outline

Introduction

Two interconnected concepts are central to work on argument structure, transitivity and case marking (including case affixes and adpositions). These concepts are semantic or participant or thematic role and grammatical function or relation. We argue in this section that grammatical functions are not as useful as is generally thought and that the concept of semantic or participant role is not nearly as hopeless as recent commentators suggest. (The term 'thematic role' will not be used here. It is in the chapter title because it is the current term in various generative models, but it is very inconvenient. The trouble is that before the term 'thematic role' was introduced in Chomskyan generative grammar the word 'theme' had for many years been in use as part of work in what is now known as information structure. Quite apart from its use in Prague School Linguistics, it was – and still is – a key term and concept in Halliday's theory of information structure, first set out in his key papers in 1967 and 1968.)

Grammatical functions

We begin with grammatical functions, which are based on grammatical criteria and not on semantics. Since at least the mid-nineteenth century they have been deployed by analysts who saw subject, direct object and so on as well-founded concepts compared with concepts such as Agent, Patient and Goal. The latter were considered to be based on semantic intuitions and not able to be applied consistently from one language to another or even by different analysts working on the same language. We will see that the definitions of grammatical functions are not entirely straightforward, that they do not carry over from one language to another, and that the concept of subject is not applicable in all languages.

Grammatical subject

A definition of subject – more accurately, grammatical subject – for English contains the following components. First, a limitation: the criteria for subjects are established for basic clauses. These are clauses with the greatest range of tense, aspect, mood and voice; they are the easiest to turn into relative or interrogative clauses; they take the greatest range of adverbs; and they are semantically more basic than other clauses. (The key article on subject is still Keenan (1976).) The referents of subject NPs exist independently of the action or process denoted by clauses (the autonomy property) – *Skilled masons built the central tower in less than a year* is a basic clause, but not *Timothy was born on Halloween.* Subjects control reflexives, control the understood subjects of infinitives, function as pivots in infinitives and coordinate constructions and control quantifier floating. The subject NP of an active clause corresponds to the NP in the *by* phrase of a passive clause. Subjects agree in person and number with the finite verb in a given clause, they typically denote agents and with respect to information structure they typically function as the theme of a clause. [For a brief but comprehensive overview with examples, see Miller (2008, pp. 98–108).]

Direct, indirect and oblique objects

Direct objects in English immediately follow the main verb in basic clauses and correspond to the subject of passive clauses. In basic clauses subject NPs typically refer to Agents and direct object NPs refer to Patients. (Agent and Patient will be defined below.)

Oblique objects are NPs preceded by prepositions: in *gave it to Rene*, *bought it for* ***Pavel***, *ran round* **the garden**, *threw it out* **the window** and *the roof of the* ***house*** the NPs in bold are all oblique objects.

Many descriptions of English and other languages employ the concept of 'indirect object' for nouns preceded by *to* and *for*, such as those in (1a–c).

(1) a. Tatiana wrote to Onegin.
    b. Magnus went to Egilsay.
    c. Frank bought a piano for Jane.

The concept of indirect object is problematical. Grammars of English would merely refer to verbs such as *tell*, *say*, *show* and *give*, which occur in the construction V NP_1 *to* NP_2 or V NP_2 NP_1: cf. *Celia gave the car to Ben* versus *Celia gave Ben the car*, where *the car* is NP_1 and *Ben* is NP_2. The indirect object was said to be the NP preceded by *to* and the relevant verbs were either listed individually or divided into classes labelled 'verbs of saying', 'verbs of giving' and so on, to avoid the label 'indirect object' being assigned to phrases such as *to Dundee* in *He went to Dundee.*

In fact, indirect objects are difficult to separate from adverbs of direction. It is sometimes suggested that the two can be distinguished on the ground that indirect object NPs contain animate nouns, whereas adverbs of place contain inanimate nouns denoting countries, towns and other places. If this were correct, we would expect inanimate nouns not to occur immediately after a verb such as *sent* in (2) and (3).

(2) a. Lucy sent a letter to Isadore.
    b. Lucy sent Isadore a letter.
(3) a. The Government sent an envoy to China.
    b. (*)The Government sent China an envoy.

China in (3b) has to be interpreted not as a geographical unit but as an organization (quasi animate) that can interact with the person sent as an envoy. The oddness of (3b) can be removed by substituting different lexical items, as in (4). Here, China is presented as a body that is to benefit from the engineers.

(4) The company sent China its senior mining engineers to help plan the new mines

(4) supports another suggestion that genuine adverbs of direction cannot occur immediately after a verb, whereas indirect objects can. (*China* is not an adverb of direction.) This suggestion is correct, but it still fails to distinguish indirect objects; many verbs are like *tell* and *show* in that they occur in the NP_1 *to* NP_2 construction but not in the double object construction. *Attributed the picture to Raphael, forwarded the letter to Winifred, presented a gold watch to the foreman, kicked the ball to John, hit the ball to Martina* and *ascribed this play to Shakespeare* are all correct, but not the corresponding examples in (5).

(5) a. *The experts attributed Raphael this picture.
b. *I forwarded Winifred the letter.
c. *The manager presented the foreman a gold watch.
d. *Kick John the ball.
e. *Monica hit Martina the ball.
f. *The critics ascribe Shakespeare this play.

The examples in (5) have been tested on many classes of students. Some have accepted some of the examples, especially (5b), but the vast majority have not accepted any of them. We cannot maintain the traditional concept of indirect object as the *to* phrase with verbs such as *give, show* and *tell*; all NPs preceded by a preposition are treated as one category, oblique objects.

Examples such as *gave Liza the doll* and *showed the lawyer the document* are said to realize the double-object construction. The question is – what kind of object? Some analyses apply the term 'indirect object' to *Liza* and there are certainly languages in which *Liza* would have a different case suffix from *doll*. In Russian, *Liza* and *kukla* 'doll' are both feminine nouns; *dala Lize kuklu* is the translation of *gave Liza the doll*, and *kuklu* has the accusative case suffix that is attached to direct object nouns, while *Lize* has the dative case suffix that, inter alia, is attached to nouns denoting recipients.

The problem for English is that in (6) the criteria for direct object apply to *Susan* and not to *money*. *Susan* immediately follows the verb and corresponds to the subject of the passive.

(6) a. Monica gave Susan the money.
b. Susan was given the money by Monica.

We can make sense of the syntax of (6a) if we treat it as a construal of an event of giving in which the recipient is presented as directly affected by the action, as a Patient. The semantics now match the syntactic status of *Susan* as direct object. *Money* can be labelled 'second object'.

Grammatical functions across languages

It looks as though grammatical functions can be recognized for English on the basis of English syntax and morphosyntax and subject and direct object can be treated as denoting respectively Agents and Patients. One question brings out a serious weakness in the concept: can grammatical functions be generalized over languages? Possibly not. For instance, grammars of French appeal to the concepts of subject, direct object and so on, but the grammatical functions of French are established on the basis of French syntax and morphosyntax. What is the justification for identifying direct objects or subjects in English grammar with direct objects or subjects in French grammar? This is analogous to the difficulties affecting analyses of parts of speech: since they are established on distributional criteria for one language at a time, how do we justify equating nouns in English with nouns in Turkish, Chinese or Dyirbal? The only reasonable answer lies in the denotation of prototypical nouns, verbs, adjectives and so on and in the speech acts that are performed with them – referring, predicating and modifying. In analogous fashion, the reason for identifying subject and direct object in English with subjects and direct object in French or Turkish is, we may suppose, the fact that we recognize prototypical Agents and Patients no matter what the language. That is, prototypical semantic roles are primary and universal, whereas grammatical functions are adequate only for one language at a time.

An additional drawback is that the major grammatical function of subject is not readily applicable to some languages. In a language such as English a number of syntactic, morphosyntactic, semantic and discourse properties converge on one noun (phrase) in a clause, as outlined earlier. That NP is what is labelled 'subject'. As demonstrated by Schachter (1977), in a language such as Tagalog the concept of subject is not applicable, as the properties that accumulate on subject NPs in English fall into two sets, which accumulate on different NPs. A third problem is that in some ergative languages, especially those of Australia, the NP that might be recognized as the subject of a clause does not correspond to the subject NPs of English and other languages of Europe.

Roles

Semantic or participant roles have not had a good press. Butt (2009, p. 33) states that while roles such as Agent, Goal/Experiencer, Theme/Patient, Instrument and Location are acknowledged by many linguists, across theories there is a huge amount of dissatisfaction with these role labels, dissatisfaction that was prompted by Fillmore (1968) and was not allayed by Dowty (1991). According to Butt (2009, p. 33), 'The problem is that while the labels are utterly intuitive and therefore quite useful at some level of description, it is very difficult to put them to practical use because the definitions provided to date are simply too vague.' (The difference between being useful at some level of description, whatever that might mean, and being put to practical use is not explained.) According to Primus, writing in the same volume (2009, pp. 265–6), the main weakness of roles is that they are not defined in terms of a limited, conceptually well-motivated set of semantic primitives. As a result 'the number of roles far exceeds the number of core syntactic functions'; analysts working with role lists 'underestimate role differences', which may lead to empirically inaccurate analyses; and role lists are unstructured sets for which analysts have to stipulate role hierarchies or mapping principles.

Butt's reference to Fillmore (1968) is correct but irrelevant, since the essential idea in Fillmore's model was that syntactic tree diagrams should focus on the dependency relations between the nouns in a clause and the head verb and that the dependency relations should be represented as labelled branches. The adequacy of the labels, which signalled participant roles, was a secondary issue. Many descriptive grammars employ the concepts of Agent, Patient and so on; the question is: what place is there for participant roles in formal models? *Quite a lot* is the answer. Roles turn up in various Chomskyan models, in Jackendoff's models and in models, such as Lexical Functional Grammar, in which argument structure is linked to syntactic structure. Jackendoff (2002, p. 142) declares 'The consensus in the field is that the order [of NP arguments in clauses] is determined by the thematic roles of the corresponding thematic arguments' and refers to, inter alios, Van Valin and La Polla (1997) and Grimshaw (1990).

The resilience of semantic/participant roles is itself an indication that the concept has a lot of intuitive appeal for analysts, and Fillmore (1968) resonated very strongly with many students in JM's classes. This is not a reason for simply accepting the concept, but it is a good reason for not throwing it away and for trying to give it a solid foundation. Another reason is that in languages such as Russian, with a rich system of case suffixes playing a central part in the syntax and semantics of the language, the relationship between semantic roles and case suffixes is an essential and intriguing issue.

Clause structure, propositions and roles

The semantic foundation of any clause is its propositional core, which has to do with the state, process or action described by a given clause and the participant roles involved in a given state, process or action. Processes and actions are typically associated with verbs, whereas states are associated with either verbs or adjectives. (Not all languages have a clear distinction between verbs and adjectives. Where the distinction is lacking, states are associated with verbs. For instance, English has the adjective *ill* as in *He is ill*, but some languages have a construction with a verb, roughly equivalent to the archaic English *He is ailing*.) Typical states are being ill or being tall; typical processes are changes of state, such as freezing (of ice) or dying; typical actions are running and cutting, causing changes of state and causing some action to happen (*make somebody do something*). The participant roles are associated with NPs.

The notions of complement and adjunct are central to discussion of the propositional core. Extending 'complement' (see pp. 42–48) to take in subject NPs, we can say that a given verb requires a certain number of NPs, or has a certain number of places for NPs. (It is immaterial whether an NP is linked to the verb by a preposition or not.) Verbs are described as 'one-place' (e.g. *John ran*), 'two-place' (e.g. *Sue sharpened the knife*) or 'three-place' (e.g. *Fiona gave the parcel to Angus*). The verb and its complements constitute the nucleus of the propositional core. It is useful to be able to refer to the 'circumstantial roles' associated with a propositional nucleus; these are expressed by adverbial phrases of time, place, manner, etc., which are typically adjuncts of a verb in that they are optional constituents. They are also optional in the propositional core. The sentence *Sue sharpened the knife in the kitchen last night* has as the nucleus of its propositional core SHARPEN (SUE, KNIFE). *In the kitchen* and *last night* are adjuncts and correspond to circumstantial roles of location and time that are outside the propositional nucleus. Their presence in the sentence and in the propositional core does not alter the fact that SHARPEN is a two-place verb.

Reasons for roles and criteria for roles

The rest of the chapter discusses the types of participant roles that are appropriate for states, processes and actions. We will deal with various questions: types of roles, how the roles can be justified, how many different roles are needed and how roles are signalled in different languages. The starting point of the discussion is English, but data from other languages will appear. The essential point to remember beforehand is that roles have to be justified on grammatical grounds. The grounds may be syntactic or morphological or may relate to tests such as the question–answer pairs to be presented below: the important thing is to have criteria. If an analyst proposes a participant role that is not signalled in the grammar of some language or supported by other tests – that is, which derives entirely from the analyst's intuitions – we must be suspicious. The validity of intuitions is not being denied, nor the fact that certain speakers of a given language will agree that they share certain intuitions. The crux of the matter is simply that intuitions are not infallible, are not always shared and do need to be justified by evidence that is public.

There are standard arguments for including roles as basic elements in syntactic theory.

- They enable us to handle constructions that have the same constituent structure but different meanings.

Consider (7) and (8).

(7) a. Barnabas liked spaghetti.
 b. Barnabas ate the lasagna.
(8) a. Sabrina made Freya her friend.
 b. Sabrina made Freya a meal.

Anticipating the discussion that follows, we need note here only that Barnabas is doing something in the situation denoted by (7b) but not in the one denoted by (7a): that is, he plays a different role in the situations described by the two sentences, although in both *Barnabas* is the subject NP. In (8a,b), *Freya* directly follows the verb inside the VP. Nonetheless, Freya plays different roles. In the situation denoted by (8a), Sabrina does something to Freya, whereas in that denoted by (8b) Sabrina does something for Freya.

- NPs can be coordinated in English (and other languages), for example, *Pavel and Rene, the snow and ice*, etc. Certain restrictions affect coordination, and examples that break the restrictions sound odd, such as (9a,b).

(9) a. The quiche and I were cooking.
b. Katarina made her mother an omelette and the kitchen a mess.

The oddness derives from the roles. In (9a), *I* refers to an Agent, but *the quiche* does not. In (9b), *her mother* refers to the recipient of the omelette, but *the kitchen* does not refer to a recipient. Coordinated NPs must have the same role or be accounted instances of zeugma.

- Roles are relevant to the neutral order of prepositional phrases, as in (10).

(10) a. Juliet went on Monday to Newcastle.
b. In Strasbourg my brother lives.
c. With roses he planted the garden last November.

(10a–c) are not acceptable as examples of neutral word order. Normal neutral word order is . . . *to Newcastle on Monday*, . . . *lives in Strasbourg* and . . . *with roses last November*. In (10a), a goal phrase – *to Newcastle* – normally precedes a time phrase – *on Monday*; in (10b) a complement place phrase normally follows the verb, and in (10c) a 'material' *with* phrase normally follows the verb and the direct object. Of course, the orders in (10a–c) are possible. They could occur, but not as first sentences in, say, a conversation, because they stress the prepositional phrases and must be used to contradict a previous part of some hypothetical conversation. The key point is that since all the phrases are prepositional phrases, there is no difference in constituent structure. What is different is the role attaching to the NP in the prepositional phrase.

- Roles are relevant to the analysis of prepositions, case affixes and verb affixes.

Both Butt (2009) and Primus (2009) complain, quite justifiably, about the lack of good clear definitions of semantic roles. To that can be added the lack of criteria for establishing roles. For example, Culicover (2009, p. 67) says that in *The dog got sick* the NP *the dog* is a Theme because it undergoes a change of state. To the best of JM's knowledge, nobody has ever argued the case for this analysis. Anderson (2006, pp. 90–1) criticizes Dowty (1989) for assigning the Agent role to *the duck* in the following examples. As we will see shortly, *the duck* is only an Agent in two of the situations denoted by the examples, but to be fair, in the light of Dowty (1991), he may have abandoned that analysis.

(11) a. The duck is swimming
b. The duck is dying

c. The duck saw the frog
d. The duck swallowed the frog

Since (11b) answers the question *What is happening to the duck?*, *the duck* is a Patient. (11a) answers the question *What is the duck doing?* (– *swimming*) and (11d) answers the question *What did the duck do?* (– *swallow the frog*). In these examples, *the duck* is an Agent. (11c) answers neither of these questions and is assigned the role of Experiencer.

Anderson (2006, p. 91) quite correctly criticizes analyses of pairs of sentences such as (12), which state that 'on an intuitive level one would assume that, for example, Max is an Agent and Mary a Recipient' in both (12a) and (12b).

(12) a. Max sold the piano to Mary for $1,000.
b. Mary bought the piano from Max for $1,000.

Anderson here takes the same line as Langacker and other proponents of Cognitive Linguistics: (12a,b) do not map directly on to the extralinguistic world but onto mental representations of it. Such representations typically allow different construals of what, in a naïve truth-conditional approach, might be considered one and the same situation. Thus, in (12a), Max is presented as the Agent, the piano as the Patient and Mary as the Goal. In (12b), Mary is presented as the Agent, the piano is again the Patient and Max is presented as the Source from which the piano moves to Mary. In fact, given the dynamics of events of buying and selling, it is perfectly possible that in the real-world situation corresponding to (12b) Mary is the Agent, persuading Max to let the piano go for $1,000 rather than Max persuading Mary to take the piano and pay $1,000.

The importance of grammatical criteria

(12a,b) illustrate another important point: roles must be established on the basis of grammatical and lexical evidence such as the occurrence of case suffixes or adpositions, word order and lexical verbs. Changes in grammar and changes of lexical verb signal a change in meaning, in the sense of a change in construal and possibly a change in primitive truth conditions too. In (12a,b), the lexical verb changes from *sold* to *bought*; *Max* is grammatical subject in (12a), but *Mary* is the grammatical subject in (12b); *Mary* is an oblique object in (12a), but *Max* is the oblique object in (12b).

Suppose we have to analyse the sentence *The doctor left the ward.* What role is best assigned to *ward*? Source might seem appropriate, given that the doctor moves from the ward to another location, but this is not supported by the grammar. (*The*) *ward* is the direct object of *left* and can only be a Patient. The Source role is justified only where there are prepositions such as *from* and *out of*: *I dashed from the room* and *I ran out of the room*. Bad methodology has led to the accusative and infinitive construction being treated as Exceptional Case Marking in Chomskyan generative grammar. In *We believed the driver to be innocent*, the driver is analysed as the subject of a clause *the driver be innocent* and the whole clause is the direct object of *believed*. In various Chomskyan models, the subject of this clause is assigned, exceptionally, accusative case, although that case is otherwise assigned to direct objects. Suppose we apply our principle that grammatical criteria are of the first importance when we are assigning participant roles. Can we provide a plausible semantic analysis? One possibility is that in this construction (see the discussion of constructions and construction meaning on pp. 102–117) *believe* acquires the construction's causative meaning: 'by our belief we put the driver into the class of innocent people.'

The examples used by Lakoff (1968) can be treated in the same fashion. The originals had Seymour cutting salami with a knife, but are brought up to date in (13).

(13) a. Sue carved the turkey with the electric knife.
b. Sue used the electric knife to carve the turkey.

Because *electric knife* denotes a kind of tool, Lakoff assumed that in both (13a) and (13b) *electric knife* has the Instrument role. (It will be proposed below, but not argued, that the instrument role is a sub-type of a more general comitative role.) Only (13a) offers syntactic support for the Instrument role – *electric knife* is an oblique object preceded by *with*. In (13b), *electric knife* is the direct object of *used* and the sentence has a passive version *The electric knife was used by Sue to carve the turkey*. (13a) certainly implies (13b), and vice-versa, but in (13b) grammatical evidence shows that *electric knife* has the role of Patient. Entailments can hold between sentences without the NPs being assigned the same role in each sentence. Anticipating the discussion below, *The gardener planted the garden with roses* entails *The gardener planted roses in the garden* but *roses* and *garden* have different roles.

The examples in (14) bear in a particularly interesting way on the the status of participant roles vis-à-vis the extra-linguistic world and reinforce the advice to take syntax and morphology seriously. The examples in (14) are very well known.

(14) a. The gardener planted rose-bushes in the garden.
b. The gardener planted the garden with rose-bushes.

(14a,b) are not identical in meaning. If we describe the conditions in which one or the other is true, it emerges that (14b) is true if the gardener filled the garden with rose-bushes, whereas (14a) leaves it open whether the rose-bushes are all over the garden or only in one part of it. (14b) entails (14a), but (14a) does not entail (14b). That is, the semantic differences are significant.

Accompanying the semantic differences are differences in syntax.

- The word order is different: *planted – roses – garden* versus *planted – garden – roses*.
- In (14a), but not (14b), *garden* is preceded by a preposition, that is, is an oblique object; *roses* is preceded by a preposition in (14b) but not in (14a).
- The preposition in (14a) is *in*, but in (14b) it is *with*.
- *Roses* is the direct object of *planted* in (14a) – witness the passive *Roses were planted in the garden by the gardener*. In (14b), it is *garden* that is the direct object, witness the passive *The garden was planted with roses by the gardener*. Being direct object is important because the referents of direct object NPs are taken to be completely affected by the action or process, unless that interpretation is excluded, say by the aspect of the verb. *The gardener was planting the garden with roses* leaves it open whether the planting was completely carried out; a continuation such as *It took him two days to do it* signals completion, *but he didn't have enough rose bushes* signals non-completion. The use of an adverb such as *partly* also signals non-completion, as in *The gardener partly planted the garden with roses*.

(14b) presents the garden as being directly operated on by the gardener: it now has the Patient role. What role goes to *rose bushes*? Again without arguing for the analysis (but see Schlesinger, 1979) we will treat *with* as signalling a general Comitative role, based on the underlying notion of 'same place'. The role structure of (14b) has the general interpretation that the gardener operates on the garden, causing it to be in the same place as roses. It might be objected that the English sentence **The garden is with rose bushes* is unacceptable (though its equivalent in other languages is not), but the NP *the garden with rose bushes* is perfectly acceptable: cf. *The garden with rose bushes is more attractive than the garden with heathers.*

Criteria for situation type and role

Three simple tests distinguish actions and processes from states and then Agents from Patients. *What happened?* enables us to sort out actions and processes from states, since only sentences describing actions or processes can be answers to the question *What happened*? Once an example is established as describing an action, the questions in (15) and (16) pick out agent and patient.

(15) What did X do?

(16) What happened to X?

Thus, *What did Jacob do*? can be appropriately answered by *He shut the safe* or *He e-mailed Grandpa. What happened to Jacob*? can be appropriately answered by *He fell off the ladder* or *He was fouled by the defender.*

Other tests for Agent are available in English. One test is whether a sentence can be incorporated into the pseudo-cleft construction *What X did was . . .*, *What X is doing is . . .* and so on. For example, *Jacob shut the safe* can be incorporated in the construction to yield (17).

(17) What Jacob did was shut the safe.

Other tests, much weaker, are whether the verb in a given sentence can be put into the progressive and whether it can be put into the imperative. *Jacob shut the safe* meets both of these criteria, as shown in (18) and (19).

(18) Jacob was shutting the safe.

(19) Shut the safe!

The progressive test is weaker because it is met by verbs that do not have an Agent role: *The patient is suffering a lot of pain, He's not understanding a single thing you say* and *You will soon be owning all the land round here* (from a TV play). We know that these verbs do not have an Agent role because the sentences are not appropriate answers to the test question: *The patient is suffering a lot of pain* is bizarre as an answer to *What is the patient doing*? (Cf. *He's annoying the nurses, He's complaining about the food*, etc.)

A final pair of tests are whether a sentence can be continued *be at it* and whether adverbs such as *enthusiastically* and *masterfully* can be inserted into a sentence. Again, *Jacob e-mailed Grandpa* meets the tests, as shown in (20) and (21).

(20) Jacob was e-mailing Grandpa when I left and was still at it when I got back.

(21) Jacob was enthusiastically e-mailing Grandpa.

Returning to the verbs that do not have an Agent role, we see that the test question *What is happening?* or *What will be happening?* separates *suffering* from *owning*. Despite its occurrence in the progressive, *own* denotes a state. *Suffer* denotes a process but not an action, as actions require Agents. If anything, *the patient* in the above example has the role of Patient: *He's suffering a lot of pain* is an appropriate answer to the question *What is happening to the patient?* Other verbs denoting processes are *freeze* (*The loch is freezing over*), *die* (*The patient is dying*) and *melt* (*The ice is melting*). Finally, not all one-place verbs take a Patient NP. The question *What is X doing?* can be answered by, for example, *X is swimming*, *X is walking in the park* and *X is working*.

Roles and role players

An important distinction separates roles and role players. So far we have demonstrated the criteria for treating nouns as denoting agents or patients. The grammar of any language permits only very general categories to be established, but broad roles on their own are not sufficient to handle all the distinctions of meaning that must be described. The semantic interpretation of a particular clause does not depend just on general participant roles; information in the lexical entries for individual nouns also contributes.

The importance of the distinction between roles and role players is illustrated by the proposal to recognize a role of Causer in addition to Agent.

(22) The Sun attracts the planets

Why call *Sun* a Causer in (22)? The justification is that the Sun is not animate, far less human, and cannot be seen as an ideal Agent. It is also true that (22) enjoys the same syntactic privileges as sentences such as *The new manager attracted more clients*. Both answer the question *What does X do?* and both occur in the pseudo-cleft construction, as in (23) and (24).

(23) a. What does the Sun do? It attracts the planets.
b. What does the new manager do? He attracts/is attracting more clients.

(24) a. What the Sun does is attract the planets.
b. What the new manager does is attract more clients.

Both sentences can be also be put into the passive. However, the Sun is clearly not as good an Agent as the manager of a hotel or store and this is reflected in the syntax. The construction *be at it* indicates the presence of a good Agent, as in *The manager attracted crowds of new clients last week and is still at it this week.* In contrast, *The Sun has attracted the planets for millions of years and is still at it* is decidedly odd. (The preceding example is only possible if the speaker or writer presents the Sun as animate: that is, if figurative language is being used.) Good Agents are signalled by adverbs such as *enthusiastically* and *masterfully*, which can be inserted into (23b) and (24b) but not into (23a) or (24a).

Prototype roles

Cruse (1973), in a very early paper that anticipates Dowty's approach though not the latter's reliance on entailments (see below), argues essentially that it is useful to work with the concept of protypical Agent and various types of non-prototypical Agents. He treats the Agent role as
composed of four strands: volitive, effective, initiative and agentive proper.

- The volitive strand has to do with an entity achieving something by exerting its willpower. Consider the examples in (25).

(25) a. Captain Oates died in order to save his comrades.
b. The fugitive lay motionless in order to avoid discovery.

Although the verbs in (25) do not denote actions, Captain Oates and the fugitive exercise their willpower and can be regarded as Agents, albeit weak Agents. Verbs such as *die* and *lie* can be put into the imperative, which is not a test for actions but is a test for volition: cf. *Die a hero's death for Sparta!* and *Lie still or they will see you!* An adverb such as *accidentally* signals that an action is not voluntary, but it can occur in imperative sentences and the latter can be given an interpretation. Thus, *Kick the defender accidentally* can be taken as an instruction to kick the defender but to make it look accidental.

- The second strand is the effective one, so-called because it relates to the production of an effect. This strand is exemplified by (26).

(26) a. This column supports the weight of the pediment.
b. The falling tree crushed the car completely.

The column produces an effect simply by being in a certain position. The tree crushed the car as a result of movement transmitted to it, for example, by the wind. No volition is involved, but note that both (26a) and (26b) can occur in the pseudo-cleft construction: *What the column does is support the weight of the pediment* and *What the falling tree did was crush the car completely.* They can be used as good answers to the questions *What does the column do?* and *What did the falling tree do?*

- The third strand is the initiative one, so-called because the person denoted by the relevant noun initiates an action, say, by giving a command but without necessarily doing anything else. This strand is exemplified by sentences such as *The guard marched the prisoners round the yard.*
- The fourth and final strand is the agentive one proper. It relates to sentences describing situations in which an object is presented as using its own energy, the object being a living creature, a machine or a natural force. Examples are given in (27).

(27) a. The computer is playing six simultaneous games of three-dimensional chess
b. The machine is crushing the wrecked car
c. The flood swept away whole villages

Prototypical Agents are those that use their own energy and volition to achieve an effect or initiate an action. This means that, until the fifth generation of Japanese robots, the best agents will be animate creatures, with humans being seen in turn as the best agents within that sub-class. To sum up: on grammatical (and other) grounds an Agent role is established. Various criteria pick out animate creatures (especially human beings) as the best prototypical agents, but the grammar of English obliges us to recognize that other types of entity can be presented as Agents, albeit weaker. Humans, animals, machines and natural forces are all types of player that can take on the agent role.

PROTO-AGENT AND PROTO-PATIENT

Dowty (1991) suggests that we can abandon the traditional set of discrete roles such as agent, patient and source, replacing them with what he calls two 'cluster concepts', PROTO-AGENT and PROTO-PATIENT, each characterized by a set of verbal entailments. The set for PROTO-AGENT is in (28) and the set for PROTO-PATIENT is in (29).

(28) a. Volitional involvement in the event or state
b. Sentience (and/or perception)
(*John sees/fears Mary, is disappointed at X, knows/believes X*)
c. Causing an event or change of state in another participant

d. Movement relative to the position of another participant
e. Exists independently of the event named by the verb

(29) a. Undergoes change of state
b. Incremental theme (filling a glass, crossing a road)
c. Causally affected by another participant
d. Stationary relative to movement of another participant
e. Does not exist independently of the event, or not all

As Dowty says, the above properties are very much like the properties set up by Keenan (1976) in his account of grammatical subject (see p. 199). Interestingly, the properties for PROTO-AGENT, particularly (28a–c), were earlier proposed by Cruse as some of the major strands in his general concept of Agent. It is satisfying to see two different approaches producing very similar results. (In fact, it is three approaches that produce similar results because Foley and Van Valin (1984) developed the concept of macro-roles, essentially general concepts of Agent and Patient.)

One of Dowty's goals is probably not achievable, getting rid of the traditional lists of discrete roles. Constructions come back into play at this point. Keeping in mind the discussion of criteria for establishing roles, in particular Anderson's critique of analyses that ignore grammatical properties, and the concept of construal, we can treat Dowty's idea as applying to major constructions involving Agents and Patients and as allowing for changes of construal leading to changes of construction, or changes of construction leading to changes of construal. An example is the historical change from *Him like pears* to *He likes pears*. In the earlier construction, *him* is not an Agent but an Experiencer and the grammatical subject is *pears*. In the later construction, *he* is the grammatical subject and is probably best treated as a very weak Agent. The construction has changed further to allow the Progressive, as *We're really liking it here*, which presents the referents of *we* as playing an active part in the situation, say, by taking part in all the activities going on. The Macdonald's slogan *I'm liking it* conjures up a picture of someone munching their burgers and expressing enjoyment, not just downing the food as quickly as possible and leaving.

A third goal of Dowty's paper is to determine, for a clause with a verb and two arguments, which argument becomes the grammatical subject and which becomes the direct object. His proposal is that the argument for which the predicate entails the greatest number of Proto-Agent properties will be lexicalized as the subject of the predicate; the argument having the greatest number of

Proto-Patient entailments will be lexicalized as the direct object. This approach looks very much like the precursor of an optimality theory treatment. (See de Hoop, 2009.)

What other roles are needed and justified by grammatical patterns (and entailments)? A general role of Comitative, encompassing Instrument and Manner. [See Schlesinger (1979), one of the few accounts of semantic roles that are based on experimental evidence as well as grammatical patterns.] A general role of Source or Ablative, encompassing Reason and Cause as well as physical starting points of journeys. A general role of Goal or Allative, encompassing the physical end points of journeys and recipients, whether of concrete entities such as money or books or of abstract entities such as advice and ideas. There is no space to discuss here whether the difference between Recipients and Patients can be handled in terms of movement into the space around a person as opposed to movement into that space and into contact with a person (see Anderson, 2006 and Jackendoff, 1983, pp. 188–211).

Roles across languages

One essential property, perhaps the essential property, of the above set of roles is that they are based on grammatical patterns. We close this discussion of semantic/participant roles by looking at two more grammatical patterns. One demonstrates that even paying attention to syntax and morphosyntax we run into complexities in the assignment of roles and the other is a good example of how sentences in one language and their translations in another language may be based on different construals.

The first pattern relates to the putative distinction between Agents and Causers (and between Agents and Natural Forces, such as water, wind, rivers, frost, rain and so on). Earlier we used the examples *The manager attracts more customers* and *The Sun attracts the planets*. The two combinations of verb and NPs share various grammatical features in English, but suppose a language turned up in which their equivalent clauses had different syntax, possibly with *Sun* requiring a different preposition, case affix or word-order from *manager*. That language would be analysed as having a narrower Agent role than English, and it would not be possible to talk of *The Sun* being presented as Agent.

Russian does have a special construction for sentences describing the operation of natural forces. Compare (30) and (31).

(30) Soldaty zatoptali carevicu.
Soldiers-nominative crushed maize-accusative-sg
'The soldiers trampled down the maize'

(31) Gradom zadavilo carevicu.
Hail-instrumental crushed maize-accusative-sg
'The hail flattened the maize'

In (30), *zadavili* is third-person plural and agrees in number with *soldaty*. *Soldaty* is nominative plural, nominative being traditionally regarded as the case of the subject noun; it agrees in number with *zadavili*, is clearly the subject of the sentence and denotes Agents. In (31), *gradom* is in the instrumental case, which is the case used for the instrumental role. If Ivan did something with a hammer, the instrumental case form *molotom* 'with a hammer' is used. *Zadavilo* is third-person singular, but is neuter gender and does not agree in gender with *gradom*. It is difficult to recognize a subject in (31), but it is not difficult to assign a role to *gradom*. Following the grammatical pattern, we do not invent a role of Causer or Natural Force. Rather we say that Natural Forces are construed as Instruments and *gradom* is an Instrument. (Schlesinger would say that it is a sub-type of Comitative.)

In connection with the above discussion of Dowty's PROTO-AGENTS, it is worthwhile pointing out that speakers of Russian can use the construction in (30) for describing hail flattening maize – *Grad zadavil carevicu*. The verb *zadavil* agrees in number and gender with *grad*, and *grad* is in the nominative case. In this construction, the Natural Force is construed as an Agent, but a weak Agent. Note that although *grad zadavil carevicu* and *gradom zadavilo carevicu* imply each other, they are not identical in meaning. The discussion forces us to say that one presents *grad* as an Agent, the other as an Instrument.

We note in passing that the rejection of the proposed Causer or Natural Force roles can be repeated for the proposed role of Result. 'Result', were it admitted to the set of roles, would be assigned to *St Paul's Cathedral*, *pattern* and *hole* in (32).

(32) a. Wren built St Paul's Cathedral
b. Siobhan carved a pattern on the piece of wood
c. The dog dug a hole in the lawn

The key point in these examples is that *build*, *carve* and *dig* denote acts of creation that bring entities into existence. The three nouns are merely Patients, though not prototypical Patients.

The final set of examples is in (33)–(36).

(33) On prokolol plastmassu igloj
he pierced plastic-accusative needle-instrumental
'He pierced the plastic with a needle'

(34) Maša maxnula rukoj
Maša waved hand-instrumental
'Masha waved (her hand)'

(35) Sobaka majala xvostom
dog wagged tail-instrumental
'The dog wagged its tail'

(36) Devočka razmaxivala palkoj
little-girl was-brandishing stick-instrumental
'The little girl was brandishing a stick'

Both the English and Russian examples in (33) have an Agent noun, a Patient noun and a noun in the role of Instrument. *Igloj* is the instrumental case form of *igla* 'needle'. In the English examples in (34)–(36), *her hand, its tail* and *a stick* are probably to be analysed as Patients. The best example is (34), which can be made passive – *A stick was being brandished by the little girl.* In the Russian examples, the corresponding nouns are in the instrumental case – *rukoj, xvostom* and *palkoj.* Following the grammatical pattern, we have to treat these nouns and their referents as having the role of Instrument. This construal of the situation can be glossed thus: 'Masha made a waving movement with her hand,' 'The dog made a wagging movement with its tail' and 'The little girl made a brandishing movement with a stick.' The alternative to this construal is to consider the instrument case suffixes as merely quirky case marking with no semantic content, a move that is ruled out by reliance on grammatical criteria as practised by Cognitive Linguistics and Localism.

Conclusion

Using grammatical criteria and working with a distinction between role players and roles, that is, distinguishing information conveyed by grammatical patterns from information conveyed by lexical items, it is possible to establish a very limited set of roles. Prototypical roles can be recognized across languages, although what looks like one and the same situation, such as brandishing a stick, may be construed differently in different languages.

On the other hand, the concepts of subject, direct object and oblique object are language-specific, given that they are established on the basis of grammatical properties and that any given language has its own unique set of grammatical characteristics.

Language Complexity

11

Chapter Outline

Introduction

The complexity of language has become a fashionable topic, with the appearance in the last two years of Miestamo et al. (2008), Sampson et al. (2008) and Givon and Shibatani (2009). Much of the research reported in these books deals with the evolution of complexity in language; the comparison of languages and what might make one language more complex than another; whether all languages are actually of equal complexity, with intricate morphology being balanced by simple syntax and vice versa. A small proportion of the research deals with the occurrence of complex syntactic structures in large databases such as the British National Corpus and the use of such structures by native speakers of English.

We will leave on one side the comparison of languages with respect to complexity but the last two topics are of interest here. They tie in with the discussion of magnasyntax (see pp. 122–127), they bear on the issue of spoken and written language and how they differ in syntax, morphology and vocabulary and they are important in connection with Chomskyan generative grammar, both with the constraints and parameters applied to structures and with the Chomskyan theory of Universal Grammar (UG) and first language acquisition. One of the arguments there is that children acquire spontaneous spoken language, which is much simpler in its syntax than written language and which contains many fixed or semi-fixed phrases. The relevance of this is that to acquire the spontaneous spoken structures, phrases and vocabulary of their native language, children do not need the very rich system of innate constraints taken for granted by Chomskyans. (As we will see, the learning of written language is a very different process.) This is an important point; the Chomskyan theory of first language acquisition was elaborated after the development of the standard model of transformational grammar. Generative grammarians deal with rules, constraints and principles for handling magnasyntax, that is, all structures from the simplest to the most complex. The theoretical apparatus of constraints, principles, etc., is then projected onto native speakers. (See the discussion of the poverty of stimulus on pp. 243–254.)

Speaking, writing and complexity

Miller and Weinert (2009) tie in syntactic complexity with written language, focusing on English but also using data from French, German and Russian. They argue that spontaneous spoken language has certain key properties and that these properties do not represent breakdowns in performance but are permanent design features that reflect the conditions in which speech is produced and interpreted.

i. Spontaneous speech is produced in real time, impromptu and with no opportunity for editing, whereas writing is generally produced with pauses for thought and with much editing.
ii. Spontaneous speech is subject to the limitations of short-term memory in both speaker and hearer: it has been said (by the psycholinguist George Miller) that the short term memory can hold 7 +/– 2 bits of information.
iii. Spontaneous speech is typically produced by people talking face-to-face in a particular context.
iv. Spontaneous speech, by definition, involves pitch, amplitude, rhythm and voice quality.
v. Spontaneous face-to-face speech is accompanied by gestures, eye gaze, facial expressions and body postures, all of which signal information.

Conditions (i)–(v) are reflected in certain linguistic properties.

a. Information is carefully staged, a small quantity of information being assigned to each phrase and clause.
b. Spontaneous spoken language typically has far less grammatical subordination than written language and much more coordination or simple parataxis.
c. The syntax of spontaneous spoken language is in general fragmented and unintegrated; phrases are less complex than phrases of written language; the clausal constructions are less complex. A central role in signalling relationships between chunks of syntax is played by deictics. (See Chapters 3, 8.)
d. The sentence is not a useful analytical unit for informal spoken language.
e. The patterns of constituent structure and the arrangement of heads and modifiers do not always correspond to the patterns recognized by syntactic theory.
f. The range of vocabulary in spontaneous language is less than in written language.
g. A number of constructions occur in spontaneous spoken language but not in written language, and vice versa.

One important property must be added to the list: many of the sequences of words produced in spontaneous spoken language are fixed phrases, either completely fixed sequences of words or templates that allow very limited substitutions or extensions. (See pp. 246–250.) The actual syntax is simple in the following sense. Fifty per cent of NPs consist of pronouns, and another 25 per cent consist of single nouns or a determiner + single noun. Details of NPs in task-related dialogues and conversation can be found in Thompson (1988) and Miller and Weinert (2009). (A wealth of examples of the complex NPs used in formal written texts can be found in Feist (forthcoming), and the difficulty of interpreting such NPs in written texts being read out is described in the discussion of unsuccessful communication between factory management and the workforce on pp. 229–232.)

The very simple structure of NPs in spontaneous speech is aptly illustrated by the little text in (1). It might seem like a counter-example, but it is taken from a humorous postcard (the words are spoken by one woman to another as they sit at the kitchen table chatting over a glass of wine and a cigarette), and the humour comes precisely from the fact that in such a relaxed setting most people cannot produce even two or three well-chosen adjectives off the cuff far less a string of nine, and even the most fluent speakers are hard pressed to produce complex syntax at the right moment in stressful situations.

(1) Then he said why was I always trying to CHANGE him and I said probably because he's such an obnoxious thoughtless selfish overbearing self-righteous hypocritical arrogant loudmouthed misogynist bastard.

Relative clauses typically have zero relativizers or are introduced by *that*, prepositions are at the end of the clause and are typically omitted. (See the account of relative clauses and magnasyntax on pp. 122–127.) Complement clauses typically have zero complementizers. The range of adverbial clauses is limited, typically clauses of time, manner and condition. The overall proportion of subordinate to main clauses is much less than in written English generally. (For details, see Miller and Weinert (2009) and the relevant sections of Biber et al. (1999). The results reported by Miller and Weinert match those reported for Italian by Sornicola (1981), for French by Blanche-Benveniste (1991) and for Russian by Zemskaja (1973). Miller and Weinert cited Mundy (1955) commenting on the looser syntactic organization of syntax in spoken Turkish. Two more recent publications, focusing on relativization and complementation with *ki*, demonstrate clearly the paratactic and sequential nature of spoken Turkish structures compared with the written Turkish structures Relative-Clause + Head Noun and Complement Clause + Verb, tightly integrated and hierarchical. (See Kerslake, 2007 and Schroeder, 2002).

Also typically missing from or rare in spontaneous spoken English, depending on the speaker, are highly integrated non-finite clauses such as free participles (*Jumping to her feet, she threw a book at the intruder*), free participles with subject NPs (*The intruder having escaped through the front door, she slammed it shut*) and full gerunds with possessive subjects (*Brown's failing to foresee the collapse has cost the country dear*). (For details and more examples, see Miller and Weinert, 2009, pp. 85–7.) A further example is the structure of the preceding sentence: a copula construction in which the complements of *be* are in sentence-initial position and the subject NP is itself very dense, consisting of the sequence *highly integrated non-finite clauses such as* followed by three conjoined NPs, each of which is followed by an example in brackets.

Complexity in corpuses of written English

Not only do speakers speaking off-the-cuff employ simple syntax, but the more complex structures common in generative analyses appear not to be much used even in written English. Karlsson (2009, p. 194) reports that the British National Corpus, the Brown Corpus and the LOB (London–Oslo–Bergen) Corpus offer only 130 instances of two levels of clause-embedding. The number may be lower, as will be explained below. (2) is straightforward: the comparison clause *than is common in modern politics* is embedded in the relative clause *into which . . . have gone*. The relative clause is in turn embedded in the subject NP *a number of speeches* of the main clause.

(2) A number of speeches into which a great deal of thought and preparation on a level much higher than is common in modern politics have gone are not reported at all . . .

Another two examples are not straightforward. In (3), the most deeply embedded clause, on Karlsson's analysis, is *in which the theme of homosexuality remains latent*. But is this clause embedded? It is certainly inside the clause *when one compares . . . with the shoddiness . . .*, but is separated from the other chunks of the clause by dashes, which signal that the clause functions as an aside. That is, the reader is invited to make a sidestep and then return to the main route through the sentence.

(3) . . . for that matter, when one compares *Swann* and *Jeunes filles* – in which the theme of homosexuality remains latent – with the shoddiness of the later volumes, one is inclined to wonder . . .

A similar problem arises with (4), in which the apparently most deeply embedded clause is *as was the way of the world*. This clause is separated by commas from the remainder of the apparent matrix clause. As in the previous example, this clause constitutes a sidestep, an optional, not strictly necessary comment by the narrator on the content of the story. The sidestep is inside a first sidestep because the clause *who . . . shamba*, separated from the rest of the main clause by commas, is a non-restrictive relative. It does not supply information that helps to pick out the referent, but throws in extra information.

(4) It was not until he was an old man that one day his son, who, as was the way of the world, had left the shamba, explained to him that . . .

If more examples can be eliminated, complex syntactic structures with two or more levels of embedding will turn out to be even rarer.

Experiments on students processing complex written language

If large databases have few or no examples of a particular construction, it is reasonable to infer that users of the language avoid it, in writing and a fortiori in speech. Experimental evidence on the above type of example is not available, but it is available for other examples. Dabrowska (1997) investigated how well different groups of native speakers of English understood complex sentences such as *Sandy will be easy to get the president to vote for* and *It was King Louis who the general convinced that this slave might speak to.* She found that university lecturers understood these and other examples better than undergraduates, who in turn understood them better than university porters and cleaners.

Chipere (2008) carried out experiments with two groups of students from a further education college. One group consisted of students of high academic ability, the other of students of low academic ability. Level of academic ability was defined in terms of grades obtained at GCSE level (the leaving certificate examinations taken at age 16 in England and Wales). In one task the students were asked to recall the given example. In a second task, they were asked to answer questions on complex sentences. For example, presented with *Tom knows the fact that flying planes low is dangerous excites the pilot*, they were asked *What does Tom know*? and *What excites the pilot*? The group with high academic ability significantly outperformed the group with low academic ability on both tasks. Some of the low academic ability group were given memory training, while the others were trained in comprehension of complex sentences. The ones who were given memory training performed much better on the recall task but did no better at comprehending the questions. The ones who were given comprehension training were better both at recalling the sentences and at answering the questions.

On the basis of the results Chipere (2009, p. 191) suggests that native speakers vary in grammatical competence, but have equal potential to acquire full grammatical competence. Sampson (2009, p. 9) mentions the difficulty in challenging the ideologically based consensus among generative linguists that 'We know that the grammars that are in fact constructed vary only slightly among speakers of the same language, despite wide variations not only in intelligence but also in the conditions under which language is acquired' (Chomsky, 1968, pp. 6–69). The extensive differences in the United Kingdom between between spoken standard and non-standard and between different non-standard varieties suggests that there are wide variations. The wide variations, observed over 36 years, in the written output of first-year students taking the same course at Edinburgh University also suggest that Chomsky was being very optimistic. In Maher and Groves (1996, p. 46), there is a photograph of Chomsky. The balloon that is linked to him contains the elegant and powerful text 'We may be materially and intellectually impoverished, physically sick, lack will and concentration, have lifelong borderline personality problems, and despite all this, the mind's cognitive system goes on building its edifice quietly, uniformly, seemingly beyond our control.' The invited inference is that everyone has the same grammar, but no evidence for this assumption has been produced and such evidence as the understanding of complex texts or the production of written texts, and pieces of research such as Philpott's (described below) all go against the assumption.

Moreover, one obstacle blocks Chipere's attempt to allow for variation in grammatical competence without challenging the consensus: the subjects in his experiments were drawn from two sets of students. It is well-known that the set of university students displays large disparities between students of high academic ability and those of low academic ability. More importantly, approximately 35 per cent of any given annual cohort of school-leavers in the United Kingdom now go on to higher education. That leaves 65 per cent who do not, whether because of insufficient ability or because of lack of interest in school or adverse circumstances at home and so on. It is from that 65 per cent that Dabrowska's porters and cleaners are drawn, and Chipere's experiments pass them by.

Spontaneous spoken language: phrases or clauses?

Chipere's book demonstrates, by accident, how crucial it is to pay attention to the linguistic experience of any group of speakers. His subjects may split into high ability and low ability groups, but they are all in higher education, which means that they had all had considerable exposure to the complex syntactic structures and vocabulary of formal writing and were reading and writing such language quite intensively. That is, they were immersed in a variety of language much denser in grammar than the typical spontaneous spoken English sketched earlier. In fact, the gap between formal written language and spontaneous spoken language may be even greater. Indeed Sornicola (1981) argues convincingly on the basis of Neapolitan Italian that much spontaneous spoken language does not even have a syntactic structure in which phrases combine into clauses or clauses into integrated clause complexes. Rather, the structure consists of blocks of syntax (phrases) with little or no syntactic linkage and requiring the listener to deploy considerable skills of inference based on contextual and world knowledge. Sornicola demonstrates that such fragments should be treated as the structures that speakers aim to produce in spontaneous speech and not as the remnants of clauses that have fallen apart as the result of performance errors. (See Miller and Weinert, 2009, pp. 58–59.)

Sornicola's account is supported by the data presented in Zemskaja (1973). Consider (5).

(5) a. moloko raznosit/ ne prixodila ešče?
milk she-delivers/ not came yet?
'the woman who delivers the milk, has she not come yet?'

b. u okna ležala/ kaprisnaja očen'.
at window she-lay/ moody very
'the woman in the bed by the window was very moody.'

(5a,b) each contain two finite verbs and two clauses, *raznosit* and *prixodila* in (5a) and *ležala* and a zero copula in (5b). If (5b) was past tense, the second clause would contain an overt form of the copula, *byla* 'was'. None of the four clauses contains a subject NP because the deictic person suffixes on the verbs point to a third person and the complete clauses, *moloko raznosit* and *u okna ležala*, provide enough information for the listener(s) to identify the referents. In a written text, there would be a subject NP modified by a relative clause, as in (6).

(6) Ženščina, kotoraja moloko raznosit, ne prixodila ešče?
Woman who milk delivers not came yet
'The woman who delivers the milk has not come yet.'

In the spoken texts in (5a,b), there is no justification for analysing *moloko raznosit* and *u okna ležala* as some kind of reduced relative clauses, but they are good main clauses. The / in the transcription indicates an intonation pattern signalling that the utterance is going to be continued and that the first clause and the following clause are connected and form a clause complex. These and the many other examples from Zemskaja (1973) have the additional advantage of belonging to informal spontaneous conversation from highly educated speakers and cannot be dismissed as instances of non-standard Russian. They are regular structures of spontaneous spoken Russian.

Two major caveats must be made at this point. The first one concerns the proportion of subordinate clauses to main clauses in different text types. According to Halliday (1989, pp. 76–91) written language is complex with highly compact and simple syntactic constructions loaded with many lexical items. In contrast, spoken language is complex in a different way, with intricate syntactic structure containing a considerable proportion of subordinate clauses. Halliday's assertion does not apply at all to the Miller–Brown Corpus of spontaneous conversations nor to the narratives analysed in Macauley (1991) nor to the French data in Blanche-Benveniste (1991) nor to Zemskaja's Russian data. It does not apply to more recent corpuses of spoken English such as the private conversations and phone-in radio programmes in the Wellington Corpus of Spoken New Zealand English and the informal conversations in the Australian English component of ICE. (His assertion does apply to, for example, monologues such as university lectures and discussion programmes with participants who are used to talking in public and who are given time to make their various contributions to the discussions. University lectures are 'semi-scripted' in that the lecturer has notes and overhead slides and nowadays of course the ubiquitous Powerpoint presentation. The studio discussions just referred to allowed much more planning time than is available in conversation or in phone-in radio programmes, where immediate responses are expected. (For a more detailed discussion of speakers and text-types, see Miller and Weinert 2009, pp. 14–22.)

Spontaneous spoken texts offer a much smaller proportion of clause complexes with subordinate clauses than, say, formal written texts or semi-scripted monologues, but it would be wrong to suppose that spontaneous spoken texts offer no clause complexes or subordinate clauses. As Fernandez (1994) observes, even informal conversation contains rehearsed chunks of language, which may range from a speaker's favourite phrases to a narrative that the speaker has told several times before. Such rehearsed chunks may indeed be complex – but they are not constructed on the spot. On the other hand, Halliday's assertion about the considerable proportion of subordinate clauses does not apply at all to the corpus of spontaneous conversations nor to the narratives analysed in Macauley (1991).

Clause combining and intonation

The second caveat concerns a very important property of spontaneous spoken language: pitch patterns can be used to signal when two or more clauses are integrated (if that term is not too strong) into a clause complex. This property is implicit in the marking used in the transcriptions in Zemskaja (1973), where single obliques, as in (5a,b) above, indicate that a particular utterance has not been completed by the speaker. This point is made explicitly in Fernandez (1994, pp. 95–6), who points out that intonation can signal the integration of two clauses as opposed to simple coordination or juxtaposition. Her (French) examples are in (7).

(7) a. T'auras pas de dessert | t'es pas venu avec nous.
'You won't have any dessert (because) you didn't come with us.'

b. Il n'a pas plu | le linge est sec
It hasn't rained (since) the washing is dry

A special pitch pattern signals that *t'es pas venu avec nous* and *le linge est sec* are not free-floating clauses, but are linked to the first clause in each example. Of course, the type of link – time, reason or concession – does have to be reconstructed by the addressee.

The most recent discussion of the use of intonation to signal the integration of two clauses into one clause complex is by Mithun (2009). Her paper is important not only because it lends support to Zemskaja and Fernandez (now Fernandez-Vest) but also because it brings data from Mohawk, a language far removed from Indo-European in geographical location and in syntax. Mithun (2009, pp. 58–9) gives two examples of pairs of clauses that differ in intonation. The first pair is in (8) and the second pair is in (9).

(8) a. 'Khe tóka' ioiánere Tóka' ne: iakenenhrénhawe'
I think it might be good. Maybe I should take the group in.

b. Iáh ki' teiotò:'on. ken' niaontié:ren'.
It is just not possible I could just do it there.
'It was impossible for me to deal with it.'

(9) a. Sok iáken' tahontásawen'. Wa'tkanón:wahkwe'ki: awèn:ke.
Then they say it started. It swirled this water.
'The water started swirling around.'

b. Sók nè:'etahatáhsawen'. wa'thahséntho'.
So then he began it He cried
'So then he started to cry'

In (8a) and (9a), there is a falling intonation from the beginning of the first clause/sentence to the end of the clause/sentence. At the beginning of the second clause/sentence, the intonation is reset and starts high again. In (8b) and (9b), the intonation is not reset at the beginning of the second clause. Rather there is a single intonation pattern that is high at the beginning of the first clause and then falls steadily till the end of the second clause is reached. In the second pair in particular, the single intonation pattern is reinforced by the clauses having the same subject.

Mithun (2009, p. 69) remarks that a common rhetorical pattern in Mohawk is for demonstratives to signal that further details are to follow. The example she gives is glossed 'We would go watch this; the men would play lacrosse,' which translates as 'We would go and watch the men playing lacrosse.' The cognitive integration by means of the demonstrative came to be reinforced by a single intonation pattern over the two clauses, as in (8b) and (9b). Fernandez (1994, p. 15) observes that discourse particles play an important role in the presentation of disconnected phrases as a coherent message. In the Finnish example in (10), the particles connect chunks of syntax that do not by themselves make up a clause conveying a proposition. (The particles are in bold.)

(10)	**Nii**	**mut**	se	oli	**nys**	se	PIRtuaika	**sitte**	joka	paikas.
	OK	but	THAT	was	now	THAT	moonshine time	afterwards	all	sides

'After that there was illicit alcohol everywhere.'

What we see is a pattern whereby clauses are not embedded one in the other but are adjacent. They are not connected by, for example, complementizers or changes of mood; that two clauses are to be interpreted as connected is signalled by intonation or by the occurrence of a cataphoric demonstrative. Demonstratives and gestures are used to signal connections between chunks of syntax that are smaller than clauses and do not combine to form a clause. These are characteristics of spontaneous spoken language; what written language has is highly integrated syntactic structures.

Studying spoken language in natural settings

Two ways of investigating the syntax of (spontaneous) spoken language are mentioned earlier. One is the analysis of corpuses of spoken language, working both with the transcription and with the audio recording (and even the video recording, if one is available, though there is a real danger of drowning in data). The recordings can be of many varieties of spoken language: dialogues and monologues; informal conversation with family or friends; discussions with colleagues, shop assistants, students and so on; lectures; task-related dialogues; story-telling and many other text types. This is the method used by, for example, Sornicola (1981), Blanche-Benveniste (1991), Thompson (1991), Chafe (1980) and Miller and Weinert (1998/2009). The second way is to focus on specific structures or even specific lexical items and collect information experimentally. This is the approach of Dabrowska (1997) and Chipere (2009).

A third method is also experimental, but the data are collected not in controlled conditions but in natural settings and in connection with real communicative practices. The investigators do not focus on specific syntactic structures exposing their subjects to variations on a theme, but information emerges about the difficulties speakers of English have dealing with formal written texts. This provides a context for the analysis of structural properties such as those sketched earlier and described in more detail in Miller and Weinert (1998/2009), Blanche-Benveniste (1991) and so on. A classic example is Heath (1983). She describes how the workforce in the Trackton mills in North Carolina go through school, learn to read and write but lose their competence in written English by never having to use it in life outside the classroom. She describes how administrative staff at the mills would read out official documents to the workers, whether agreements relating to insurance or to loans. When members of the African American community in Trackton received letters from the local authorities, say concerning children going to school or going for medical check-ups, the documents were interpreted by groups of adults, and crucial input came from adults who had already experienced such events and were able to relate their experiences to otherwise mysterious parts of the local authority texts. One set of people in Trackton had no difficulty with complex written texts: the people with post-school education working in the professions or in management at the mill or elsewhere and so on. The account in Heath fits with and indirectly supports the findings of Dabrawska and Chipere.

Another investigation (carried out in the United Kingdom) lends even stronger support to Dabrowska and Chipere. In the summer and autumn of 1997 and in the winter of 1997–98 Rebecca Philpott carried out research into communication at the factory where she had a summer job. The research was written up as Philpott (1998). Philpott investigated the attempts by the management to keep the workforce informed about events in the factory, the current trading position and forthcoming developments. The information was conveyed via presentations by a member of the management team. The core of each presentation was a set of overhead projection slides; additional notes were written by the factory manager and read aloud by the presenter. The text on the slides and all the additional notes were read verbatim, to guard against discrepancies in the information given out at the different briefing sessions.

The language of the text was highly condensed partly because of the limited space on the slides and partly because of the use of technical business language. The condensing was manifested principally in very dense NPs, as in the sample overhead slide in (11). The names of products have been replaced by dummy labels.

(11) The warm weather continued to depress soup sales.
X sales were 5% above the April 1996 level but year to date are 7% down on last year and 15% below a datum which assumed a major boost from the relaunch.
Canned Vegetables sales were better in April, 1% above last year, so year-to-date are 13% down on last year and 6% below datum.
While X is currently being relaunched with a new pack design, the full boost to volume will come towards the end of the year because of difficulties in developing sufficiently impactful advertising. Our plans for the year had assumed heavy advertising from April, so there has been a substantial reduction in the sales forecast. Partially offsetting this is a major sampling exercise.

depress soup sales is a technical phrase, not a use of *depress* which is found in non-business contexts. *year to date* is likewise a technical term, along with *datum. a datum which assumed a major boost* is highly technical and formal. The lexical item *assume* with this technical sense occurs again in *Our plans for the year had assumed heavy advertising.* Other awkward phrases are *the full boost to volume* and *developing sufficiently impactful advertising* and *a substantial reduction in the sales forecast.* The final sentence is an example of a relatively rare construction with the complement of *is* in sentence-initial position, *Partially offsetting this.* (This looks like a Progressive, but the structure is unacceptable in the normal word order: **A major sampling exercise is offsetting this.*)

Another overhead slide had a *respectively* construction. These are never easy to interpret.

(12) Sales and profits are down about 5% and 10% respectively on the first four months compared to the equivalent period last year

Because Philpott was young, had been working at the factory and knew many of the workers, was sociable and, being 'just a student', was not perceived as a threat or as some kind of spy, she was able to persuade a good number of workers to take part in an interview. As part of the interview, she took an excerpt from the overhead slides and asked the subjects to answer questions on its content. The excerpt is in (13).

(13) X sales were 5% above the April 1996 level but year to date are 7% down on last year and 15% below a datum which assumed a major boost from the relaunch.

Philpott asked her subjects to say which of the following four propositions were true.

- Sales of the product are above the level they were at in April 1996
- Sales are down on the same time last year
- Sales are currently below the projected target
- This target was set, thinking that sales would be improved because of a relaunch of the product

The interview revealed a high level of discomfort with formal written language and its interpretation. More than half the subjects did not even attempt the exercise. Of those who did, some got none of the propositions correct. Some subjects, however, did gain high scores, including full marks. Many subjects took a long time to complete the test, with the average time being just over 10 minutes. An unexpected obstacle was that many subjects paraphrased the sentences ideally in speech, but refused to write this version down and even the most verbose subjects asked for confirmation that what they had written was correct. (Some men provided further evidence for the by now well-known phenomenon of women in many households being the users of written language. During the interview, the men commented that their wives always did the writing at home.) Other questions asked the subjects whether particular excerpts were more abstract or hypothetical than ordinary language. Terms such as *abstract*, *hypothetical* and *ordinary language* simply sowed confusion. To sum up, Philpott's research showed that not only are complex structures avoided in spontaneous speech but many speakers (of English in her study but her findings apply generally) cannot interpret them in writing and indeed avoid writing any texts at all.

How (written) language becomes complex

The above account of language code, communication and a factory workforce is a valuable reminder that language codes do not become elaborate and complex all by themselves. The users of language codes elaborate them for particular practices and the elaboration may affect syntax and vocabulary. All this is well-known to sociolinguists concerned with standard and non-standard language. As recounted to students taking introductory courses in sociolinguistics, where a number of varieties co-exist in a political unit, one variety is selected as the standard and is codified and elaborated for particular purposes. The reality is that whatever group of speakers has political, military and economic power use their variety and impose its use in formal, public situations. The variety begins to be analysed and described; the describers often do their work with a view to 'improving' the language and creating standard grammatical norms. Particular groups of users elaborate the language for particular purposes such as the keeping of records, the writing of laws, the language of different types of poetry and so on.

Deutscher (2000) contributes to the view of Guiraud (1963) and Palmer (1954) with his work on Akkadian, a language whose written tradition lasted for 2,000 years. He demonstrates that the earlier written records contain simple non-recursive structures but none that we would recognize as complement clauses. Finite complement clauses emerged slowly, possibly to satisfy communicative needs in Babylonian society. Sampson (2009, pp. 16–17) states that it would be impossible to provide an adequate Old Chinese translation for the opening sentence of the United Nations Charter. That sentence has an extremely involved syntax with several layers of subordination, and Old Chinese did not have such syntactic devices. Modern Chinese, a language with an extremely long tradition of being written and elaborated, can be used to provide an adequate translation. Sampson (2009, p. 16) refers to Gil's contention that official, formal written Indonesian is to some extent an artificial construct, created to mirror the logical properties of European languages.

Complex written language, then, is developed by groups of users collaborating in particular tasks and language practices and emerges gradually. The gradual emergence of complex, elaborated sentence structure in written language has been observed for various languages with long traditions of writing.

The development of sentence structure is discussed, for example, by Palmer and Guiraud. Palmer (1954, p. 119) remarks that complex sentences in written Latin prose were consciously developed by generations of writers and that the resulting body of rhetorical conventions had to be taught. Once the vernacular Romance languages had broken away from Latin, the organization of clauses into sentences had to be established for each vernacular Romance language as it began to be used as a vehicle for prose literature. Guiraud (1963, p. 113) observes that the Old French literary language was very close to the spoken language, having an essentially paratactic organization of clauses into larger units. Such a syntax 'n'a jamais eu l'entraînement ou la pratique qui l'auraient pliée à l'expression d'une pensée élaborée; elle ignore l'articulation logique de la démonstration scientifique ou les méandres de l'argumentation philosophique'. ['has never had the training or practice that would have formed it to the expression of elaborated thought; it is unaware of the logical structure of scientific argument or the meanderings of philosophical discussion'. JM]

It is significant that Guiraud mentions the uses to which language is put by literate human beings; French syntax did not develop a complex, hypotactic organization of clauses by some mysterious process but through the conscious efforts of certain literate people to convert French into an instrument suitable for the purposes served by Classical Latin.

It must be emphasized that neither Palmer nor Guiraud suggests that the development of subordinate clauses was subsequent to the development of written Latin and written French. Rather they allude to the organization of several or many clauses into a sentence and the way in which the conventions governing this organization were developed by the users of a given written language. They also allude to the special development of language by scientists for the accurate description of scientific data, experiments and theories, which is quite in accord with the comments by Ong (1982) on the role of the Royal Society in Britain in the late seventeenth century in encouraging the emergence of a special scientific language and the logical presentation of hypotheses, data and conclusions. Jocelyne Fernandez-Vest (personal communication) points out that a similar observation can be made about the Old Swedish legal language, which was based on the paratactic organization of clauses in the spoken language. Over time, this legal language was elaborated and provided with the hypotactic organization of clauses into sentences typical of elaborated written language.

Two general points come out of the above. The first is simply that Jackendoff (1993, p. 32) is mistaken when he asserts that 'the earliest written documents already display the full expressive variety and grammatical complexity of modern languages.' The earliest Sumerian records, for instance, are of booty, grain stores, royal possessions, floods, astronomical observations and so on (Goody, 1977, pp. 90–9). That is, they are lists, and lists offer little opportunity for elaborating syntax. Ong (1982) sets out the properties of the language of the Old Testament that indicate that the syntax and discourse organization of this collection of texts have many characteristics of the texts produced in oral societies. Crucially, no elaborated syntax. (Sampson, 2009, pp. 6–7 reports that his reference to Ong produced a furore on the *Linguist List*, with claims that Old Hebrew had much more in the way of clause subordination than Ong imagined. Ong, however, was not making any claims about Old Hebrew in general but about a particular set of texts.) Jackendoff's assertion is also countered by the work of Palmer and Guiraud referred to above.

The second point concerns language as a social and cultural phenomenon and as a psychological (and biological) phenomenon. Pinker (1994, p. 18) declares that language is no more a cultural invention than upright posture and is not a cultural artefact that we learn the way we learn to tell the time. The declaration contains a large grain of truth in that the processes by which humans handle sequences of symbols can certainly be regarded, in Pinker's words, as a distinct piece of the biological make-up of our brains, but the various genres, registers and their corresponding syntax and vocabulary are cultural artefacts (and in particular, the elaborated syntax that marks off written language from spontaneous spoken language). These have been consciously developed and elaborated by certain users of written language and developed in different ways in different cultures. Examples are the longer sentences, almost the equivalent of paragraphs, written by Pepys and Jane Austen, say, compared with the shorter sentences of modern novelists such as Penelope Lively and Susan Hill. (See the discussion in Miller and Weinert, (2009), pp. 41–5). Modern texts of all sorts offer examples of text sentences that do not contain a finite verb; Miller and Weinert present examples from French and Russian and see pp. 25–26 for examples of text sentences from contemporary English. Also supporting the idea that language is in (possibly large) part a social phenomenon are, again, the researches of Palmer and Guiraud, Gil's argument about the conscious development of formal, written Indonesian (see above) and the comments of Lewis (1953) that a tighter, more 'European' sentence structure was replacing the rambling structure of traditional Turkish written sentences, made possible by the many non-finite nominal constructions. A more accurate statement would have been that influential and probably younger users of written Turkish were adopting a new type of sentence structure.

The above paragraphs deal with the elaboration of syntax as a conscious social activity among influential groups of writers. Mair and Leech (2006, p. 336) propose that an opposing language practice (also consciously adopted) is now reducing the degree of elaboration in the written syntax of English. One example of change in language practices is what Mair and Leech (2006, p. 336) call 'colloquialization', the use in written language of features associated with spoken language: semi-modals – *you want to do it this way*, the *get* passive, *that* or zero relative clauses, and singular *they*. None of these is new; in fact, the last three are attested in the early seventeenth century. Some of them have their own functions and meanings: singular *they* enables writers to avoid the clumsy *he or she*, the *get* passive is dynamic and is frequently, but by no means exclusively, used for adverse events and *that* is the norm in restrictive relative clauses in American English. Not all these changes represent a reduction in elaboration; a long passive is equally complex whether it contains *be* or *get*. But relative clauses with zero or *that* complementizers are less complex than ones with *wh* (see the discussion of relative clauses on pp. 122–127), and the use of *they* enables writers to get rid of awkward phrases such as *he or she* or *his or hers*.

Complexity of grammar is an intricate topic that connects directly with the contrast between spontaneous spoken language and formal written language and with the controversial topic of linguistic competence and whether all the native speakers of a given language have the same level of competence. The contrast between spontaneous spoken language and written language is generally taken as demonstrated. The question of equality of competence is left open, but it is clear that speakers who do not have long exposure to written language cannot deal with its structures when they are listening to a text. Amount of exposure to written language is one of the central issues in the following chapter on first language acquisition and how quickly children acquire a knowledge of their native language.

12 First Language Acquisition

Chapter Outline

This final chapter offers a critical account of theories of first language acquisition. From pp. 2–11 it picks up the discussion of what syntax is (descriptive syntax vs theory of the language faculty) and from the previous chapter it picks up the topic of language complexity. The central idea is that the Chomskyan theory of first language acquisition is not adequate because it does not take into account the characteristics of spontaneous spoken language, which is what children are exposed to in large measure, and it does not reckon with the properties of written language, the nature of written texts and the way in which children arrive at some command of writing and reading. A more satisfactory theory of language acquisition looks more likely to emerge from the approach advocated by researchers such as Tomasello.

There are five strands to the discussion:

- the age by which children have acquired what knowledge of their native language, with particular attention to literacy in the broadest sense;
- the ideas of poverty of stimulus and negative evidence;
- the projection onto children (and adult speakers) of the intricate analyses devised by analysts (i.e. analysts working with any generative model) to handle magna-syntax, from the simplest, most frequent structures to the most complex and rare;
- the frequency of fixed or semi-fixed phrases
- the acquisition of language in context.

Boeckx (2006, p. 2, fn1) bemoans the 'sad situation' in which not everybody accepts the hypothesis that he and many others consider demonstrated beyond all doubt: that humans could not acquire their native language unless their linguistic ability were supported by 'some innate component'. Boeckx does not argue the case in detail, 'merely pointing [out] that the arguments raised against an innate language faculty are extremely weak and very often incoherent (see, for example, Cowie 1999).' Boeckx' comments are misplaced, since there is general agreement among linguists and psycholinguists that children require some sort of innate faculty to acquire language. Where people diverge is over the properties of the innate faculty: is it richly endowed with information about universal constraints on possible syntactic structures and co-referential relations? Is it simply the ability to recognize recurrent bundles of stimuli (of whatever sort), to build hypotheses about the interpretation of the bundles in terms of categories and to test the hypotheses against more data?

Tomasello (2003, pp. 3–4) suggests that, while children do not have the Chomskyan innate language faculty, they do have considerably more than the basic mechanisms of simple association and blind induction for the learning of patterns. He attributes two important sets of skills to children, the ability to read the intentions of others and the ability to find patterns in the stimuli they receive. Young children quickly come to follow the attention and gesturing of other persons to distant objects and events, to direct the attention of others to distant objects and events and to learn the intentional acts of others, including their communicative acts underlain by communicative intentions. They also have the ability to form perceptual and conceptual categories of similar objects and events, to form sensory-motor schemas from recurrent patterns of perception and action; to analyse the distribution of various kinds of perceptual and behavioural sequences, and to create analogies across two or more complex wholes, based on the similar functional roles of some elements in those differing wholes.

The acquisition of meaning is likewise to be grounded in experience. Tomasello (2003, p. 54) suggests that whatever representations underlie children's use of relational words and verbs can be specified in terms of space, time, causality and objects (and perhaps possession). These are all concepts that can be constructed by young children from their own experience. For instance, the action of giving can be conceptualized as a sequence of steps: a person may be co-located with or possess an object but someone else comes to be co-located with or possess that object. This view of how abstract meanings are constructed on the basis of concrete relational meanings is eminently compatible with the localist and Cognitive Linguistic analysis of case relations, aspect and so on, mentioned on p. 215, which is based on general properties of syntax, morphology and meaning across languages.

The approach outlined by Tomasello underpins this account of spoken and written language and the account in Miller and Weinert (2009). Since our focus here is on the properties of spoken and written language, the contrast between Tomasello's approach and the Chomskyan approach will not be explored further, but one item from Boeckx (2006, p. 8) requires a comment. Boeckx describes Minimalism as asking to what extent the architecture of previous generative models follows from general properties of optimal, computationally efficient systems. He draws a parallel between Minimalism and modern theoretical physics and declares that the minimalist programme has a particularly strong commitment to the Galilean vision of natural phenomena and theory construction: 'That is, minimalists endorse the belief (held by all major proponents of modern science, from Kepler to Einstein) that nature is the realization of the simplest conceivable mathematical ideas, and the idea that a theory should be more highly valued if it "give[s] us a sense that nothing could be changed"'. [The quote is from Weinberg (2001, p. 39).] The trouble is that the generally received view has been that language is not an optimal, computationally efficient system but a system with a great deal of redundancy. And it is all very well having a theory that gives the sense that nothing could be changed but if that theory fails to relate in any convincing way to the properties and the acquisition of spoken language, and if it fails to take into account the differences between spoken and written language, the Galilean vision requires that it be revised or even abandoned.

How long does it take children to acquire their native language? Pinker (1994, p. 44) refers to 'the third year of life during which children suddenly begin to speak in fluent sentences, respecting most of the fine points of their community's spoken language'. What constructions are included in a community's spoken language is not specified, but later in the book, Pinker (1994, p. 273) declares that it is safe to say that all languages are acquired with equal ease before the child turns four, except for constructions that are rare, are used predominantly in written language or are mentally taxing, such as *The horse that the elephant kicked kissed the pig.* This view is standard in publications on Principles and Parameters and Minimalism. For instance, Adger (2003, p. 8) follows Pinker in stating that most children have a command over the core structures of their language by the time they are three. He supplies the examples in (1a,b), which were produced by a child at the age of 3 years and 2 months

(1) a. Can I put my head in the mailbox so the mailman can know where I are and put me in the mailbox?
(2) b. Can I keep the screwdriver just like a carpenter keep the screwdriver?

The difficulty with Pinker's statement is that the syntax learned after the age of four is presented as an exception, but the exception is enormous. It includes gapping and accusative-and-infinitive structures, full gerunds and free participles, WH relative clauses, certain types of adverbial clause, such as clauses of concession, complex NPs, particularly of the sort found in formal writing, and the large numbers of Greco-Latinate verbs with their peculiar syntax. (See Miller and Weinert, 2009, pp. 81–132 for the syntax of written and spoken language and pp. 133–89 for NPs in written and spoken language.)

The difficulty with Adger's examples in (1) and (2) is that they are relevant data only on the assumption that all humans have the same linguistic competence. If that assumption is not accepted (see Sampson, 2009), we must ask why it is legitimate to generalize from one child to all children on the basis of a couple of examples. Adger does not define what he means by 'core structures'; a definition or at least a list is essential, given the account of relative clauses on pp. 104–106, which shows that it can be tricky deciding what counts as a single construction. In earlier models of Chomskyan generative grammar, the core grammar of a language consisted of the constructions based on what were taken to be the innate principles and parameters of Universal Grammar, which included the constructions subject to constraints on movement. wh relative clauses are in this set of constructions, but wh relative clauses are typical of written language and it looks as though there are many wh relative clause constructions, not just a single over-arching one.

By what age have children acquired their native language?

Haegeman (1991, p. 16) says 'By the age of six a child exposed to English will have constructed the grammar of his language ... [However] we go on learning new words throughout our lives. In addition, we also learn certain less usual constructions of the language. These exceptional or marked patterns of the language are not taken to be part of the core grammar'. It is certainly true that children acquire a large range of syntactic structures and vocabulary by the time they are four, but there remains a vast range of written syntax, derivational morphology and vocabulary which children still have to master and which are neither trivial exceptions to the general grammar nor rare and exceptional patterns. They constitute a large mass of material that children learn over a number of years, that children acquire at different rates, that children typically do not command until the final year of secondary education or the first year of higher education or even later and that many children do not acquire at all.

Some researchers have looked at the knowledge of English displayed by schoolchildren. Perera (1984) provides a mass of data, which has not been taken into account by any proponents of the Chomskyan view of first language acquisition. Her data was presented in Miller and Weinert (2009, pp. 397–8) and are reproduced here.

i. studies have shown that only half of a set of ten year olds could accurately interpret the structure Subject–Verb–Second Object–Direct Object as in *We showed her the book*;
ii. eleven year olds regularly use adverbs in verb phrases, as in *have been always trying*, but six year olds rarely do;
iii. the sequence Determiner–Noun–Prepositional Phrase is rare between the ages of five and twelve;
iv. the ability to handle a range of pre- and post nominal modifiers is only reached about age fifteen or sixteen;
v. apart from set phrases such as *mum and dad*, co-ordinated Noun Phrases are not used extensively before age five and only become frequent between the ages of eight and thirteen; unsurprisingly, since speakers avoid complex subject Noun Phrases, the earliest coordinated Noun Phrases function as Direct Object;
vi. concealed negatives are difficult – only 44% of a sample of seven year olds understood the sentence *Tom's mother was anything but pleased*, only 58% understood *If only David had known, the dog was quite tame,* and only 38% understood *Mary's dress was neither new nor pretty*;
vii. the full passive appears late in children's speech – one study found that only 30% of a sample of eleven year olds used a full passive;
viii. children under eleven do not use finite or non-finite clauses as Subject;
ix. WH complements of indirect speech may have the word order of interrogatives as in *I can't remember what was it about* – as opposed to *I can't remember what it was about*. [Perera treats this as an error but see the discussion on pp. 4–6 and pp. 18–20.]

x. the verbs that take finite complement clauses belong to a limited set - mainly *tell*, *know*, *show*;
xi. in one study, free relative clauses after verbs like *ask*, as in *Ask Helen which book to read*, were misunderstood by 30% of a sample of nineteen year olds;
xii. adverbial clauses of time, reason and condition are found in children's speech, but adverbial clauses of result, place, manner and concession are much rarer;
xiii. even when children can use various adverbial clauses of time, they do not always understand the relationship between the main clause and adverbial clause;
xiv. one study found that only 40% of a sample of nine year olds used relative clauses in subject noun phrases;
xv. primary schoolchildren generally do not use relative clauses introduced by *whom*, *whose* or preposition plus a relative pronoun, as in *the shop in which we bought it*.

(xv) confirms our discussion of relative clauses on pp. 104–106, but it also shows that by age six, contrary to Haegeman's statement, children have not mastered wh relatives, which are part of Chomskyan core grammar. In fact, Perera's work in schools shows that most children up to the age of 12 do not use these wh constructions. (iii), (iv) and (xiv) are compatible with the findings of Biber that in informal spoken language NPs are very simple. A look at the age ranges is instructive: children aged 6 and 11 typically cannot handle complex NPs, but children reach the age of 16 before they can produce and interpret complex NPs. (x) is an indication of a characteristic that is now familiar: constructions that would be freely generated by rule in a generative grammar of English are in children's speech and writing more like templates that allow a minimum amount of manoeuvring. Point (xii) accords with the types of adverbial found in spontaneous spoken English by Miller and Weiner (2009).

Perera collected data from a large sample of primary-school children and secondary-school students and many studies, such as the one by Crain and Nakayama referred to on pp. 104–106, collect data from smaller sets of subjects. Intensive work on the language of individual speakers (in this case, children) is also valuable, since it gives a view in depth that complements the broad but superficial perspective offered by large samples. Carr (2007, p. 674) reports that the theory of language, which he calls Radical Internalism, is hard to reconcile with the linguistic competence of an 8-year-old child, bilingual in French and English, whose language development Carr was following in detail. Radical Internalism, essentially the Chomskyan theory, takes language to be an innately endowed, specifically linguistic module in the mind/brain.

Language has a reality independent of languages and is universal, ranging over all individuals with the relevant innate endowment.

The 8-year old child studied by Carr had not mastered the following apparently basic points of French grammar:

- the use of the complementiser *ce que* 'that which', as in *Je sais ce qu'il a dit* 'I know that which he has said, I know what he said'.
- the use of the subjunctive. The present subjunctive is required in certain subordinate clauses in spoken and written French but the past subjunctive is a characteristic of formal written French.
- the future tense.

According to Carr the lack of mastery of the above points is not related to the child's bilingualism; his teachers report that his control of French is on a par with that of his monolingual peers. Carr (2007, p. 675) argues that language acquisition, contrary to the beliefs of Chomsky, Pinker, Haegeman, Adger and Chomskyans in general, is slow because of the complexity of language. (He refers to Dabrowska's research on the language acquisition of a boy with Polish as his native language. The boy did not have adequate mastery of the genitive case until age 10, the genitive being a central case in Polish.) His observations lead him to the opinion that some speakers never master all the complexity, especially the dense subordinate-clause structures. This latter view is entirely compatible with the research of Philpott and Brice Heath. (See pp. 230–232.) Carr's observations also lead him to the conclusion that different children take different paths to language acquisition. This variation does not sit with the Chomskyan theory, since innate endowment is said to be invariant across the species. (The variation is implicit in the neglected work of Anne Peters (1983), who proposed that many children do not acquire small linguistic units, which they then combine into larger ones but instead use large units as a whole for specific purposes, learning gradually how the large units break down into smaller ones.)

Poverty of stimulus

Chomsky (1986a, pp. xxv–xxvii) sets out the essentials of the Chomskyan theory of first language acquisition. What Chomsky calls 'Plato's problem' is to explain how humans know so much about their native language, given that the evidence available to them is so sparse. Applied to language, the problem is the poverty of stimulus: children learn their native language from allegedly meagre, degenerate data; learning it, furthermore, without instruction or negative evidence, that is, evidence that particular sequences of morphs and words are ungrammatical. The data to which children are exposed, so the Chomskyan theory runs, do not provide anything like enough evidence for children to work out the correct and complex structures which they nonetheless use unerringly, applying computationally complex structure-dependent rules. The solution to the problem, in the Chomskyan theory of first language acquisition, is to assume that humans are endowed with an innate language faculty that determines the operation of various constraints on possible syntactic structures without exposure to E-language, or external linguistic data. Some minor, variable, properties are switched on by exposure to whatever language a particular child is acquiring. These essentials continue to be an integral component of the Minimalist Program, whose ambition, according to Boeckx (2006, p. 10), is to construct explicit models of the three factors influencing language design: the genetic component (the innate language faculty), experience (exposure to specific E-language), and the general properties of well-designed, optimal systems.

The line taken here is that the concept of poverty of stimulus and the claim that children are exposed to meagre, degenerate data are unsustainable. This becomes quite obvious when we take into account the properties of spontaneous spoken language, the properties of (formal) written language, the ways in which children gain knowledge of spoken and written language and the ages at which they do so. On the last point, we simply refer readers to the previous section. Children do not learn the majority of the syntactic structures of their native language by age three or age six and many constructions are not mastered till the late teens. Perera (1984), Carr (2007) and Dabrowska (2005) supply solid evidence that language learning takes place quite slowly.

What children typically acquire in the first three years of life is knowledge of the spontaneous spoken variety of their native language. (There are of course children with parents who read stories and rhymes to them every day. Such children pick up words and phrases and even whole clauses that might be quite untypical of everyday speech. We return to this topic below.) As argued on pp. 220–222 in connection with language complexity, and as described in detail in Miller and Weinert (2009), Zemskaja (1973), Blanche-Benveniste (1991) and many others, the syntax of spontaneous spoken language is very simple. Miller and Weinert (2009) proposed, possibly controversially, that the extendability and complexity of clauses and phrases is severely limited.

On the basis of the data they examined – which was analogous to data examined in the above references – the following statements apply.

i. A subject NP contains at most one out of the set {determiner, quantifier, numeral} together with a full noun; alternatively, a subject NP contains a pronoun;
ii. Other NPs may contain at most a determiner/numeral/quantifier/two adjectives and a noun. The noun may be followed by one prepositional phrase or one relative clause. (But see Perera's points (iii), (v), (xiv), (xv).)
iii. A main clause may be preceded or followed by only one adverbial clause, of time, reason or condition.
iv. The main verb in a main clause may be followed by only one complement clause, and the verb governing the complement clause is one of a very small set – see Perera's point (x).
v. Subordinate clauses are not embedded in other subordinate clauses

The structures are so simple that they can be acquired via straightforward learning mechanisms. But how degenerate are the spoken data that children are exposed to? Of course, speakers suffer from slips of the tongue that result in grammatical infelicities, Spoonerisms, choice of wrong lexical item (usually connected in sound or sense to the one the speaker should have chosen); the evidence is that in informal circumstances, talking to close family or friends about uncomplicated topics, speakers do not produce degenerate data. That is, they successfully perform the rules of the grammar of whatever variety they speak of whatever language. The language of the various databases of informal conversation examined by Miller and Weinert (2009) is not degenerate. Only once in the 250,000 words of the Miller-Brown Corpus of spontaneous conversation is there a serious breakdown of syntax – interestingly, at a point where the speaker is trying to express a complex set of conditions by means of relatively complex syntax. The relevant excerpt is in (3).

(3) a26 no if we can get louise i mean her mother and father louise's parents would give us they've got a big car and keep the mini for the week but louise isn't too keen on the idea so
m39 what on driving the
ms38 no because louise is frightened to drive
a27 but she likes the big car better than the mini actually because the austin it's got power steering she finds the mini difficult to drive

Miller–Brown Corpus, conversation 12

Presumably <a26> wanted to say something along the lines of 'if we could get louise's mother and father to give us their big car and take the Mini for the week [that would be good], but louise isn't too keen on the idea so [we're stuck with the Mini]. The other participants in the conversation do not notice the disjointed syntax, the conversation continues without hesitations and <a> has her syntax back in order for her next turn, which is also relatively complex in content. In fact, JM did not notice the disjointed syntax when listening to the recording for the first time but only when he came to transcribe it.

Labov (1972, p. 203) goes so far as to say that the ungrammaticality of everyday speech is a myth. In his empirical studies, 75 per cent of utterances corresponded directly to well-formed sentences. That figure rose to 98 per cent when cases of ellipsis were excluded, along with instances of stammering and false starts. Labov says that a great many other linguists have confirmed his view that when non-academic speakers are talking about subjects they know well, such as personal experiences, only 10 per cent of utterances need to be edited to qualify as corresponding to well-formed sentences. When speakers try to express complex ideas in impromptu talk, such as conversations at conferences, syntactic structure can go awry, but children do not participate in such gatherings.

The other side of the coin is that the grammar of written language can be very complex and dense. As Biber (1988) has shown, there are many types of written text, with academic monographs and papers among the most complex. The language of books intended to be read to 3-year-olds is quite simple, while the language of books intended for older children can be quite complex. But this type of written language, unlike spoken language, is not evanescent and is certainly not degenerate, since it is carefully written, scrutinized by editors and checked by copy editors. Children's books are not read once and discarded. Well, they can be, but many children read books over and over again till they have large chunks of text in their memory. (And children typically complain instantly if a tired parent tries to skip a paragraph or turn two pages at once.)

Fixed phrases

Children who are read to have phrases and clauses in their memory and can in turn use these chunks or bits of the chunks. These might be called idiosyncratic formulae. The pervasiveness of fixed phrases has slowly been discovered over the last twenty-five years. Bolinger (1976) was already suggesting that ready-made chunks of unanalysed language are as important as productive rules, and even earlier Lyons (1968, p. 416) wrote 'There is a good deal of our everyday use of language which is quite properly described in "behaviourist" terms, and can be attributed to our "acting out" of particular "roles" in the maintenance of socially-prescribed, "ritualistic" patterns of behaviour.' Lyons related fixed phrases to the acting out of everyday routines of interaction and to speech acts, but Peters (1983) saw basic first language acquisition as involving, in large measure, chunks of language learned whole, and Pawley and Syder (1983, p. 209) argued that any speaker of English has stored in memory a large number of phrases and clauses. They suggest that ordinary, mature English speakers probably know several hundreds of thousands of sentence-length expressions: examples are *I thought better of it*, *It doesn't bear thinking about*, *Think twice before you VP*, *I (just) can't think straight* and so on (Pawley and Syder, 1983, p. 213). Pawley and Syder observe that such prefabricated patterns are easily encoded and permit the speaker to attend to the task of constructing the larger discourse. Equally, they lessen the decoding burden for listeners. These advantages are illustrated in (4), an excerpt from a discussion programme broadcast by Scottish Television.

(4) Presenter 1 — you said that you know there was a time when you thought you might leave him and that he had a drink problem I mean do you take any responsibility for your marriage going the way it did?

Roseanne 1 — well obviously it takes two to tango but ehm I went to the Marriage Guidance Council he wouldn't go I went to Al Anon we went to one meeting together and to Alcoholics whatever it was counselling session and he came out that woman's bloody daft

Presenter 2 — . . .

Roseanne 2 — I said that woman is a professional and eh you know we kept trying to make a go of it and be pleasant we went quite a few holidays together we had a good lifestyle but he just seemed to

Fixed phrases are *had a drink problem*, *it takes two to tango*, *counselling session*, *is a professional*, *make a go of it* and *had a good lifestyle*. *Had a drink problem* is a euphemism for *was dependent on alcohol* or *was suffering from alcoholism* or *was an alcoholic*. It has the light verb *had*. and the everyday nouns *drink* and *problem*. *it takes two to tango* is a convenient shorthand for complex expressions conveying a complex idea: when a problem has to be solved in a situation involving two people, both persons have to be reasonable, make compromises and cooperate. If one of the persons fails to do this, there is no agreement and no positive action. *is a professional* is shorthand for '*has had a proper training and gained a qualification and has experience of analyzing a given type of situation and offering advice.* Moreover professionals conduct themselves in an appropriate manner during interviews with clients and may have to follow a code of conduct. Professionals provide objective and accurate assessments of what needs to be done'. *had a good lifestyle* is shorthand for 'had sufficient income to have a solid house, good furniture, an expensive car, to visit the cinema, theatre or clubs and go on regular holidays (overseas, in the UK context). *to make a go of it* in this context is to work together in an unsatisfactory situation to keep the relationship alive by overlooking unpleasant incidents and trying to cajole one's partner into a reasonable course of action. These examples illustrate very neatly how fixed phrases enable speaker and listener to deal with complex ideas in straightforward language, thereby reducing their cognitive load and keeping the discussion flowing.

Cruse (1986, pp. 37–48) demonstrated that while the syntax of idioms is not completely frozen, it has very limited flexibility. Idioms are not easily interrupted by adverbs – Cruse cites the doubtful examples *?Arthur has a chip, apparently, on his shoulder* and *?We took them, after a shaky start, to the cleaners*; a WH cleft highlighting an entire idiom is fine – *What John did was pull his sister's leg* – but a WH cleft highlighting the object of *pull* will not do – **What John pulled was his sister's leg.* The latter example is of course quite acceptable in its literal interpretation. In the same spirit, Nattinger and Decarrico (1992) developed the notion of 'lexical phrases', prefabricated chunks of language which come partially or completely assembled, but open to analysis by grammatical rules. Wray (2002) demonstrates the central role of fixed phrases in normal adult language, aphasia, and first and second language acquisition.

Fixed phrases are very important for theories of first (and indeed second) language acquisition because they raise questions about a central tenet of Chomskyan generative grammar mentioned at the beginning of this chapter, that children acquire computationally complex structure-dependent rules. The enormous number and variety of fixed phrases suggest an alternative view: much of language is formulaic and imitation, combined with the learning and manipulation of formulas, plays an important part in first language acquisition. This alternative view is supported by three developments in recent work: research into the acquisition of language that highlights the role of imitation and formulas; recent syntactic research focusing on the power of lexical items and the central position of the lexicon in generative models and recent syntactic research focusing on units that are larger than single words but have to be analysed and learned as single units.

We return to fixed phrases. Earlier we examined public fixed phrases, that is, fixed phrases that are known to many if not most speakers of English and are listed in dictionaries and collections of idioms. There are also private or semi-private fixed phrases, that is, sequences of morphemes and words that are not idioms but are used over and over again by adult speakers as well as by children learning their first language or a second language. An interesting example comes from Blanche-Benveniste (1991), interesting not only in being French but in being an instance of those apparently mundane constructions, relative clauses. Blanche-Benveniste applies the label 'fixed phrase' or 'formula' to examples containing the French pronoun *lequel*, which can function as an interrogative or a relative pronoun. Consider (5).

(5) a Tu choisiras lequel?
you will-choose which-one?
b vous avez une canalisation de gaz sur laquelle il y a un doute
you have a pipe of gas on which there-is a doubt

Examples such as (5b) are said by Blanche-Benveniste to be used by speakers who are highly educated and/or used to public speaking. Most speakers, however, use the pronoun in a small set of formulas built round a small set of lexical items, as in (6).

(6) a. le milieu, le groupe, dans lequel je vis
the milieu the group in which I live
b. la mentalité, l'ambiance, dans laquelle il a été élevé
the outlook, the ambiance in which he was brought-up
c. la raison pour laquelle il le fait
the reason for which he it is-doing
d. le secteur dans lequel il intervient
the sector in which he is-intervening

The significance of large numbers of fixed phrases is that they point to a larger role in language processing for storage and retrieval. It has long been recognized (see, for example, Crick, 1979) that there are serious limitations on processing capacity compared with storage. (One major development in computing hardware over the past twenty years has been the application of nano-technology to produce smaller and smaller chips with greater and greater capacity for the storage of information.) Human beings have great facility for memorizing facts and retrieving them, but are patently not so adept at producing complex syntax impromptu in real time. (Humans differ with respect to memory capacity, speed of storage, length of storage and accuracy of retrieval from memory. A person's memory can be trained, but differences are not removed.) A model of language acquisition that gives a major role to storage of lexical items and a very large number of fixed phrases does not need to invoke a rich and powerful faculty of language.

Generative analyses and the language of children

The simple structure of clauses and phrases in spontaneous spoken language together with the fixed phrases presents a striking contrast with the examples used by Chomskyans to demonstrate the need to appeal to an innate, rich faculty of language and a Universal Grammar of intricate constraints. Boeckx (2006, pp. 23–4) wonders what data could lead children to generate examples such as (7).

(7) Will the man who is tall leave now?

The generalization, for linguists, is [Move the main clause Aux to the front]. Suppose the declarative clause were *The man who is tall will leave now.* This sentence contains two constituents that can move to the front of clauses to produce interrogatives, *is* (*The man is tall* and *Is the man tall*?) and *will* (*He will leave* and *Will he leave*?). How does the child know that in (7) *will* has to move to the front and not *is*, (8) being ungrammatical?

(8) *Is the man who tall leave now?

Boeckx argues that children could not get at the correct rule if they only used simple, well-formed bits of the language as data. But that is precisely what they hear (says Boeckx), since they do not come across incorrect examples such as (8), that is, they have no negative evidence. Boeckx comments that it is quite possible that examples like (7), though well-formed, are too complex to be part of children's linguistic input; children will simply skip over a structure that is too complex and will certainly not produce one. In other words, says Boeckx, this suggests that children do not arrive at the right rule solely on the basis of the linguistic input of the target language but are guided by some biological feature of children rather than by some property of the linguistic input.

There is another answer that does not appeal to as yet mysterious biological properties. It lies in the discussion of the NP-Clause construction on pp. 29–31. (7) is not a typical structure of spontaneous spoken language. The declarative version, *The man who is tall will leave now*, has a complex subject NP, which is very rare in spontaneous spoken language. The structure would be *The man who is tall he'll leave now*, or more likely *The guy who's tall he'll leave now*. The corresponding interrogative is *The guy who's tall will he leave now*?

Of course, children will eventually come across sentences such as (7), but they will do so when they come in contact with written language. This brings us to two crucial points. One is that children, say of three or four, listening to a story containing such interrogative and declarative sentences will either skip the material that is above their heads or interpret it on the basis of extra-linguistic context, for instance, the story up to that point and the events in the story immediately after that point. Consider the examples in (9), repeated from Miller and Weinert (2009, pp. 410–11).

(9) a. Here is a car to put in the garage
b. Oh – you've found a block to put on top of the tower
c. Here is biscuit to give to the doggie

The important property of these examples is that the interpretation is heavily supported by the extra-linguistic context. Young children taking their first steps in language have a small world and talk about events as they are on-going – often driving parents mad by stating the obvious, over and over. Children quickly learn that toy cars go into garages and that they do not go into the garages by themselves but have to be pushed in. Blocks can be put one on top of the other to form towers, and the child or its carers have to manipulate the block. Biscuits are edible, and dogs eat biscuits. That is, children can call on their knowledge of the extra-linguistic world to interpret examples such as those in (9). Even if a given child does not understand the syntax, it can pick up the crucial items *car, garage; block, tower; biscuit, doggie*. In the child's world, the relationship between the relevant entities is clear-cut. If it is not, the carer will demonstrate the relationship, and from these small beginnings the child will eventually come to complex examples, but probably not before age eight or later, depending on a given child's reading experience.

The second crucial point is that many children only come across written language in school; even children who are regularly read to and who may be able to read before they go to school have to work at written language, completing sentences, producing appropriate complete sentences, answering questions in complete sentences, circling examples of nouns, verbs, adjectives, and over a number of years learning how to produce integrated syntax, combining finite and non-finite clauses into complex sentences and learning to read and interpret such sentences. All this work involves various types of negative evidence, from suggestions as to how a given pupil's text can be rephrased and made clearer to demonstrations of how to use free participles, say, and wh relative clauses of the more intricate kind, and adverbial clauses of concession and so on. All the work on syntax is part of a bigger exercise: extending children's vocabulary and their appreciation of different types of text from poetry to the language in which scientific experiments are written up. Children are exposed to lots of negative evidence as well as positive examples of difficult syntactic structures.

Do children get any negative evidence at all before they go to school? It is generally accepted that the parents of pre-school children do correct what they consider incorrect grammar, but equally it is a truism that such young children pay no attention to corrections. On the other hand, children are forced to act if their addressees do not understand what has been said; if a simple repetition does not produce results, the grammar, and perhaps the vocabulary, has to be recast. This could be considered an indirect sort of negative evidence.

An unattractive feature of the Chomskyan approach to first language acquisition is the projection on to language learners of the principles and constraints required for the handling of magnasyntax. Models designed to generate any structure from the simplest to the most complex end up with whatever complex apparatus is necessary to generate the most complex examples. The essential point made earlier is that the complexity is irrelevant to children, who deal with spontaneous spoken language. Note too the skewing that occurs when first language acquisition theorists or specialists in generative syntax get the data wrong. This point was made on p. 5 in connection with strong and weak features in Minimalism. This is relevant to young learners, since knowledge of features is part of the Universal Grammar ascribed to them. It is also relevant in another connection; children are not exposed only to examples such as *I wondered who Medea had poisoned* and *I enquired when we could leave* but to the versions declared unacceptable by Adger (2003, p. 357), *I wondered who had Medea poisoned* and *I enquired when could we leave.* Another strong possibility is that young children do not encounter such indirect questions or, if they do, do not stop to analyse the syntax. A third possibility is that children encounter such examples only in stories and work out the meaning from the content of the story.

Horrocks (1988, p. 154) is an example of how the pervasive influence of magnasyntax leads to inappropriate adult data being cited in connection with children's language acquisition. Horrocks discusses the invented example *Graball found a new set of clients to fleece.* Horrocks wonders how children might learn that *Graball* is understood as the subject of *fleece* and *set of clients* as the object (alternatively, Agent and Patient). How could children interpret the sentence correctly without prior knowledge of principles of interpretation? If they got it wrong, how would they know that they had got it wrong? Can it really be true, he asks, that every 2-year-old has gone through a conscious process of working out what sentences of this sort might mean in principle and then discounting all but the correct interpretation?'

A first reaction might be that Horrocks' concern is misplaced, since no 2-year-olds who would pay any attention to his example. (*Clients, fleece* – only in 'Mary had a little lamb', *set*?) A second reaction is that in, say, a Mister Men book, a 3-year-old – better, a 4- or 5-year-old – might meet a sentence such as *When Mr Bump had annoyed all the people in Bluetown, he went to Greentown and found lots of other people to annoy.* As with the examples earlier involving cars and garages, biscuits and doggies, the 4- or 5-year-old can work out from the preceding story the relationship 'annoy' between Mr Bump and lots of other people.

Horrocks (1988, p. 156) discusses coordination and how young children know that questions such as *Who do you love me and, Mummy*? are odd. From a pragmatic perspective, there is good reason not to end utterances with *and. and* sets up an expectation that more information is to follow; carers who break off an utterance on *and* are probably going to say something else, or have changed their minds, and the child who finishes an utterance with *and* will be asked to supply the extra information. Typical language games run thus, with the carer asking the questions and the child giving the answers: *Who's coming to see you*? *Granny. Uhuh, and*? *Grandpa. Uhuh, and*? *Aunt Lucie* and so on. We do not need to look for purely syntactic constraints when there are perfectly good pragmatic reasons why children discover early in life that utterances should not finish with *and.*

Manzini (1990) affords a final example of magnasyntax misapplied in discussions of child language acquisition. She adduces the examples *John and*

Peter like each other's pictures and *John and Peter thought that each other's pictures were on sale.* (Examples with *each other* also feature in Maher and Groves.) These examples are central for a grammar that is to handle the syntax and semantics of *each other*, but this is not a construction that older children use, far less young children. (Of course children do use *each other*, but in examples such as *we kicked each other.*) The examples that young children hear are on the lines of *they're very like each other*, with *each* and *other* adjacent, not in a possessive construction and not in a separate clause from the their antecedent.

We have argued that various assumptions made by Chomsky and others are incorrect: that for written language it is not true that children are exposed to meagre, degenerate data; that for written language children do have access to previously presented data; that for written language children do receive overt instruction. With respect to spontaneous spoken language, the incidence of ungrammatical structures has been greatly exaggerated and the absence of overt instruction exaggerated. The structures of spontaneous spoken language, as demonstrated in Chapter 11 and elsewhere in the book, are much less complex than the structures of written language. Children do not acquire their first language in a vacuum but in a rich social environment, in a relatively limited universe where referential tasks are severely limited in scope. Given what we know about spontaneous spoken language, the hypothesis of a rich innate set of principles is too extreme; what is needed is a theory mixing hypothesis formation, rote learning and social interaction.

Appendix

Appendix 3.1

S1A-057(A) 3 How's mum and firstname1

S1A-057(B) 4 Oh they're alright I've been to see them this morning and there's a crowd of visitors there so

S1A-057(A) 6 Who was there

S1A-057(A) 7 Ah mother and father and Mother and brother and firstname2 and firstname3

S1A-057(A) 10 firstname3 was there firstname3 rang me this morning actually

S1A-057(B) 12 Yes She said she'd been in touch with you this morning

S1A-057(A) 14 Mmm And fullname4 Do you know firstname4

S1A-057(B) 16 No I don't think I do

S1A-057(A) 17 She rang as well and firstname5 rang

S1A-057(B) 18 Oh yes Did you know there was a fire on the harbour bridge

S1A-057(A) 21 No What happened

S1A-057(B) 22 Oh the workmen were doing some work on it and apparently the what do they call that that ox oxywelding caught fire and they went for the fire extinguishers and when they got the fire extinguishers there was nothing in the fire extinguishers sothey couldn't put out the fire

S1A-057(A) 28 Yeah

S1A-057(A) 29 Oh really

S1A-057(A) 30 Where abouts was the fire On the road Or up on the top

S1A-057(B) 33 No Up on the top I think

S1A-057(A) 34 On the very top

S1A-057(B) 35 Somewhere up on the top I think I don't know I didn't hear much about it but anyway that was the harbour bridge

S1A-057(A) 39 And how long what how did they get it off How did they get that get the fire out

S1A-057(B) 42 Well they had to call the fire brigade but it held up all the traffic

S1A-057(A) 45 This morning

S1A-057(B) 46 Yes

S1A-057(A) 47 Was this this morning In peak hour

S1A-057(B) 48 Yes

S1A-057(B) 49 This was not very long ago Only about well it probably would've been in peak hour but it was on the actually it was it wasn't on the news I don't think

S1A-057(B) 52 It was a news flash between the news reports that I heard it

S1A-057(B) 53 Mmm Yes

S1A-057(A) 54 Oh

S1A-057(A) 55 So who else was ov who who was firstname6 and firstname7 there were they

S1A-057(B) 57 Yes

S1A-057(A) 58 Oh and how's firstname1 Is he alright today

S1A-057(B) 60 Yes He's sitting out on the chair and

S1A-057(A) 61 Has he still got a drip

S1A-057(B) 62 No He didn't have the drip Well I don't think so

S1A-057(B) 64 I didn't see any drip but I didn't stay I just went sort of in and out and when they were all there I took the flowers and put them in water for them

S1A-057(A) 68 Oh

S1A-057(A) 69 Did mum

S1A-057(A) 70 Ho what flowers

S1A-057(B) 71 We got about three bunches of flowers that we bought them

S1A-057(A) 73 What did ah mum have a drip in

S1A-057(B) 74 Yes She's still got it

S1A-057(A) 75 Did they say how long she's gonna be in hospital for

S1A-057(B) 76 Well I really wasn't talking to anybody this morning but see they've gotta get her back on food and see how that goes

S1A-057(A) 79 Yeah

S1A-057(A) 80 Did you get in contact with the doctor

S1A-057(B) 81 No I haven't seen the doctor

S1A-057(A) 82 Oh

S1A-057(B) 83 It's hard to see the doctor unless you're there right when he's there you don't see him

S1A-057(B) 84 And I'd rather talk to doctor ah surname8 is it surname8

S1A-057(B) 86 What's the his

S1A-057(A) 87 Yeah

S1A-057(A) 88 Names

S1A-057(B) 89 Yeah What's the doctor's name

S1A-057(A) 90 The one who operated on mum I think it was surname8 'cos firstname1's got Dr surname9

S1A-057(B) 93 Yes

S1A-057(B) 94 Yes

S1A-057(B) 95 Yes But it's hard to get to see the doctors 'cos they're so busy and getting around to being busy they're building another hospital

S1A-057(B) 98 In the southwest I think In the southwest

S1A-057(A) 100 Yeah

S1A-057(A) 101 They're clo

S1A-057(A) 102 They're closing Balmain ye yesterday when I went down there

S1A-057(A) 103 Oh well they're not closing it but they're not doing any operations

S1A-057(B) 105 Really

S1A-057(B) 106 And it's going to take in Concord Balmain and another couple of hospitals I think to service the area

S1A-057(A) 109 Really

S1A-057(A) 110 'Cos it's a long way

S1A-057(B) 111 That's when you go out the Hume highway you go through Gordon don't you

S1A-057(A) 113 Yeah Oh no You don't have to go that way

S1A-057(A) 114 You can go the back way

S1A-057(B) 116 Yes It's still a long way when they've got hospitals already here for convenience

S1A-057(A) 118 Yeah

S1A-057(B) 120 Did you get in touch with firstname1

S1A-057(A) 121 Yep

S1A-057(B) 122 Is he coming in to see mum

S1A-057(A) 123 Yeah He's I don't think he could handle coming in yesterday but um ah he's gonna come in today with firstname2

S1A-057(B) 127 Oh that's good Yes And did he work at the weekend firstname1

S1A-057(A) 130 Yeah He worked on Saturday ah Saturday and Sunday and um and then I'm going to get him to come in on Saturday for four hours 'cos I'm gonna go shopping

S1A-057(A) 134 So I'm gonna work from ten till one and then he's gonna work from one till five and then firstname2 will probably work on Sunday

S1A-057(B) 137 Mmm

S1A-057(B) 138 Mmm That's good

S1A-057(B) 139 Mmm

S1A-057(B) 140 I see I see said the blindman but he couldn't see at all

S1A-057(B) 141 Oh anyway I've got some pumpkin and some cauliflower and I'm going to make pumpkin soup and cauliflower soup for the weekend

S1A-057(A) 144 Is that for when mum and firstname1 come out

S1A-057(B) 146 Yes But you can have some if you like pumpkin soup and cauliflower soup

S1A-057(B) 148 Do you

S1A-057(A) 149 Are you making two different soups or putting them both in one

S1A-057(B) 151 No Making two different ones

S1A-057(A) 152 Oh I like pump I like pumpkin soup

S1A-057(B) 153 Yeah And if there's any over it can be frozen

S1A-057(A) 155 We usually freeze it don't we though

S1A-057(B) 156 Oh yes but in the deep freeze

S1A-057(A) 157 Oh we don't have any

S1A-057(B) 158 Yes you do You've got a freezer at the top of the fridge

S1A-057(B) 159 That freezer

S1A-057(A) 160 Oh I thought you meant a big freeze like a

S1A-057(B) 161 No The freezing compartment at the top of the fridge

S1A-057(B) 163 You put it in there I've got some little plastic containers to put it in so there's just enough for one serving

S1A-057(A) 167 Oh New conversation on same tape

Appendix 3.2

S2B-036(A) 175 There are many factors which determine how dangerous a snake is

S2B-036(A) 176 Even the most toxic snake with the longest fangs and the worst temper can hardly be considered dangerous if it doesn't come into contact with humans

S2B-036(A) 179 Unfortunately Australia's most dangerous snake is found all too commonly in our backyards

S2B-036(A) 181 Until 1954 a full bite from a taipan meant certain death

S2B-036(A) 183 Although it was the most urgently needed taipan anti-venom was one of the last to be developed

S2B-036(A) 184 Fortunately taipan venom isn't the most potent but in all other aspects it rates equal with or above Australia's other venomous snakes and has earned the reputation as the most dangerous snake in Australia

S2B-036(A) 188 It's the longest of the venomous snakes and this is an advantage when striking

S2B-036(A) 190 If cornered it will go on the attack Its length means it can strike high making the bite more effective

S2B-036(A) 193 Unlike their cousins the vipers which can fold their fangs back they have permanently erect fangs which limits the length that they can grow

S2B-036(A) 195 They average about 4 to 5 millimetres

S2B-036(A) 196 The taipan's fangs can grow to be 12 millimetres that's about the length of my fingernail which makes for greater killing power

S2B-036(A) 198 Like the snake the taipan uses a strike and release method of attack

S2B-036(A) 200 Unlike the snake it will bite repeatedly

S2B-036(A) 201 Its long fangs mean the venom can be injected to a far greater depth and therefore have a greater effect

S2B-036(A) 203 In one reported attack a 12-year-old boy died less than an hour after being bitten 12 times by a taipan

S2B-036(A) 206 Taipans are most commonly found in well-grassed tropical woodlands but their preferred diet of small rodents birds and the occasional bandicoot means they're often found near farm outbuildings and even urban backyards

S2B-036(A) 210 In comparison the tiger snake isn't considered as dangerous as the taipan yet it accounts for far more bites than any other snake in Australia

S2B-036(A) 212 This tiger snake is shedding its skin

S2B-036(A) 213 The process called sloughing happens about five times a year

S2B-036(A) 214 Immature snakes slough as they grow but in adults it occurs to replace damaged and worn skin

S2B-036(A) 216 The eastern tiger snake is found from the south-eastern corner of Queensland down through New South Wales and most of Victoria and up into South Australia the most densely populated corner of the continent

S2B-036(A) 220 This brings it into contact with humans far more often than most snakes

S2B-036(A) 221 When it does come into contact with us it's unlikely to flee

S2B-036(A) 222 If you do happen to find a snake in a building discretion is the better part of valour

S2B-036(A) 224 Don't try to remove it Just give it a wide berth and it will usually go out the way it came in

S2B-036(A) 226 An overexcited snake is more likely to attack so if it comes towards you simply move quietly out of the way

S2B-036(A) 227 It's probably just curious or even lost

S2B-036(A) 228 This is a Chapel Island tiger snake

S2B-036(A) 229 Its darker colour is due to its cold habitat in the Bass Straight

S2B-036(A) 230 When it feeds it works its jaws in a chewing motion

S2B-036(A) 231 The fangs are very small but the venom is extremely potent

S2B-036(A) 232 By injecting large amounts the venom quickly begins the process of breaking down the food

S2B-036(A) 234 The fangs also aid in the act of swallowing

S2B-036(A) 235 The snake literally walks along its victim forcing it down its throat

Epilogue

In the Introduction, written in November 2009, I mention the inspiration and encouragement I gained from the work of Claire Blanche-Benveniste. This Epilogue is being written at the beginning of June 2010, almost 6 weeks after her death, a huge loss, especially to scholars working on spoken language. I only met Claire Blanche-Benveniste once, in April 2000. In the course of our conversation, she mentioned how difficult it had been to have her research taken seriously, as it focused on spontaneous spoken French and not on literary texts. Ten years on the situation has improved, but not as much as might have been hoped. The three central ideas presented in the Introduction have progressed at different rates. Descriptive grammars of many languages continue to appear in impressive numbers. The tenet that meaning is central to the understanding of grammatical patterns, indeed is their raison d'être, has been adopted by many researchers, particularly by adherents of Cognitive Linguistics.

Less headway has been made by the idea that spontaneous spoken language is important for core theoretical areas such as syntax, language acquisition, typology, language evolution and language variation. Variationists focus on non-standard varieties of a given language or on text types; they have not so far given the same attention to the contrasts, indeed tensions, within any literate society between the grammatical and discourse patterns of spontaneous speech and the grammatical and discourse patterns of formal writing. This potential strand of variation theory connects directly with theories of first language acquisition; any adequate theory of first language acquisition must take account of these contrasts and tensions. All these points were recognized by Claire Blanche-Benveniste. Hopefully, this book will continue her work and propel spontaneous spoken language a little further into the various theoretical arenas.

References

Aarts, B. (2004), 'Modelling linguistic gradience'. *Studies in Language* 28, 1–49.

Aarts, B. (2007), 'In defence of distributional analysis, *pace* Croft'. *Studies in Language* 31/2, 431–43.

Abney, S. P. (1987), 'The English noun phrase in its sentential aspect'. Ph.D. thesis, Massachusetts Institute of Technology.

Adger, D. (2003), *Core Syntax. A Minimalist Approach*. Oxford: Oxford University Press.

Anderson, J. M. (1971), *The Grammar of Case*. Cambridge: Cambridge University Press.

Anderson, J. M. (1973), *An Essay Concerning Aspect*. The Hague: Mouton.

Anderson, J. M. (2006), *Modern Grammars of Case*. Oxford: Oxford University Press.

Anderson, S. R. (2008), 'The logical structure of linguistic theory'. *Language* 84/4, 795–814.

Austin, P. (1981), *A Grammar of Diyari, South Australia*. Cambridge: Cambridge University Press.

Baker, M. (1996), *The Polysynthesis Parameter*. Cambridge: Cambridge University Press.

Ball, R. (2000), *Colloquial French Grammar. A Practical Guide*. Oxford: Blackwell.

Bard, E. G., Robertson, D. and Sorace, A. (1996), 'Magnitude estimation of linguistic acceptability'. *Language* 72, 32–68.

Barlow, M. and Kemmer S. (eds) (2000), *Usage-Based Models of Language*. Stanford: CSLI.

Bavin, E. L. (2006), 'Syntactic development'. In Brown, K. (ed.), *Encyclopaedia of Language and Linguistics, Volume 12* (second edition). Oxford: Elsevier, pp. 383–90.

Bauer, W. with W. Parker, Te Kareongawai Evans and Te Aroha Noti Teepa (1997), *The Reed Reference Grammar of Maori*. Auckland: Reed Publishing.

Bennett, M. (1992), *Scottish Customs from the Cradle to the Grave*. Edinburgh: Polygon.

Biber, D. (1988), *Variation Across Speech and Writing*. Cambridge: Cambridge University Press.

Biber, D., Johansson, S., Leech, G., Conrad, S., and Finegan, E. (1999), *Longman Grammar of Spoken and Written English*. London: Longman.

Blackman, R. (1908), *Composition and Style. A Literary Handbook*. Edinburgh: John Grant.

Blanche-Benveniste, C. (1991), *Le Français Parlé: Etudes Grammaticales*. Paris: Editions du Centre National de la Recherche Scientifique.

Bloomfield, L. (1933), *Language*. London: George Allen and Unwin.

Boeckx, C. (2006), *Linguistic Minimalism. Origins, Concepts, Methods, and Aims*. Oxford: Oxford University Press.

Bolinger, D. (1976), 'Meaning and memory'. *Forum Linguisticum* 1, 1–14.

Börjars, K. (2006), 'Description and theory'. In B. Aarts and A. McMahon (eds) *The Handbook of English Linguistics*. Oxford: Blackwell, pp. 9–32.

Bosworth, J. and Toller, N. (1972), *An Anglo-Saxon Dictionary*. Oxford: Oxford University Press.

Bowe, H. J. (1990), *Categories, Constituents and Constituent Order in Pitjantjatjara, An Aboriginal Language of Australia*. London: Routledge.

Brazil, D. (1995), *A Grammar of Speech.* Oxford: Oxford University Press.

Bresnan, J. (1982), 'The passive in lexical theory'. In J. Bresnan (ed) *The Mental Representation of Grammatical Relations.* Cambridge, MA: MIT Press, pp. 3–86.

Bresnan, J. and Grimshaw, J. (1978), 'The syntax of free relatives in English'. *Linguistic Inquiry* 9, 331–91.

Brown, G., Anderson, A., Shillcock, R. and Yule, G. (1984), *Teaching Talk: Strategies for Production and Assessment.* Cambridge: Cambridge University Press.

Brown, G., Currie, K. L. and Kenworthy, J. (1980), *Questions of Intonation.* London: Croom Helm.

Brown, K. and Miller, J. (1996), *Concise Encyclopedia of Syntactic Theories.* Oxford: Elsevier.

Burchfield, R. W. (1981), *The Spoken Word: A BBC Guide.* London: BBC Publications.

Burchfield, R. W. (1996), *The New Fowler's Modern English Usage. Third Edition.* Oxford: Oxford University Press.

Butt, M. (2009), '*Modern approaches to case: an overview*'. In A. Malchukov and A. Spencer (eds) *The Oxford Handbook of Case.* Oxford: Oxford University Press, pp. 59–71.

Calude, A. (2008), 'Demonstrative clefts and double cleft constructions in spontaneous spoken English'. *Studia Linguistica* 62/1, 78–118.

Cameron, D. (1995), *Verbal Hygiene.* London: Routledge.

Cann, R. (1993), 'Patterns of headedness'. In G. G. Corbett, N. M. Fraser, and S. McGlashan (eds), *Heads in Grammatical Theory.* Cambridge: Cambridge University Press, pp. 44–72.

Carr, P. (2005), 'Philosophy of linguistics'. In Brown, K. (ed.), *Encyclopedia of Language and Linguistics, Volume 9 (second edition).* Oxford: Elsevier, pp. 331–7.

Carr, P. (2007), 'Internalism, externalism and coding'. *Language Sciences* 29, 672–89.

Carter, R. and McCarthy, M. (1997), *Exploring Spoken English.* Cambridge: Cambridge University Press.

Carter, R. and McCarthy, M. (1999), 'The English *get*-passive in spoken discourse: description and implications for an interpersonal grammar'. *English Language and Linguistics* 3/1, 41–58.

Chafe, W. (ed.) (1980), *The Pear Stories: Cognitive, Cultural and Linguistic Aspects of Narrative Production.* Norwood, NJ: Ablex.

Cheshire, J. (2005), 'Syntactic variation and spoken language'. In L. Cornips and K. P. Corrigan (eds) *Syntax and Variation. Reconciling the Biological and the Social.* Amsterdam: John Benjamin, pp. 81–106.

Cheshire, J., Edwards, V. and Whittle, P. (1993), 'Non-standard English and dialect levelling'. In Milroy, J. and Milroy, L. (eds), *Real English. The Grammar of Dialects in the British Isles.* London: Longman, pp. 53–96.

Chipere, N. (2009), 'Individual differences in processing complex grammatical structures'. In G. Sampson, D. Gil, and P. Trudgill (eds) *Language Complexity as an Evolving Variable.* Oxford: Oxford University Press, pp. 178–91.

Chomsky, N. A. (1957), *Syntactic Structures.* The Hague: Mouton.

Chomsky, N. A. (1965), *Aspects of the Theory of Syntax.* Cambridge, MA: MIT Press.

Chomsky, N. A. (1968), *Language and Mind.* New York: Harcourt, Brace and World.

Chomsky, N. A. (1986a), *Knowledge of Language: Its Nature, Origin and Use.* Westport, CT: Praeger.

Chomsky, N. A. (1986b), 'Principles and parameters in syntactic theory'. In N. Hornstein and D. Lightfoot (eds) *Explanation in Linguistics. The Logical Problem of Language Acquisition.* London: Longman, pp. 32–75.

Chomsky, N. A. (1995), *The Minimalist Program.* Cambridge, MA: MIT Press.

Clark, B. (2005), 'Linguistics as a science'. In Brown, K. (ed.), *Encyclopedia of Language and Linguistics, Volume 7 (second edition).* Oxford: Elsevier, pp. 227–34.

Collins, P. and Hollo, C. (2000), *English Grammar. An Introduction.* Basingstoke and London: Macmillan Press.

Collins, P. and Peters, P. (2008), 'Australian English: morphology and syntax'. In K. Burridge and B. Kortmann (eds) *Varieties of English 3: The Pacific and Australasia.* Berlin: Mouton de Gruyter, pp. 341–61.

Comrie, B. (1985), *Tense.* Cambridge: Cambridge University Press.

Corbett, C., Fraser, N. M., and McGlashan, S. (1993), *Heads in Grammatical Theory.* Cambridge: Cambridge University Press.

Cornips, L. and Corrigan, K. P. (eds.) (2005), *Syntax and Variation. Reconciling the Biological and the Social.* Amsterdam: John Benjamin.

Coulthard, R. M. and Robinson, W. P. (1968), 'The structure of the nominal group and the elaboratedness of code'. *Language and Speech* 11/4, 234–50.

Cowie, F. (1999), *What's Within? Nativism Reconsidered.* Oxford: Oxford University Press.

Crain, S. and Nakayama, M. (1987), 'Structure dependence in grammar formation'. *Language* 63, 522–43.

Crick, F. H. C. (1979), 'Thinking about the brain'. *Scientific American* 9, 219–32.

Croft, W. (2001), *Radical Construction Grammar. Syntactic Theory in Typological Perspective.* Oxford: Oxford University Press.

Croft, W. (2007), 'Beyond Aristotle and gradience. A reply to Aarts'. *Studies in Language* 31/2, 409–30.

Croft, W. and Cruse, D. A. (2004), *Cognitive Linguistics.* Cambridge: Cambridge University Press.

Cruse, D. A. (1973), 'Some thoughts on agentivity'. *Journal of Linguistics* 9, 11–23.

Cruse, D. A. (1986), *Lexical Semantics.* Cambridge: Cambridge University Press.

Crystal, D. (1976), 'Neglected grammatical factors in conversational English'. In S. Greenbaum, G. Leech, and J. Svartvik (eds), *Studies in English Linguistics.* London: Longman, pp. 153–66.

Crystal, D. (1987), *The Cambridge Encyclopedia of Language.* Cambridge: Cambridge University Press.

Culicover, P. (2009), *Natural Language Syntax.* Oxford: Oxford University Press.

Dabrowska, E. (1997), 'The LAD goes to school: a cautionary tale for nativists'. *Linguistics* 35, 735–66.

Dabrowska, E. (2005), 'Productivity and beyond; mastering the Polish genitive inflection'. *Journal of Child Language* 32, 191–205.

Dahl, Ö. (1999), 'Perfect'. In K. Brown and J. Miller (eds) *Concise Encyclopedia of Grammatical Categories.* Oxford: Elsevier, pp. 290–1.

De Cat, C. (2007), 'French dislocation without movement'. *Natural Language and Linguistic Theory,* 25, 485–534.

De Hoop, H. (2009), 'Case in Optimality Theory'. In A. Malchukov and A. Spencer (eds) *The Oxford Handbook of Case.* Oxford: Oxford University Press, pp. 88–101.

Denison, D. (1993), *English Historical Syntax.* London: Longman.

Denison, D. (1998), 'Syntax'. In S. Romaine (ed.) *The Cambridge History of the English Language. Volume IV 1776–1997.* Cambridge: Cambridge University Press, pp. 92–329.

Deutscher, G. (2000), *Syntactic Change in Akkadian: The Evolution of Sentential Complementation.* Oxford: Oxford University Press.

Dickens, C. (1853), *Bleak House.* (References to the 1996 Penguin Classics edition.)

Dixon, R. M. W. (1972), *The Dyirbal Language of North Queensland.* Cambridge: Cambridge University Press.

Donaldson, T. (1980), *Ngiyambaa. The Language of the Wangaaybuwan.* Cambridge: Cambridge University Press.

Dougherty, R. (1970), 'Recent Studies in Language Universals'. *Foundations of Language* 6, 505–61.

Dowty, D. (1989), 'On the semantic content of the notion "thematic role"'. In G. Chierchia, B. H. Partee, and R. Turner (eds) *Properties, Types and Meanings, 2: Semantic Issues.* Dordrecht: Kluwer, pp. 69–129.

Dowty, D. (1991), 'Thematic roles and argument selection'. *Language* 62, 547–619.

Elson, B. and Pickett, V. (1967), *An Introduction to Morphology and Syntax* (fifth edition). Santa Ana, CA: Summer Institute of Linguistics.

Elsness, J. (1997), *The Perfect and the Preterit in Contemporary and Earlier English.* Berlin: Mouton de Gruyter.

Fernandez, M. M. J. (1994), *Les Particules Enonciatives.* Paris: Presses Universitaires de France.

Fillmore, C. J. (1963), 'The position of embedding transformations in a grammar'. *Word* 19, 208–31.

Fillmore, C. J. (1968), 'The case for case'. In E. Bach and R. Harms (eds), *Universals in Linguistic Theory.* New York: Holt, Rinehart and Winston, pp. 1–88.

Foley, W. A. and Van Valin, R. D., Jr. (1984), *Functional Syntax and Universal Grammar.* Cambridge: Cambridge University Press.

Gazdar, G., Klein, E., Pullum, G. K., and Sag, I. A. (1985), *Generalized Phrase Structure Grammar.* Oxford: Basil Blackwell.

Gee, J. P. (1974), "Get passive": on some constructions with "Get". Bloomington, Indiana: Indiana University Linguistics Club.

Ginzburg, J. and Sag, I. A. (2001), *Interrogative Investigations: The Form, Meaning and Use of English Interrogatives.* Stanford, CA: CSLI Publications.

Givon, T. (1990), *Syntax: A Functional–Typological Introduction.* Amsterdam: John Benjamins.

Givon, T. and Shibatani, M. (2009), *Syntactic Complexity. Diachrony, Acquisition, Neuro-Cognition, Evolution.* Amsterdam: John Benjamin.

Givon, T. and Yang, L. (1994), 'The rise of the English *Get*-passive'. In B. Fox and P. J. Hopper (eds) *Voice. Form and Function.* Amsterdam: John Benjamins, pp. 119–49.

Goldberg, A. (1995), *Constructions: A Construction Grammar Approach to Argument Structure.* Chicago: University of Chicago Press.

Goody, J. (1977), *The Domestication of the Savage Mind.* Cambridge: Cambridge University Press.

Green, M. (2006), 'Levels of adequacy, observational, descriptive, explanatory'. In K. Brown (ed.), *Encyclopedia of Language and Linguistics, Volume 7* (second edition). Oxford: Elsevier, pp. 49–51.

Grévisse, M. (A. Goosse). *Le Bon Usage.* Paris and Louvain-la-Neuve: Duculot.

Grimshaw, J. (1990), *Argument Structure.* Cambridge, MA: MIT Press.

Gronemeyer, C. (1999), 'On deriving complex polysemy: the grammaticalization of *get*'. *English Language and Linguistics* 3/1, 1–39.

Gropen, J., Pinker, S., Hollander, M., Goldberg, R., and Wilson, R. (1989), 'The learnability and acquisition of the dative alternation in English'. *Language* 65, 203–57.

Guiraud, P. (1963), *Le Moyen Français*. Paris: Presses Universitaires de France.

Haegeman, L. (1991), *Introduction to Government and Binding Theory*. Oxford: Basil Blackwell.

Hale, K. (1981), *On the Position of Warlpiri in a Typology of the Base*. Bloomington, IN: Indiana University Linguistics Club.

Hale, K. (1982), 'Preliminary remarks on configurationality'. In J. Pustejovsky and P. Sells (eds). *NELS* 12, 86–96.

Hale, K. (1983), 'Warlpiri and the grammar of non-configurational languages'. *Natural Language and Linguistic Theory* 1, 5–47.

Halliday, M. A. K. (1967a), 'Notes on transitivity and theme in English. Part 1'. *Journal of Linguistics* 3, 37–81.

Halliday, M. A. K. (1967b), 'Notes on transitivity and theme in English. Part 2'. *Journal of Linguistics* 3, 199–244.

Halliday, M. A. K. (1968), 'Notes on transitivity and theme in English. Part 3'. *Journal of Linguistics* 4, 179–215.

Halliday, M. A. K. (1989), *Spoken and Written Language*. Oxford: Oxford University Press.

Harris, Z. S. (1946), 'From morpheme to utterance'. *Language* 22, 161–83. Reprinted in M. Joos (ed.) (1957) *Readings in Linguistics I*. Chicago and London: University of Chicago Press.

Haspelmath, M. (1993), 'Passive participles across languages'. In B. Fox and P. J. Hopper (eds) *Voice. Form and Function*. Amsterdam: John Benjamins, pp. 151–77.

Haspelmath, M. (1997), *Indefinite Pronouns*. Oxford: Oxford University Press.

Hawkins, P. (1969), 'Social class, the nominal group and reference'. *Language and Speech* 14/4, 125–35.

Hays, D. (1964), 'Dependency theory: a formalism and some observations'. *Language* 40, 511–25.

Heath, S. B. (1983), *Ways with Words*. Cambridge: Cambridge University Press.

Held, W. H., Schmalstieg, W. R., and Gertz, J. E. (1987), *Beginning Hittite*. Columbus, OH: Slavica.

Henry, A. (1995), *Belfast English and Standard English: Dialect Variation and Parameter Setting*. New York: Oxford University Press.

Henry, A. (2002), 'Variation and syntactic theory'. In J. K. Chambers, P. Trudgill, and N. Schilling-Estes (eds) *The Handbook of Language Variation and Change*. Oxford: Blackwell, pp. 267–82.

Henry, A. (2005), 'Idiolectal variation and syntactic theory'. In L. Cornips and K. P. Corrigan (eds) *Syntax and Variation. Reconciling the Biological and the Social*. Amsterdam: John Benjamin, pp. 109–22.

Hockett, C. F. (1958), *A Course in Modern Linguistics*. New York: Macmillan.

Holthausen, F. (1963), *Altenglisches Etymologisches Wörterbuch*. Oxford: Oxford University Press.

Horrocks, G. (1988), *Generative Grammar*. London: Longman.

Huddleston, R. (1984), *Introduction to the Grammar of English*. Cambridge: Cambridge University Press.

Huddleston, R. (1988), *English Grammar. An Outline*. Cambridge: Cambridge University Press.

Huddleston, R. and Pullum, G. K. (2002), *The Cambridge Grammar of the English Language.* Cambridge: Cambridge University Press.

Hudson, R. A. (1987), 'Zwicky on heads'. *Journal of Linguistics* 23, 109–32.

Hudson, R. A. (1990), *English Word Grammar.* Oxford: Blackwell.

Hudson, R. A. (1998), *English Grammar.* London: Routledge.

Hudson, R. A. (2007), *Language Networks: the New Word Grammar.* Oxford: Oxford University Press.

Jackendoff, R. S. (1976), 'Toward an explanatory semantic representation'. *Linguistic Inquiry* 7, 89–150.

Jackendoff, R. S. (1990), *Semantic Structures.* Cambridge, MA: MIT Press.

Jackendoff, R. S. (1993), *Patterns in the Mind.* New York: Harvester Wheatsheaf.

Jackendoff, R. S. (2002), *Foundations of Language.* Oxford: Oxford University Press.

Jacobs, R. A. and Rosenbaum, P. S. (1970) *English Transformational Grammar.* Waltham, MA: Xerox College Publishing.

Jakobson, R. (1936), 'Beitrag zur allgemeinen Kasuslehre: Gesamtbedeutungen der russischen Kasus'. *Travaux du Cercle Linguistique de Prague* 6, 240–83.

Jelinek, E. (1984), 'Empty categories, case, and configurations'. *Natural Language and Linguistic Theory* 2/1, 39–76.

Jespersen, O. (1924), *The Philosophy of Grammar.* London: Allen & Unwin.

Jespersen, O. (1961a), *A Modern English Grammar on Historical Principles. Part III. Syntax Second Volume.* Reprinted 1974. London: George Allen and Unwin.

Jespersen, O. (1961b), *A Modern English Grammar on Historical Principles. Part IV. Syntax Third Volume.* Reprinted 1970. London: George Allen and Unwin.

Jucker, A. H. (1992), *Social Stylistics: Stylistic Variation in British Newspapers.* Berlin: Mouton de Gruyter.

Kapanadze, M. and Zemskaja, E. O. (1979), *Teksty.* Moscow: Nauka.

Karlsson, F. (2009), 'Origin and maintenance of clausal embedding complexity'. In G. Sampson, D. Gil, and P. Trudgill (eds) *Language Complexity as an Evolving Variable.* Oxford: Oxford University Press, pp. 192–202.

Keenan, E. L. (1976), 'Towards a universal definition of "subject"'. In C. N. Li (ed.) *Subject and Topic.* New York: Academic Press, pp. 303–33.

Keenan, E. L. and Comrie, B. (1977), 'Noun phrase accessibility and universal grammar'. *Linguistic Inquiry* 8, 63–99.

Kennedy, A. L. (1994), *Looking For the Possible Dance.* London: Minerva.

Kerslake, C. (2007), 'Alternative subordination strategies in Turkish.' In J. Rehbein, C. Hohenstein and L. Pietsch (eds) *Connectivity in Grammar and Discourse.* Amsterdam: John Benjamins, pp. 231–58.

Kimball, J. (1973), 'Get'. In J. Kimball (ed.) *Syntax and Semantics 2.* New York: Academic Press.

Klein, W. (1992), 'The present perfect puzzle'. *Language* 68, 525–52.

Kurath, H. and Kurath, S. M. (1963), *Middle English Dictionary.* Ann Arbor: University of Michigan.

Labov, W. (1972), 'The logic of non-standard English'. In P. Giglioli (ed.) *Language and Social Context.* Harmondsworth: Penguin, pp. 179–215.

Labov, W. (1975), *What Is a Linguistic Fact?* Lisse: Peter de Ridder.

Lakoff, G. (1968), 'Instrumental adverbs and the concept of deep structure'. *Foundations of Language* 4, 4–29.

Lakoff, G. (1970), *Irregularity in Syntax*. New York: Holt, Rinehart and Winston.

Lakoff, G. (1987), *Women, Fire and Dangerous Things. What Categories Reveal About the Mind.* Chicago: University of Chicago Press.

Lakoff, R. (1971), 'Passive resistance'. Papers from the 7th Regional Meeting, Chicago Linguistic Society, pp. 149–82.

Langacker, R. W. (1982), 'Space grammar, analyzability, and the English passive'. *Language* 58, 22–80.

Langacker, R.W. (1987), *Foundations of Cognitive Grammar. Volume 1: Theoretical Prerequisites. Volume 2: Descriptive Application.* Stanford: Stanford University Press.

Langacker, R. W. (1991), *Concept, Image and Symbol. The Cognitive Basis of Grammar.* New York: Mouton de Gruyter.

Lapteva, O. A. (1976), *Russkij razgovornyj sintaksis.* Moscow: Nauka.

Leech, G. N. (1971), *Meaning and the English Verb.* London: Longman.

Leech, G., Myers, G., and Thomas, J. (1995), *Spoken English on Computer.* Harlow: Longman.

Levin, B. and Rappaport Hovav, M. (2005), *Argument Realization.* Cambridge: Cambridge University Press.

Lewis, G. L. (1978) *Turkish Grammar.* Oxford: Clarendon Press.

Linell, P. (1988), 'The impact of literacy on the conception of language: the case of linguistics'. In R. Saljö (ed.), *The Written World.* Berlin: Springer, pp. 41–58.

Lyons, J. (1968), *Introduction to Theoretical Linguistics.* Cambridge: Cambridge University Press.

Lyons, J. (1975), 'Deixis as the source of reference'. In E. L. Keenan (ed), *Formal Semantics of Natural Language.* Cambridge: Cambridge University Press, pp. 61–83. Reprinted in Sir John Lyons (1991), *Natural Language and Universal Grammar.* Cambridge: Cambridge University Press, pp. 146–65.

Lyons, J. (1977a), *Semantics. Vol. 1.* Cambridge: Cambridge University Press.

Lyons, J. (1977b), *Semantics. Vol. 2.* Cambridge: Cambridge University Press.

Macaulay, R. K. S. (1991), *Locating Dialect in Discourse.* Oxford: Oxford University Press.

McCarthy, M. (1998), *Spoken Language and Applied Linguistics.* Cambridge: Cambridge University Press.

McConvell, P. (1988), 'To be or double be? Current changes in the English copula'. *Australian Journal of Linguistics* 8, 287–305.

Maher, J. and Groves, J. (1996), *Chomsky for Beginners.* Duxford, Cambridge: Icon Books.

Mair, C. and Leech, G. (2006), 'Current changes in English syntax'. In B. Aarts and A. McMahon (eds) *The Handbook of English Linguistics.* Oxford: Blackwell, pp. 318–42.

Manzini, R. (1990), 'Locality and parameters again'. In I. Roca (ed.) *Logical Issues in Language Acquisition.* Dordrecht: Foris, pp. 137–56.

Massam, D. (1999), '*Thing is* constructions: the thing is, what's the right analysis?' *English Language and Linguistics* 3/2, 335–52.

Matthews P. H. (1979), *Generative Grammar and Linguistic Competence.* London: George Allen and Unwin.

Matthews, P. H. (1981), *Syntax.* Cambridge: Cambridge University Press.

Matthews P. H. (2007), *Oxford Concise Dictionary of Linguistics* (second edition). Oxford: Oxford University Press.

Michaelis, L. A. (1994), 'The ambiguity of the English present perfect'. *Journal of Linguistics*, 30, 111–57.

Michaelis, L. A. (2006), 'Tense in English'. In B. Aarts and A. McMahon (eds) *The Handbook of English Linguistics.* Oxford: Blackwell, pp. 220–43.

Miller, G.A. and Johnson-Laird, P. (1976), *Language and Perception.* Cambridge, Mass.: Harvard University Press and London: Cambridge University Press.

Miller, J. (1973), 'A generative account of the 'category of state' in Russian'. In F. Kiefer and N. Ruwet (eds) *Generative Grammar in Europe.* Dordrecht: D. Reidel, pp. 333–59.

Miller, J. (1985), *Semantics and Syntax: Parallels and Connections.* Cambridge: Cambridge University Press.

Miller, J. (2000), 'The Perfect in spoken and written English'. *Transactions of the Philological Society*, 98/2, 323–52.

Miller, J. (2003), 'Syntax and discourse in Modern Scots'. In J. Corbett, J. D. McClure, and J. Stuart-Smith (eds) *The Edinburgh Companion to Scots.* Edinburgh: Edinburgh University Press, pp. 72–109.

Miller, J. (2008), *An Introduction to English Syntax.* Edinburgh: Edinburgh University Press.

Miller, J. (2009), '*Like* and other discourse markers'. In P. Peters, P. Collins and A. Smith (eds), *Comparative Studies in Australian and New Zealand English. Grammar and Beyond.* Amsterdam, John Benjamin, pp. 317–37.

Miller, J. (2011) 'Contemporary English'. In L. Brinton and A. Bergs (eds) *Historical Linguistics of English. Volume 2.* Berlin: Mouton de Gruyter.

Miller, J. and Weinert, R. (2009), *Spontaneous Spoken Language. Syntax and Discourse* (second edition). Oxford: Clarendon Press.

Milroy, L. (1987), *Observing and Analysing Natural Language.* Oxford: Basil Blackwell.

Mithun, M. (2009), 'Re(e)volving complexity: adding intonation'. In T. Givon, and M. Shibatani (eds) *Syntactic Complexity. Diachrony, Acquisition, Neuro-Cognition, Evolution.* Amsterdam: John Benjamin, pp. 53–80.

Morozova, T. S. (1984), 'Nekotorye osobennosti postroenija vyskazyvanija v prostorečie'. In E. A. Zemskaja and D. N. Šmelev (eds), *Gorodskoe prostorečie.* Moskva: Nauka, pp. 141–62.

Mundy, C. S. (1955), 'Turkish syntax as a system of qualification'. *Bulletin of the School of Oriental Studies* 17, 277–305.

Mustanoja, T. (1960), *A Middle English Syntax.* Helsinki: Société Néophilologique de Helsinki.

Naismith, R. (1985), *Buildings of the Scottish Countryside.* London: Victor Gollancz.

Nattinger, J. and DeCarrico, J. (1992), *Lexical Phrases and Language Teaching.* Oxford: Oxford University Press.

Newmeyer, F. J. (2003), 'Grammar is grammar and usage is usage'. *Language* 79, 682–707.

Ochs, E. (1979), 'Planned and unplanned discourse'. In T. Givon (ed.), *Syntax and Semantics xii. Discourse and Syntax.* New York: Academic Press, pp. 51–80.

Ong, W. (1982), *Orality and Literacy.* London: Routledge.

Onions, C. T. (1904), *An Advanced English Syntax.* Oxford: Oxford University Press.

Palmer, L. R. (1954), *The Latin Language.* London: Faber and Faber.

Pawley, A. and Syder, F. (1983), 'Two puzzles for linguistic theory: nativelike selection and nativelike fluency'. In J. C. Richards and R. W. Schmidt (eds) *Language and Communication.* London: Longman, pp. 191–226.

Payne, J. (1993), 'The headedness of noun phrases: slaying the nominal hydra'. In C. Corbett, N. M. Fraser, and S. McGlashan (eds), *Heads in Grammatical Theory.* Cambridge: Cambridge University Press, pp. 114–39.

Pensalfini, R. (2004), 'Towards a typology of configurationality'. *Natural Language and Linguistic Theory* 22, 359–408.

Pereltsvaig, A. (2008), 'Split phrases in colloquial Russian'. *Studia Linguistica* 62/1, 5–38.

Perera, K. (1984), *Children's Writing and Reading.* Oxford: Basil Blackwell.

Peters, A. (1983), *The Units of Language Acquisition.* Cambridge: Cambridge University Press.

Peters, P., Collins, P., and Smith, A. (eds) (2009), *Comparative Studies in Australian and New Zealand English. Grammar and Beyond.* Amsterdam: John Benjamin.

Philpott, R. (1998), 'Spoken and written language in employee communication'. MA dissertation, Department of Linguistics, University of Edinburgh.

Pinker, S. (1994), *The Language Instinct. The New Science of Language and Mind.* Harmondsworth, Middlesex: Allen Lane, Penguin Books.

Pollard, C. and Sag, I. A. (1994), *Head-Driven Phrase Structure Grammar.* Stanford: CSLI; Chicago and London: University of Chicago Press.

Postal, P. M. (1970), 'On so-called pronouns in English'. In R. A. Jacobs and P. S. Rosenbaum (eds) *Readings in English Transformational Grammar.* Waltham, MA: Ginn and Company, pp. 56–82.

Primus, B. (2009), 'Case, grammatical relations, and semantic roles'. In A. Malchukov and A. Spencer (eds) *The Oxford Handbook of Case.* Oxford: Oxford University Press, pp. 261–75.

Quirk, R. and Greenbaum, S. (1973), *University Grammar of English.* London: Longman.

Quirk, R., Greenbaum, S., Leech, G. N., and Svartvik, J. (1985), *A Comprehensive Grammar of the English Language.* London: Longman.

Radford, A. (1988), *Transformational Grammar: A First Course.* Cambridge: Cambridge University Press.

Robinson, J. J. (1970), 'Dependency structure and transformational rules'. *Language* 46, 259–85.

Ross, J. R. (1967), 'Constraints on variables in syntax'. Ph.D. dissertation, Massachusetts Institute of Technology.

Ross-Hagebaum, S. (2004), 'The *That's X is Y* construction as an information structure amalgam'. *Proceedings of the Berkeley Linguistics Society*, 403–14.

Sampson, G. (2007), 'Grammar without grammaticality'. *Corpus Linguistics and Linguistic Theory* 3/1, 1–32.

Scatton, E. A. (1984), *A Reference Grammar of Modern Bulgarian*. Columbus, OH: Slavica.

Schachter, P. (1977), 'Reference-related and role-related properties of subjects'. In P. Cole and J. Sadock (eds) *Grammatical Relations. Syntax and Semantics 8*. New York: Academic Press, pp. 279–306.

Schlesinger, I. M. (1979), 'Cognitive and linguistic structures: the case of the instrumental'. *Journal of Linguistics* 15, 307–24.

Schmalstieg, W. R. (1983), *An Introduction to Old Church Slavic*. Columbus, OH: Slavica.

Schroeder, C. (2002), 'On the structure of spoken Turkish.' *Essener Linguistische Skripte-elektronisch* 2, 73–90. http://www.elise.uni-essen.de.

Searle, J. R. (1969), *Speech Acts*. Cambridge: Cambridge University Press.

Shaumjan, S. K. (1965), *Applikativnaja Grammatika*. Moscow: Akademija Nauk.

Siewerska, A. (1984), 'Phrasal discontinuity in Polish'. *Australian Journal of Linguistics* 4, 57–71.

Smitterberg, E. (2000), 'The progressive form and genre variation during the nineteenth century'. In R. Bermudez-Otero, D. Denison, R. Hogg, and C. B. McCully (eds), *Generative Theory and Corpus Studies. A Dialogue from 10 ICEHL*. Berlin: Mouton de Gruyter, pp. 283–97.

Sode-Woodhead, K. (2001), 'Making suggestions in business meetings'. University of Edinburgh, Ph.D. thesis.

Sonnenschein, E.A. (1921), *A New English Grammar*. Oxford: Oxford University Press.

Sornicola, R. (1981), *Sul Parlato*. Bologna: Il Mulino.

Ščerba, L. V. (1928), 'O častjax reči v russkom jazyke.' Russkaja Reč', Novaja Serija, Moscow. ('On parts of speech in Russian'). Reprinted in Ščerba, L. V., 1957, *Izbrannye Raboty po Russkomu Jazyku*.

Thompson, S. A. (1988), 'A discourse approach to the cross-linguistic category "adjective"'. In J. A. Hawkins (ed.), *Explaining Linguistic Universals*. Oxford: Oxford University Press, pp. 167–85.

Thubron, C. (1987), *Beyond the Great Wall*. London: Heinemann.

Tixonov, A. N. (1960), *Kategorija Sostojanija v Sovremennom Russkom Jazyke*. Samarkand. 'The Category of State in Modern Russian'.

Trask, R. L. (2001), *Mind the Gaffe. The Penguin Guide to Common Errors in English*. London: Penguin Books.

Traugott, E. (1972), *The History of English Syntax*. New York: Holt, Rinehart & Winston.

Trudgill, P. (1983), *Sociolinguistics*. Harmondsworth: Penguin Books.

Van Valin, R. D., Jr. and LaPolla, R. J. (1997), *Syntax: Structure, Meaning and Function*. Cambridge: Cambridge University Press.

Vargas, F. (2008), *Un Lieu Incertain*. Paris: Viviane Hamy.

Vinogradov, V. V. (1938), *Sovremennyj Russkij Jazyk*. Moscow. ('Modern Russian')

Wackernagel-Jolles, B. (1971), *Untersuchungen zur gesprochenen Sprache: Beobachtungen zur Verknüpfung spontanen Sprechens*. Göppingen: Alfred Kümmerle.

Weinberg, S. (2001), *Facing Up*. Cambridge, MA: Harvard University Press.

Weinert, R. and Miller, J. (1996), 'Clefts in spoken discourse'. *Journal of Pragmatics* 25, 173–202.

Wray, A. (2002), *Formulaic Language and the Lexicon*. Cambridge: Cambridge University Press.

Zemskaja, E. A. (1973), *Russkaja razgovornaja reč*. Moscow: Nauka.

Zwicky, A. (1985), 'Heads'. *Journal of Linguistics* 21, 1–29.

Index